URBAN MINISTRY

IN A NEW MILLENNIUM

Urban
Ministry
in a New Millennium

David Claerbaut

Authentic
MEDIA

World Vision

Published in Partnership with World Vision Resources

Authentic Media
We welcome your comments and questions.
129 Mobilization Drive, Waynesboro, GA 30830 USA authenticusa@stl.org

and 9 Holdom Avenue, Bletchley, Milton Keynes, Bucks, MK1 1QR, UK
www.authenticbooks.com

If you would like a copy of our current catalog, contact us at:
1-8MORE-BOOKS
ordersusa@stl.org

Urban Ministry in a New Millennium
ISBN: 1-932805-35-4

Published in partnership with World Vision
P.O. Box 9716, Federal Way, WA 98063 USA
www.worldvision.org

Unless otherwise indicated, Scripture quotations are taken from the *Holy Bible*,
New Living Translation, copyright © 1966. Used by permission of Tyndale
House Publishers, Inc., Wheaton, Illinois 60189. All rights reserved.

Cover design: Paul Lewis
Interior design: Angela Duerksen
Editorial team: Bette Smyth and Carolyn Ziegler

Printed in the United States of America

In memory of

Erwin Claerbaut

and

Bill Leslie,

*a layperson and a pastor,
two pioneers whose earthly labors
in urban ministry are done*

Contents

PREFACE

Urban Ministry in a New Millenium has its roots in my original book, *Urban Ministry*. That book grew out of my teaching association with the late urban pastoral legend, Bill Leslie. When looking for textbooks for a course on urban ministry back then, there was little from which to choose. One either used a secular text that outlined the issues facing the urban poor (Michael Harrington's *The Other America*, for example) or a book heavy on theology and ministry but light on an understanding of the city itself and its impact on ministry. Being an urban sociologist, I began writing what amounted to a primer on urban sociology seen through the lens of ministry in the inner city. From that effort *Urban Ministry* was born. I was flattered by how well it was received.

This book takes urban ministry into the new millennium. The discerning reader will notice that the references include current research as well as resources from decades ago. There are very important reasons for this. First, the book attempts to provide a historical perspective on the city, the church, and urban ministry, enabling the reader to see the hand of change in each. In addition, however, some of the best urban-sociology treatments, as well as some of the finest literature specific to urban ministry, began appearing in the late 1970s. Much of this classic, timeless, and unmatched literature has disappeared or been ignored over the years. Urban pioneers have died (and with them many of their ideas), valuable reports and research has been lost, churches have changed, and books are out of print. Where relevant and contemporarily important, some of that material is included here to give the reader a sense of depth and a fuller perspective.

Change, however, remains the only constant in life. As such, this book brings urban ministry into the now. It examines urban ministry in the context of the globalization and regentrification that currently dominate the contemporary American city, in addition to presenting the latest models of community development.

As in the case of the earlier volume, I have attempted to make the book applicable—conceptually and practically—to pastors who lack background in urban sociology, to seminarians, to parachurch workers, and to other "first-entry" people. Though much of the material may be familiar to urban veterans and particularly to African-American church people who have a rich heritage of effective urban ministry, I trust that some of the concepts, models, and strategies will be helpful to that audience as well. Moreover, I have been careful to present the materials in such a way that they will be useful regardless of the reader's position on any liberal-conservative theological continuum.

In addition to the research, this book contains a number of references to my own experiences and observations. I have worked and worshiped in major cities throughout my adult life and have been a scholar and participant in urban ministry for several decades. As such, I have formed some opinions as to the central issues facing the urban church and pastor of today.

One term that needs to be defined is *urban ministry*. This term encompasses the urban church and ministry. Although the urban church can be defined in a variety of ways, a good working definition is "a community, usually organized formally, of God's people in the city." Ministry is carried on both *within* to the members and *without* to the world. Ministry has six facets:

1. Worship—adoration of God

2. Evangelism—reaching those on the outside with the gospel

3. Discipleship—developing mature followers of Christ

4. Fellowship—care and intimacy among the members

5. Stewardship—responsible earthly citizenship aimed at advancing justice and improving the quality of life in the neighborhood, city, and world

6. Service—addressing immediate physical, social, and spiritual needs of those within and without in a non-paternalistic parallel fashion.

These six facets of ministry are stressed in different proportions in various churches. Traditional churches have tended to envelop all six ministries. Growing churches, however, tend to focus primarily on one or two of the facets, thus developing a distinctive identity. These churches can often be divided into three categories: *Experiential* churches highlight worship and evangelism through creative and conventional approaches. *Relational* churches emphasize discipleship and fellowship. *Task* churches focus on stewardship and service.

Urban ministry is an exceedingly broad topic. Although this book deals occasionally with experiential and relational categories as well as ministries of worship, evangelism, discipleship, and fellowship, its chief focus is on the task of the church and its ministries of stewardship and service. In addition, it emphasizes life and ministry among the poor of the inner city, where the problems are the most severe and the challenge to ministry is the greatest. However, with the explosive increase in the number of churches in changing neighborhoods and urban processes permeating all of society, I trust the material discussed in this book will be applicable to ministry in a variety of contexts.

ACKNOWLEDGMENTS

I want to thank Dr. Clinton E. Stockwell, Executive Director of the Chicago Semester. Clinton is a friend whose knowledge of cities and urban ministry is unsurpassed. This book could not have been done without his help

URBAN MINISTRY: BIBLICAL MANDATE 1

It has been said that Christianity has failed to make an impact in three major areas: the Hindu culture, the Islamic society, and the major cities. Our concern here is the city: the gospel must penetrate the city if it is really to penetrate all of society, for the city is the soul of the society. Cities determine the destiny of nations. To remove the cities is to excise the central nervous system of the global society. There is, then, a very practical mandate to serve the city.

THE CITY—WAVE OF THE FUTURE

Urbanization is an irreversible trend. At the beginning of the twentieth century, about 8 percent of the world's population lived in cities. By the early 1980s half of the world's population resided in urban areas. And the beat goes on. Demographers project that almost all of the world's population growth over the next thirty years will be in urban areas. By 2004 nine cities in the United States had populations in excess of a million people. The nation's top ten cities numbered nearly 25 million. In fact, over 75 percent of the U.S. population lives in urban areas (population 2,500 minimum). The United States is now a nation of strip cities and urban sprawl, with metropolitan areas in the East running almost uninterrupted from Boston to New York, on through Philadelphia

1

and Baltimore, and into Washington, D.C. (More than 30 million people live in the New York-Philadelphia corridor alone.) The urban expanse is apparent from Chicago to Milwaukee in the Midwest and in the West from Sacramento to San Francisco, on down through Los Angeles, and on to San Diego close to the Mexican border.[1]

The city is not, however, just a place with certain structures and forms; it is a set of processes that flow out through suburbia and into rural communities. Farmers, who once viewed themselves as self-sufficient, are caught up in the process of urbanization. For example, when the federal government establishes sanctions against the sale of farm products to other countries, the backing up of the futures markets is felt in the harvest fields. In addition, an ever-greater proportion of the farmers' crops feed city dwellers. People in small towns also feel the effect of urbanization as major food chains replace corner grocery stores. Moreover, what once were exclusively urban problems—such as drug abuse, housing shortages, unmarried cohabitation, unemployment, lack of care for the elderly, and poverty—are now felt in every locale, urban or rural.

To understand the city is to understand the future. A world-class city is a microcosm of the world. A city dweller has the opportunity to become truly international and cross-cultural. Long ago, Lewis Mumford put aside the old separation of urban from rural, arguing that the entire planet was becoming an inter-related village. He said that beyond place, the city is an organ for developing and expressing the new human personality—the "world person."[2] Today we speak of globalization and first-tier global cities. These reflect the centrality of the city in what is now a multinational and international economic and political system.

Major cities do indeed mirror the world's population and are becoming ever-greater manifestations of a global way of life. Take Chicago, for example. The Windy City has seventy-seven definable neighborhoods located within just 224 square miles making it one of the last truly traditional U.S. cities. Founded in

1837 with only 4 thousand citizens, by 1850 the "foreign" population exceeded the native-born population. At the turn of the new millennium, Chicago was accommodating more than 30 thousand immigrants annually (with Los Angeles taking in twice that number and New York over 80 thousand).[3] Chicago reflects the world's population among its 2.8 million residents.[4] It is roughly a third Caucasian and a third African American, with nearly 750 thousand legal residents of Hispanic ancestry. In addition, there are 150 thousand others, consisting largely of various Asian and Middle Eastern populations. Chicago once had more Native American living in its Uptown community than anywhere else in the country, with the possible exception of some reservations. Although that number has dropped, it still has a Native American presence. Moreover, the metropolitan area (city and suburbs) has more than 8 million residents, many of Irish, Polish, Italian, and other Caucasian descent.

Amid the glamour and globalization of the city—worldwide—is also suffering. Poverty is increasingly concentrated in the city. Population experts project that by 2025 the world's urban population could reach 5 billion, with two-thirds of that number in poor countries. In fact, the projection is that a quarter of the world's poor will live in depressed urban areas. In 1998, according to the World Bank, 1.2 billion people (about 25 percent of the developing world's population) consumed less than a dollar a day per capita. As for the United States, in 2004 nearly 80 percent of its poor were urbanized. They are in spiritual need, for their inner lives—their souls—are dying. But they also have social, physical, and political needs. People in these cities, especially the inner cities, are experiencing crowded conditions, powerlessness, and ill health. They need whole-person care. Hence, the church in the city faces an awesome challenge. This challenge—to extend service to the social as well as the spiritual realm—is a most appropriate one, for it is biblical.

Yet urban ministry has faced controversy. For decades Christians, especially evangelicals, have battled over the issue of evangelism versus social concern. These two ministries have often been viewed as opposed to one another. Those who espoused evangelism felt that to care for temporal needs was to be concerned with the part of the person that would die anyway. What was needed was concern for the eternal soul. Those who espoused social concern argued that soul-winning may be of value, but in a world in which people are not eating properly, are housed in substandard conditions, are jobless, and do not receive adequate health care, presenting Christ remains an abstract answer to a more immediate need. David Moberg states that when the church remains silent on difficult social issues, "it renounces its claim that it ministers to 'the whole man.'" And yet, as he unconditionally warned, social services should not be used as "bait" to win souls.[5] And so the debate has continued. Many conservatives see social activists as apostate, while those who have social concerns are tempted to become non-spiritual in their efforts.

This is a sad situation for all involved. As John Perkins said so prophetically, neither the liberal nor the evangelical church has functioned as a complete church. Much of their energy has been drawn away in criticizing each other, and the result has been less-than-effective spiritual ministries.[6] In fact, resistance to social concern among some Christians has had a large part in the tendency of churches to abandon the city. Roger Greenway laments that "by their locations, their architecture, their liturgy, their sermons, and their entire program, urban Protestant churches have conveyed the message to the masses that these churches are not for them."[7]

Humans were created to be whole persons, with physical, mental, relational, and spiritual dimensions. Deprivation in any of these dimensions has a deadening effect on the others, since all parts are interrelated and interactive. Suffering physically makes it difficult to function well psychologically and interactively. Severe emotional disabilities are sometimes translated into physical disabilities. Loneliness is detrimental to psychological and physical health. A spiritually sterile life is often revealed in depression, isolation, and a low energy level. Just as theologically we cannot divide people into component parts, so also in ministry we must not dissect but rather serve whole persons. The soul without the body is a ghost; the body without the soul is a corpse.

BIBLICAL MANDATE

The biblical mandate for urban ministry can be seen in two topics. First is the Scripture's appeal to the city itself—with all its institutions—by the Old Testament prophets and New Testament apostles.

Second, and far more weighty and complex, is God's concern for justice for the poor and oppressed. His concern that the powerless members of society be treated fairly and with compassion is seen in numerous passages in both testaments and in the practices of the Israelite culture and the early church. Finally, and most powerfully, God's concern has been demonstrated fully in Jesus Christ.

The Concept of the City in Scripture

The city with all its institutions is treated as a single entity in many scriptural passages. Urban expert Raymond Bakke claims to have found 119 cities mentioned in Scripture. In the Old Testament the prophets were involved not only in evangelization but also in urban planning. Jonah called Nineveh—as a city, including its king—to repentance. Babylon, the symbol of collective evil, was such a successful target of evangelism that its lifestyle and even its government were affected.[8] Joseph and Daniel did key urban planning while occupying powerful political positions. Jeremiah modeled sainthood in an alien city. Nehemiah was the architect of true urban renewal in Jerusalem.

In the New Testament the city becomes more central still. Jesus visited Jerusalem, the major city of the time, perhaps five times. He also spent time in Nazareth, Bethany, Capernaum, and other cities. "I must preach the Good News of the Kingdom of

God in other places, too," he says in Luke 4:43. "Jesus was clear about his calling and his vocation as one anointed to proclaim the gospel to the poor in the cities," states urban expert Clinton Stockwell.[9] Hope for the cities, though primarily spiritual, also entailed a new social order—one that included women, the poor, the oppressed, the outcast, the diseased, those unwelcome in the religious and political society of Christ's day. Only the pure and unblemished could even enter the temple, and the Romans, who controlled the Jewish colony, were no less elitist in their secular culture.

In the New Testament the early church made evangelism in the city one of its highest priorities. Paul's epistles as well as the book of Acts tell the story of how the faith and the church grew in the cities of the ancient world. Their example was Christ who grieved over Jerusalem. Barnabas developed a missionary church in Antioch, an ethnically segregated city of 600 thousand, and the apostle Paul proved to be an urban strategist as he did his evangelism.[10] He would begin by visiting the temple and presenting the gospel to his fellow Jews. He also fearlessly engaged diversity, encountering any and all Gentiles who might give him a hearing. He went to Athens, the intellectual capital of his day, and Corinth, a seaport city with a bawdy, free-wheeling culture typical of Greenwich Village or Miami's South Beach. In fact, to live a sensual life in Paul's day was to "live like a Corinthian." As for ancient Rome, where Paul also worked tirelessly even as a prisoner, the city was characterized by apartment-living with units almost as densely situated as in present-day New York City. The majority of Rome's 1.6 million citizens lived in five- and six-story apartment buildings, and the early church evangelized the area effectively.[11]

As zealous as Paul was to announce the resurrection of the Christ, he burned through myriad social barriers along the way.[12] "Paul challenged authorities, bridged nation-states, linked and unified ethnic groups, mollified the class structure by welcoming slaves and free, men and women, Jews and national groups into a new community."[13] Shirley Jackson Case of the University of Chicago noted that Christianity triumphed in part "because it reached the cities, included a diversity of people, and met the spiritual and material needs of the poor and marginal of the Greco-Roman society."[14]

Material needs were clearly important. In Acts 11 Luke tells of a prophet named Agabus who, by direction of the Holy Spirit, predicted a severe famine over the Roman world. "The believers in Antioch decided to send relief to the brothers and sisters in Judea, everyone giving as much as they could. This they did, entrusting their gifts to Barnabas and [Paul] to take to the elders of the church in Jerusalem" (11:29–30).

According to the famous Jewish historian Josephus, food shortages were common in the middle of the first century, something to which Paul refers frequently in his letters.[15] Once, after meeting with the church leaders in Jerusalem, he writes, "The only thing they suggested was that we remember to help the poor, and I have certainly been eager to do that" (Gal. 2:10). At the conclusion of Romans, Paul states, "Before I come, I must go down to Jerusalem to take a gift to the Christians there. For you see, the believers in Greece have eagerly taken up an offering for the Christians in Jerusalem, who are going through such hard times. They were very glad to do this because they feel they owe a real debt to them. Since the Gentiles received the wonderful spiritual blessings of the Good News from the Jewish Christians, they feel the least they can do in return is help them financially" (15:25–27). Paul wanted to build a bridge to unite these two ancestral groups in an effort to construct a worldwide church, one that met temporal as well as spiritual needs.[16]

In 2 Corinthians 8:1–9 Paul lauds the Macedonian believers for their generosity despite severe poverty. Out of joy they gave, despite "deep poverty," beyond what they were seemingly capable. He then urges the Corinthians to excel in the "gracious privilege of sharing." "You know how full of love and kindness our Lord Jesus Christ was," he writes, that "though he was very rich, yet for your sakes he became poor, so that by his poverty he could make you rich."

The prophets and apostles involved themselves in the life of the city and its institutions without compromising their faith or values. They are examples of urban involvement rather than exodus.

Concern for the Poor and Oppressed

The theme of justice for the poor and oppressed is of particular import in Scripture. Over four hundred verses indicate God's concern for the poor, and over eighty verses underscore divine concern for justice.

> Oh, the joys of those who are kind to the poor. The LORD rescues them in times of trouble. (Ps. 41:1)

> Those who oppress the poor insult their Maker, but those who help the poor honor him. (Prov. 14:31)

> Those who shut their ears to the cries of the poor will be ignored in their own time of need. (Prov. 21:13)

> Whoever gives to the poor will lack nothing. But a curse will come upon those who close their eyes to poverty. (Prov. 28:27)

> The godly know the rights of the poor; the wicked don't care to know. (Prov. 29:7)

> And if you do good only to those who do good to you, is that so wonderful? Even sinners do that much! And if you lend money only to those who can repay you, what good is that? Even sinners will lend to their own kind for a full return. "Love your enemies! Do good to them! Lend to them! And don't be concerned that they might not repay. Then your reward from heaven will be very great, and you will truly be acting as children of the Most High, for he is kind to the unthankful and to those who are wicked. You must be compassionate, just as your Father is compassionate. (Luke 6:33–36)

If anyone has enough money to live well and sees a
brother or sister in need and refuses to help—how can
God's love be in that person? Dear children, let us stop
just saying we love each other; let us really show it by our
actions. (1 John 3:17–18)

The gospel challenges the worship of wealth in every form in
a society in which the poor live proximal to the rich. "If the rich
young ruler," notes Stockwell, "was challenged to sell his possessions and give to the poor, it is a challenge also to create social
arrangements so that, even if there are poor people, there cannot
be poverty." While Christ stated that the poor will be with us
always, his example indicated that there must be provisions made
to care for them. The Deuteronomy 15 passage to which Jesus was
referring mandates the Jewish society to provide for the poor.[17] As
longtime advocate of the poor, Ronald Sider loves to say, "God is
on the side of the poor."[18]

Decades ago, in the spirit of this concern for the poor, Senator
Mark Hatfield of Oregon introduced a resolution urging the
Congress of the United States to assert that every person has a
right to a nutritionally adequate food supply. The basis for this
resolution was that God, who possesses the earth and its fullness,
regularly proclaims in Scripture the high value he places on human life.[19]

"Justice is a part of the gospel," writes Stockwell.[20] Many
evangelicals make an artificial separation between proclaiming
the gospel and doing justice. The Bible links the spreading of the
spiritual gospel with doing justice and making peace. "The LORD
has already told you what is good," writes the prophet Micah,
"and this is what he requires: to do what is right, to love mercy,
and to walk humbly with your God" (Micah 6:8). Jesus speaks not
of the poor in spirit but the *poor*—women, children, orphans, and
those on society's outside owing to prejudice, ethnic origin, or
lifestyle (Luke 4:18).

Walter Brueggemann rightly maintains that what distinguished
Jesus from the other prophets of his time was his "alternative con-

9

sciousness," one that aligned him with the poor and the oppressed as opposed to the rich and powerful.[21] Furthermore, scholars have suggested that the Greek word *euangelion* indicates the connection of verbal declaration with *praxis* or action. In Genesis the statements of God in creation are inextricably linked to action—a speaking into being.[22] Indeed, the Incarnation is the ultimate connection of the Word and action (in the flesh). We are to give bread, rather than the stone of the empty word (Matt. 7:9).

Justice for the oppressed is a major scriptural issue, described in terms of God's particular concern for the powerless.

For the LORD loves justice, and he will never abandon the godly. (Ps. 37:28)

Happy are those who deal justly with others and always do what is right. (Ps. 106:3)

Evil people don't understand justice, but those who follow the LORD understand completely. (Prov. 28:5)

Speak up for those who cannot speak for themselves; ensure justice for those who are perishing. Yes, speak up for the poor and helpless, and see that they get justice. (Prov. 31:8–9)

Learn to do good. Seek justice. Help the oppressed. Defend the orphan. Fight for the rights of widows (Isa. 1:17).

"He made sure that justice and help were given to the poor and needy, and everything went well for him. Isn't that what it means to know me?" asks the LORD. (Jer. 22:16)

The LORD has already told you what is good, and this is what he requires: to do what is right, to love mercy, and to walk humbly with your God. (Mic. 6:8)

"When you put on a luncheon or a dinner," [Jesus] said, "don't invite your friends, brothers, relatives, and rich neighbors. For they will repay you by inviting you back. Instead, invite the poor, the crippled, the lame, and the blind. Then at the resurrection of the godly, God will reward you for inviting those who could not repay you." (Luke 14:12–14)

Both in the law of Moses and later through the prophets, God warned his people that judgment would result from their refusal to show justice to the poor, the oppressed, and the powerless.[23]

> You must not oppress a stranger in any way; remember, you yourselves were foreigners in the land of Egypt. You must not exploit widows or orphans; if you do so in any way, and they cry to me for my help, I will surely give it. And my anger shall flame out against you, and I will kill you with enemy armies, so that your wives will be widows and your children fatherless. (Exod. 22:21–24)

Isaiah castigated the city of Jerusalem for its corruption:

> See how Jerusalem, once so faithful, has become a prostitute. Once the home of justice and righteousness, she is now filled with murderers. Once like pure silver, you have become like worthless slag. Once so pure, you are now like watered-down wine. Your leaders are rebels, the companions of thieves. All of them take bribes and refuse to defend the orphans and the widows. (Isa. 1:21–23)

And he foretold God's judgment on Judah:

> Destruction is certain for the unjust judges, for those who issue unfair laws. They deprive the poor, the widows, and the orphans of justice. Yes, they rob widows and fatherless children! What will you do when I send desolation upon you from a distant land? To whom will you turn for help? Where will your treasures be safe? (Isa. 10:1–3)

Jeremiah renders a similar message to the denizens of Jerusalem:

> "Like a cage filled with birds, their homes are filled with evil plots. And the result? Now they are great and rich. They are well fed and well groomed, and there is no limit

to their wicked deeds. They refuse justice to orphans and deny the rights of the poor. Should I not punish them for this?" asks the LORD. "Should I not avenge myself against a nation such as this?" (Jer. 5:27–29).

These were more than individual sins. They were systemic, institutional evils. The poor were to be protected by those in authority. When they were not, the prophets became their advocates. Psalm 82 offers a call to the nations. It is subtitled "Justice as the Order of the Universe" in the *HarperCollins Study Bible*. "How long will you judges hand down unjust decisions? How long will you shower special favors on the wicked?" the psalmist asks. "Give fair judgment to the poor and the orphan; uphold the rights of the oppressed and the destitute. Rescue the poor and helpless; deliver them from the grasp of evil people" (Ps. 82: 2–4).

Jeremiah warned the people that their only hope for escape was to change their ways: "I will be merciful only if you stop your wicked thoughts and deeds and are fair to others; and if you stop exploiting foreigners, orphans, and widows; and if you stop your murdering; and if you stop worshiping idols as you now do to your own harm" (Jer. 7:5–6).

Through Amos, God inveighed against not only the oppression of the poor (Amos 2:6–7) but also the exploitation of the dispossessed by the rich (6:1–7), calling rich women "fat cows" (4:1). He noted the injustice in the court system as well (5:10–15), and God made his anger known about this evil (5:21–24).

With some irony the writer of Ecclesiastes notes that a bureaucracy for which no one is willing to take responsibility perpetuates the evil of oppression.

If you see a poor person being oppressed by the powerful and justice being miscarried throughout the land, don't be surprised! For every official is under orders from higher up, and matters of justice only get lost in red tape and bureaucracy. (Eccl. 5:8)

In the New Testament James cautions the powerful about the outcome of their exploitation:

> Your gold and silver have become worthless. The very wealth you were counting on will eat away your flesh in hell. This treasure you have accumulated will stand as evidence against you on the day of judgment. For listen! Hear the cries of the field workers whom you have cheated of their pay. The wages you held back cry out against you. The cries of the reapers have reached the ears of the Lord Almighty. You have spent your years on earth in luxury, satisfying your every whim. Now your hearts are nice and fat, ready for the slaughter. You have condemned and killed good people who had no power to defend themselves against you. (James 5:3–6)

Standing idly by is not acceptable. There is no evidence that the rich man (Dives) oppressed Lazarus the beggar—he just ignored him (Luke 16). Clark Pinnock, in observing the eternal destiny of Dives, feels the story "ought to explode in our hands when we read it sitting at our well-covered tables while the third world stands outside."[24] Harvie Conn says that injustice is "apostasy; the rejection of the poor, the rejection of God."[25]

So obvious is God's concern for justice that the Israelite culture and the early church were to be characterized by egalitarianism and human rights. There was to be no special regard for status groups and class distinctions.

In the Old Testament no elite class was to control the real estate, nor was there to be a system of riches for a few with only crumbs for the masses. Legal statutes were designed to protect criminals from excessively cruel and inhuman treatment and to protect minorities, widows, orphans, and slaves. Industry was to be furthered and slothfulness condemned. Slavery was restricted so that savage and dehumanizing forms of furthering economic ends were minimized.[26]

The principle of stewardship in the protection of the poor and disadvantaged was so pervasive that it was unlawful to charge the poor interest on loans (Ex. 22:25; Deut. 23:20). Every seven years all debts were forgiven (Deut. 15:1–6), and the fields were left fallow so the poor could go out and gather the increase (Ex. 23: 11; Lev. 25:6). Moreover, the poor were allowed to glean fields after a harvest and eat anything in the field the harvester was unable to take with him. Every fiftieth year was the Year of Jubilee when all land was returned to its original owner. This principle underscored the point that God's people are stewards of all—even land—but God is the owner (Lev. 25).

The principle of service was found in mandatory almsgiving. Almsgiving was classified as a form of justice and 10 percent was expected to be given to the poor every third year (Deut. 14:28).

There is evidence that the moral law of Moses was not abrogated in the New Testament (Matt. 5:17–20; Rom. 8:4). The disciples shared a common fund (John 12:6) and received resources from the women who followed Christ (Luke 8:3). The early church shared everything (Acts 2:43–47; 5:1–11; 6:1–7), and Paul regularly emphasized caring for the poor (Rom. 15:22–28; Gal. 2:10); in fact, he was arrested while sharing financial aid with the saints in Jerusalem (Acts 24:17).

The poor are rarely if ever blamed for their poverty in Scripture. To treat them respectfully, to accommodate their needs, to create social structures that maintain and preserve their lives and safety are not matters of charity but matters of justice.

The most powerful example of God's concern for justice is found in the ministry of Jesus Christ. Christ spent large amounts of time feeding the hungry, healing the sick, and delivering the demon-possessed. He defined his own mission by saying,

> The Spirit of the Lord is upon me; he has appointed me to preach Good News to the poor; he has sent me to heal the brokenhearted and to announce that captives shall be released and the blind shall see, that the downtrodden

shall be freed from their oppressors, and that God is ready
to give blessings to all who come to him. (Luke 4:18–19)

In these words he is referring to Isaiah's prophecy and the
social tyranny of the Old Testament days.

Christ's humble social status indicates God's understanding of
and deep concern for people of every stratum. According to Sider,
Christ's parents were very poor, and Christ was a refugee and then
an immigrant entering Galilean society (Matt. 2:19–23). He was not
paid for his public ministry and had no home of his own (Matt. 8:
20). He also placed his disciples in poverty (Luke 9:20; 10:4).[27]

Jesus referred to his identification with the have-nots in
answering the messengers of John the Baptist when they asked
whether he was the Christ (Matt. 11:2–6). Paul emphasized this
identification when he wrote, "Though he was very rich, yet for
your sakes he became poor" (2 Cor. 8:9). John said, "We know
what real love is because Christ gave up his life for us. And so
we also ought to give up our lives for our Christian brothers and
sisters" (1 John 3:16).

Any comprehension of the biblical command for love as
expressed in Mark 12:28–31 and John 13:34–35 convinces us that
Christians must be actively involved in their neighbors' lives. To
imitate Christ necessarily involves concern for all the aspects of
the lives of others (Eph. 5:1–2). In fact, acts of compassion done
to others are viewed by Christ as acts of worship to him. And neglect of the needy and oppressed is regarded as abandoning Christ
(Matt. 25:31–46). If the incarnation of Christ is taken seriously,
then the church must see itself as continuing the incarnation. The
Christian church must act as Christ's hands, feet, and eyes in the
world. It must both preach a message and perform a ministry—just
as Christ did.

Spiritual and Social Reconciliation

Christianity is relevant when its love ethic is infused into all
spheres of human existence. When people enter into a relationship with Christ, they are to be godlike in all their relationships.

This makes a Christian an evangelist, reconciler or peacemaker, prophet, reformer, and agent of relief and ministry. The Christian is called to a vertical relationship with God and a horizontal relationship with fellow human beings. The calling to horizontal and vertical relationships is inseparable. These relationships are twin dimensions of the Christian experience. This is evident in the prophets (Isa. 1:12–17; Amos 5:21–24; Micah 6:6–8), in Christ himself (Matt. 25:31–46; Luke 10:25–37), in Paul (Rom. 13:8–10; 1 Cor. 13:4–7; Gal. 5:22–23), in James (James 2:8, 14–17), and in John (1 John 1:3–4, 7; 3:14–18; 4:20–21).[28]

A key mandate in Scripture, then, is spiritual and social reconciliation: bringing alienated people back into harmony vertically with God and horizontally with others. Because human beings are cast in the image of the divine, it is only natural that they be completed by a relationship with God. Even if churches were successful in elevating the standard of living of every one of their people to a middle-income status, there would remain a gnawing hunger for a sense of completeness. The evangelical mandate is the spiritual glue that holds the church together. It is the stuff of commitment and dedication to discipleship, of living out the Christian life in fellowship and likemindedness.[29]

Social concern—stewardship and service—complements evangelism in that it helps people understand the love of God. In addition, social ministries remove temporal barriers such as hunger and emotional problems. Quests for justice and peace overturn oppressive forces that destroy people's lives and reduce their ability to respond to the person of Christ. But again, most importantly, social concern exemplifies the caring love of God.

If the church is to take its mandate seriously, it will have to transcend social barriers—racial, economic, linguistic, cultural, sexual, and age—in order to meet the challenge. To do this reconciling, the church must go to people where they are. Howard Rice stresses this by saying that if we really believe God dwells with people, then we have to go to the cities where most of them are.[30] For the church in the city, this means locating in and among the poor. All too often, however, middle-class Christians move out as the poor move into a community. Then, several years later, those same Christians go back to try to evangelize the present inhabitants. It is no wonder that the poor have little respect when those doing missionary work did not want to live with them in the first place.[31] When the church does demonstrate genuine social commitment, however, its spiritual message gains credibility.

In summary, the scriptural mandate is both spiritual and social reconciliation. In fact, evangelism undergirds social concern. Social improvement alone leaves a person incomplete without knowing Christ. Moreover, people who are spiritually transformed are able to make commitments toward transforming their society. A Christian commitment can provide the spiritual power and energy necessary to endure in advancing social justice. And a Christian commitment encourages the believer to live like Christ, who modeled social concern and care in his daily life and ministry.[32]

IMPLICATIONS FOR MINISTRY

Once convinced of the divine mandate favoring social justice, it is important to reflect soberly on how that social concern should be made manifest and how to work out a set of principles that should guide these stewardship and service ministries.

Types of Social Concern

Social concern is often of three general kinds. One is *social reconciliation,* or peacemaking. Both a stewardship and service ministry, reconciliation focuses on healing attempts to reach across the barriers of economics, race, and community to love and care for people regardless of social category. It means, especially, identifying with the poor and oppressed. It may involve being a lightning rod for many of their frustrations and angers as the church seeks to alleviate alienation and separation among peoples.

The church is then challenged to break out of its own tight fellowship to embrace the poor and dispossessed who are just outside the door, to reach out to heal the individual and social hurts in their community. Jacques Ellul states that the Christian must listen and identify with the poor. Nicholas Wolterstorff, in referring to Ellul, emphasizes the importance of Christians siding with the cause of the oppressed. It is only if Christians make the cause of the poor and oppressed their cause that they can feel they are loving their neighbor and seeking a condition of genuine peace.[33]

A major step for the church is to embrace diversity. The once-visible walls of racial and ethnic segregation continue to crumble throughout urban and suburban areas of the United States. Churches need self-consciously to aim at being multicultural in composition. If a church is ethnically homogeneous the question arises: Is this merely a de facto form of segregation, or is the church—however unintentionally—inhospitable to the stranger?

This is not a call for head counts and quotas. It is a call for self-examination. Is our God too white? Too married? Too young? Too middle class? Or too rich?

The second kind of social concern is *social relief.* This service ministry includes such deeds of mercy as giving the cup of cold water. It can take the form of working with senior citizens, tutoring neighborhood youth, providing legal aid or psychological counseling, and so forth. Churches can provide their members with spiritual gifts inventories to help them discover a gift that can be used in a service area. As important as relieving suffering is—something Christ spent much of his time doing—there is a need to address causes as well. There is plenty of need for relief. Victims of homelessness, alcoholism and other addictions, emotional and mental disorders, sexual abuse, domestic violence, joblessness, illiteracy, and other maladies are not in short supply. Their needs stare at, challenge, and disturb those of us who live more similarly to Dives than Lazarus.

But the call goes deeper, because relief has its limits. It cannot address the root causes of the victimization we witness. In addition, it places the recipients in a subordinate—client or patient—status, one that does not empower those on the receiving end, but rather creates dependencies. As such, relief ministries, as loving and Christlike as they may be, often reinforce the very power differentials that foster the conditions out of which dependency comes. According to the famous reformed theologian Abraham Kuyper, relief ministry falls short of genuine Christian love. If we feed the poor from the crumbs that fall from our affluent tables, then "all such charity is more like an insult that beats in the bosom of the poor man (or woman)."[34] As such, Kuyper calls for more than charity. He advocates a reworking of the social order.

This brings us to the third kind of social concern: *social reform*. Relief deals with the symptoms of society's malignancies. Reform addresses the basic unjust conditions and systems that oppress and dehumanize people. Its emphasis is on institutions. Reform is necessary if social progress is to be made, and, even more importantly, if Christ is to be seen as Lord over social and institutional life and activity as well as over individual lives. Reform also moves beyond a provider-client (or recipient) relationship to one of building an inclusive community. It challenges unjust institutions and empowers the powerless. According to Lowell Livezey of the University of Illinois at Chicago, reform ministry moves beyond the use of human capital (the knowledge and skills of the people in the community that they will use for their own betterment) to building community and enhancing social capital (the shared knowledge, beliefs, and commitments that are the glue of the community at large).[35]

In fact, the Bible's version of relief was larger in scope than what we see today. First, it was aimed at building an inclusive community. The poor were not to be marginal citizens in the community, but integral parts of the larger unit. Moreover, the poor were to be welcomed as equals rather than as deficient organisms in the social order. Finally, giving to the poor was an expectation, not an act of compassion. It was part of the very sense of citizenship and the society's definition of justice. In the New Testament church, the early believers eschewed wealth and held everything in common, making certain no one was in need (Acts 2:44–45). Referring to Acts 4:34, Stockwell notes that the church made certain "there was not a needy person among them."[36]

Urban ministry, then, to be complete must reach reform. Reform engages what the famous sociologist C. Wright Mills called the sociological imagination. "Perhaps the most fruitful distinction with which the sociological imagination works is between 'the personal troubles of the milieu' and 'the public issues of social structure.' This distinction is an essential tool of the sociological imagination and a feature of all classic work in social science."[37] In brief, the sociological imagination moves us beyond the visible symptoms standing before us in human flesh to the causes of social victimization.

One type of reform ministry is called *advocacy*. Advocacy occurs when those with resources and commitment to justice attempt to change social systems, laws, and policies that create oppression. Many church-based organizations engage in advocacy. In Chicago alone there is the Interfaith Council for the Homeless, Protestants for the Common Good, the Chicago Religious Task Force on Central America, the Justice Coalition of Greater Chicago, the Community Renewal Society, the Metropolitan Alliance of Congregations, and the United Power for Action and Justice, among others. These organizations have full-time staff that work on housing, finance reform, welfare reform, jobs, and more. Though these organizations are theologically diverse, urban pastors can gain up-to-date information and direction from organizations like these in dealing with any problem afflicting their own church communities.

Another type of reform involves *community organization*. There was not a better community organizer than Nehemiah, as recorded in the books of Ezra and Nehemiah. When the exiles returned from Babylon, rebuilding a sense of community was a daunting challenge. The problem was intensified by the authorities, who had levied a heavy tax on the people: "'We have mortgaged our fields, vineyards, and homes to get food during the famine.' And others said, 'We have already borrowed to the limit on our fields and vineyards to pay our taxes. We belong to the same family, and our children are just like theirs. Yet we must sell our children into slavery just to get enough money to live. We have already sold some of our daughters, and we are helpless to do anything about it, for our fields and vineyards are already mortgaged to others'" (Neh. 5:3–5).[38]

Nehemiah was angry. He took the complaints of the people to those in power and sought redress. He urged a repeal of the tax law and a removal of the debts incurred by those unable to meet the tax burden. Nehemiah also organized the community, rebuilt the walls of the city, restored the temple, and developed a political economy that insured that the needs of the people would be provided by the common treasury. He did this as an act of worship. "The people and the Levites must bring these offerings of grain, new wine, and olive oil to the Temple and place them in the sacred containers near the ministering priests, the gatekeepers, and the singers. So we promise together not to neglect the Temple of our God" (Neh. 10:39).

Kuyper felt strongly about the importance of reform. He believed that charity that did not go beyond the symptoms of social problems was not truly Christian love.[39] Moreover, the biblical model is not the social-service model of today. Charity was extended to the poor as a way of inviting them to be equals at the fellowship table, and such activity was expected as a way of insuring that justice was being dispensed. In other words, giving to the poor is to be done without strings because it is right in its own sake. Rev. James Harper of Chicago's Center for Street People told author Clinton Stockwell that he dispensed food, shelter, and clothing to the homeless for just two reasons: to improve the quality of their lives for that day and to extend the length of their lives only slightly.[40]

Using a health model, the church has to be a healing force among its own members and for the community at large. Much of this is of a relief nature, in which individuals are ministered to by the church with both practical assistance and spiritual hope. Where possible, it needs also to be engaged in both a surgical and preventive-health role, that of organizing the community in quest of justice. It is surgical in that this often means confronting and removing toxic forces. It is preventive in its vigilance and desire to prevent oppressive activities from victimizing the community.[41]

Institutions and systems are vitally important. The apostle Paul writes of the age being dominated by principalities and powers that oppose Christian ideals. In our time, examples include a society that tolerates poverty and denigrates those who are poor; a two-track justice system that provides one route for the rich and powerful and another for the poor and indigent; and a nation that is, on one hand, experiencing an unparalleled explosion of knowledge and, on the other hand, allowing millions of inner-city youth to drown in a Dark Ages-like abyss of illiteracy.

God's directive through Jeremiah was that the Israelites work for the welfare of the alien city Babylon, because their own welfare as exiles was tied to that of the city (Jer. 29:7). This reminds us that we need to do this reconciling, relieving, and reforming in the city. God's grace may come in the form of food for the hungry, justice for the oppressed, and love for the rejected. Such a perspective moved an elderly Jesuit priest in India to say, "I bring God to the people in the form in which God is absent. Here, it is water."[42]

Implementing Social Ministries

The work of the individual urban church is facilitated when there is a commitment to urban ministry on the part of a larger body. Over the years there have been many examples of church alliances (often denominational structures) that coordinate social ministries as well as encourage one another through a larger fellowship. Dennis Shoemaker suggested that denominations entering urban ministry focus their resources on no more than three critical urban churches. Shoemaker pointed out several ingredients for maximum future effectiveness. First, careful evaluation should be made, followed by careful statistical research. Then the results should be practically applied to urban strategies. Finally, a plan that will garner the support of both urban and suburban churches should be developed. Measurement of success should be determined on the basis of meeting people's needs rather than increasing numbers.[43]

The beginning for any urban church is a commitment to turf. The Central Presbyterian Church in Atlanta began its involvement with the community in 1858 and over the decades opened its doors to everyone—from mourners at the funeral of Martin Luther King, Jr. to protesting farmers. The key is that Central decided to be central to the city.

Simply staying in the community physically is not enough. To ignore a community's needs for ministry is tantamount to moving. Turf commitment must generate turf awareness. This means getting to know the members of the community, the agencies located there, and those who have power in it. Realistic assessment is imperative. Once such knowledge is obtained, the church needs to determine where it can align with other institutions to bring about change and where it may have to act independently. In either case, the prior issue of accurate diagnosis, based on possession of the facts of the turf, cannot be overestimated.[44] Churches can use a census tract map and other census data to assess the demographic nature of its community. Often community organizations and associations will be happy to provide up-to-date information on a neighborhood.

Resources for beginning urban ministry are available. Publications running back to the late 1970s, denominational publications, current community-development models, and much Internet information are available. One of the best clearinghouses for urban-ministry materials is SCUPE (Seminary Consortium for Urban Pastoral Education) in Chicago.

CONCLUSION

Tragically, the unchecked materialism of our age engulfs the church as well as the larger society. Biblical injunctions against materialism seem to go largely unheeded. Yet, Ezekiel 16:49 declares that the major sin of Sodom was its insensitivity to the poor and deprived within that decadent city. A reading of Matthew 18–20 is both unsettling and illuminating in its presentation of what God's standards are in contrast to those of the prevailing culture.

Although the business of breaking away from the status quo is a thorny one, it must be confronted. As John Perkins advocates, the church must model what society should be rather than occasionally critiquing what it is.

In a society that affirms the separation of church and state, it is perhaps most prudent if the church attempts to accomplish reform by regularly reminding the institutions of power of their obligation to dispense justice. There must be regularized vigilance here, such that the church knows how to encourage those political forces that affirm justice and rightness and also how to oppose those that seek only manipulation. This does not mean being a naive pawn of a political party or candidate. Rather, it means studying the issues and problems and then affirming positions and programs that bring justice and reconciliation. Often there may be no clear road to take, as the issues may be muddied and the political choices a matter of Tweedledee and Tweedledum. If so, the church should be aware of that too and see what alternatives are available. In short, although it may be wise not to align itself officially with any mainline party or candidate, thus preserving apolitical integrity, it is important that the church educate itself on key issues advocating social justice and human rights.

To carry out the biblical mandate of social concern, it is important that church members study significant social and community issues and confront the congregation with the data. Such investigations and reports will likely give rise to debate, but they should also produce ideas for creative actions to be taken. Study groups should report and speak to, not for, the church. They are not the church but informers of it. Nonetheless, such lay activity builds consciousness among attenders that the church is concerned about social issues and that it is the obligation of the members to become active in efforts to bring reconciliation, relief, and reform.

THE GLOBAL CITY AND THE INNER CITY 2

There are two types of cities in the United States: traditional cities and emerging cities. Traditional cities are older urban entities, with roots going back often a century or longer. Many of them are in the northeast quadrant of the United States. New York, Boston, Cleveland, Cincinnati, Detroit, Philadelphia, and Chicago are examples of traditional cities.

The traditional cities grew in response to economic forces rather than through rational urban planning. They tended to shoot up where natural resources such as waterways and raw materials made industrial expansion most attractive. Early opportunities for unskilled labor brought floods of immigrants into the rapidly growing cities. These cities continued to grow because they became centers of industry, transportation, and communication. In short, they became the nerve centers of society.

Emerging cities are newer cities. These include Seattle, San Antonio, Phoenix, and Indianapolis, among others. The advantage the emerging cities enjoy is that they are often, at least in part the product of careful urban planning. Whereas, the traditional cities are the urban equivalent of the suddenly large family outgrowing its overused house, the emerging entities are more similar to a family whose growth and size have been more controlled. The willy-nilly yet explosive growth of the traditional cities resulted in space soon becoming a premium. Later, when these municipalities sought to rebuild their tax bases by revitalizing their downtown areas for business and attracting middle-class residents, the only way they could do this was by claiming huge chunks of valuable real estate through eminent domain and expelling the poor inhabitants of that land as they built more affluent structures for incoming businesses and residents.

The emerging cities, though not without problems, tended to foresee the need for a vital downtown area. Hence, many of these cities allocated prime space for the building of sports complexes for their professional teams along with hotels and huge, multi-level shopping centers before the areas became ghettoized.

Today large portions of U.S. cities—and particularly traditional ones—continue to experience decline in response to ever-changing economic forces. Problems of poverty and unemployment continue to plague millions. In the late 1970s, one out of every six U.S. families was on public aid, with one of three on the brink. Nothing much has changed. The percentage of the population living below the poverty level is the same as thirty-five years ago. Moreover, the United States has the highest poverty rate of any industrialized nation in the world, and many of these indigent people are located in urban squalor.

DECLINE OF THE CITY

To bring us up to date, it is helpful to trace the history of urban decline. In the 1960s and '70s, the social decline and transition in the traditional cities was the result of shifts in the U.S. economy. More spacious and desirable opportunities opened up in the suburbs or urban fringes, and the affluent headed in that direction, while a poorer class of urbanites pushed into the vacant area. This became an ongoing process of exit and entry such that neighborhood and community transition was simply an urban fact of life.

Chicago's infamous Cabrini-Green community was an outgrowth of transition. In the 1960s, this community, within a mile of the city's superrich, was a mixed community and a steppingstone to a better life for immigrants and African Americans from the South. When federal housing rules began forcing people to leave the area once they made a decent living, leaders and role models left, and the transition stage to an all-black poverty population was on. Transition soon became post-transition, and with the death of Martin Luther King in 1968, a tougher, more angry group of African Americans began filling the community. By the 1980s the public aid system, a way in which at least some were able to fight their way out of poverty, was becoming increasingly unpopular politically. As federal subsidies began evaporating, management and maintenance of the public housing structures slacked off, and the decline accelerated. A drug culture began to sprout, gang life intensified, shootings increased, and incarcerations accumulated as the community deteriorated beyond any hope of reclamation.[1]

The African American community of Sandtown in Baltimore was also a place of hope in the 1960s. Churches, shops, movie theaters, and living units were full. Soon the manufacturing jobs began leaving as businesses relocated. A lessening of residential segregation opened housing opportunities, and many upwardly mobile African Americans moved out. Once again, the assassination of King proved critical, as riots further destroyed a once-healthy community. The destruction was evident in the numbers, as Sandtown's population hit a low of 15,000 in 1980, down from a peak of 45,000 just after World War II. More than a thousand Sandtown homes were vacant. The community continued to deteriorate, such that in one block, half of the twenty-three connected dwellings were vacant, and those were hard to isolate because slum landlords had neglected the upkeep of the others. The dimly lit streets were home to break-ins, fires, and open drug trafficking. All the while, the middle class, dismayed at the deteriorating nature of the city left in droves, and Baltimore's population fell to under 650,000 from a high-water mark of nearly a million in 1950.[2]

Urban deterioration from the 1960s forward followed a pattern. As the affluent moved out, businesses headed for suburban developments and malls. The absence of businesses and a strong middle class eroded the tax base such that, without governmental aid, cities headed for bankruptcy.

In addition to the erosion of the tax base caused by the exodus of the affluent and businesses, the tax measures themselves killed urban communities. In Philadelphia, for example, the schools stayed closed one September while the city sank its money into measures that actually benefited the suburbs. This practice was true of many cities. It was primarily city money that paid for sports stadiums, airports, art centers, and theaters. Yet it was the suburbanite population that had the money to go to the ballpark and travel on the jets; and it was to satisfy the more-affluent tastes that art exhibits and professional theaters were built. As important as cultural refinements and entertainment opportunities are, their value is tarnished when they reflect economic exploitation. An angry Anthony Campolo wrote in 1979, "We have two names for welfare, don't we? When white suburbanites are on the receiving end, it's called 'public service.' God is not mocked."[3]

In the same spirit as Campolo, the outspoken Michael Harrington, in his sociological classic *The Other America,* claimed that what we have is socialism for the rich and free enterprise for the poor.[4] By this he meant that while middle-class Americans regularly complain about socialist welfare programs for slum dwellers, the fact is that the more affluent receive the thumping majority of the tax dollars. That the poor receive very little can still be observed in how much of each tax dollar goes into highway construction, higher-education facilities, salaries of governmental employees, and maintenance and renovation of parks and other recreational facilities used by the larger society. Although some argue that the middle class should receive more tax benefits because they pay the preponderance of the taxes, the point is that they do.

In fact, political pressure from power brokers has long been such that it is almost impossible to get legislation that will deliver benefits to the needy without skimming the cream for the rich. In

California the hazard-insurance legislation directed at the burned-out Watts area in the 1970s was written in such a way that the nonpoor could get low-cost insurance as well. The result was that insured Bel Air mansions were built on mudslides and hills that had been burned regularly. Hence, benefits ostensibly for the poor enriched the wealthy.

In addition to erosion of the city's tax base and unjust allocation of tax benefits, the city's finances continue to be affected by earnings taken out of the city by many suburbanites who make their living in the city. They drive in on public expressways and city streets that are paid for by city taxes, drink city water, flush city toilets, and walk on city pavements, but they pay taxes, build modern schools, and acquire goods and services in a suburban municipality. All the while, the poor remain in a colony of misery, walled in by poverty and a lack of opportunity.

F. K. Pious Jr. claimed that 85 percent of urban decline can be traced back to three pieces of legislation.[5] The first was the Homeowner Loan Act of June 13, 1933. Along with the Federal Home Loan Bank Act of July 22, 1932, this Act replaced the five-year renewable mortgages with fifteen- to thirty-year mortgages. This legislation made the privately funded building and loan entities into predecessors for the present quasi-socialized savings and loan associations. Though the purpose of the Act was to help the housing industry mired in the Depression, the effect was to sponsor the building and sale of freestanding, owner-occupied dwellings while ignoring the needs of multiple-family rental housing. Because available land for free-standing dwellings tended to be in the suburbs while the large rental housing was in the city, the legislation had a suburban bias.

The second piece of legislation was the Serviceman's Readjustment Act of June 22, 1944. The GI Bill financed the suburbs by having the government guarantee money lent by banks and savings and loan associations to GIs. Housing starts, almost all suburban, zoomed. No comparable program, involving owning or renting, existed for the city.

The Federal Aid Highway Act of June 29, 1956, was the third factor. This Act led to the bankrolling of the 42,500-mile Interstate Highway System and other highway projects. Federal transportation planners damaged the city by cutting up city neighborhoods and paving them over, thus lifting valuable land from the tax rolls. The effect was a simplified transportation into the city for suburbanites who held city jobs while stifling mass transit, a key to urban health.

With suburban growth and urban decline, Pious said that the middle class "smelling the meat acookin' elsewhere, wisely left, and refugees from rural poverty and Southern discrimination flowed in to occupy what was already abandoned territory."[6]

With jobs leaving the city along with its middle-class residents, the focus in many cities shifted to one of cultural pluralism. The ethnic village became the goal, with neighborhoods retaining strong ethnic roots to a subcultural tradition—African-American, Mexican, Puerto Rican, Chinese—while building a sustainable community base that functioned effectively in the larger urban environment.

REGENTRIFICATION AND GLOBALIZATION

Since the mid-1980s, however, there has been a major new force operative in the major cities. It is called *regentrification*, a process by which the affluent begin moving back into the cities. Major cities, wanting to attract a larger tax base and better business core, began renovating their downtown areas. New hotels were built and sports stadiums were planted in the city centers. In short, the downtown areas have been transformed into showpieces. Today the city has become the center of cultural, entertainment, and economic activity with opulent living spaces readily available by sweeping out and rezoning what were once manufacturing areas in favor of lofts, condominiums, and other living units close to the stimulating night spots. Hence, suburban empty-nesters, yuppies, and the newly rich have been flocking back into the city to enjoy its excitement and opportunities without incurring long commutes.

Much of the initial regentrification occurs close to the downtown area in what once were low-income communities. Chicago's Cabrini Green public-housing community is an example. In the 1970s it held nearly 20,000 people in its high-rise, mid-rise, and row houses. By 2005 perhaps 5,000 were left. Its story is a virtual case study in regentrification. Cabrini-Green was once a poverty-ridden public-housing project with an infamous reputation. In 1970 two Chicago policemen were gunned down by sniper fire; in 1981 Mayor Jane Byrne actually moved into the community to stem the violence; in 1992 a seven-year-old boy was shot to death while walking to school holding his mother's hand; in 1997 a nine-year-old girl was raped and left for dead in a smelly tenement stairwell. Cabrini-Green, however, was located near the now redeveloped, spectacular Windy City downtown, and the noose of affluence began settling around its geographical neck.[7]

The city of Chicago wanted it both ways. It began knocking down project buildings and allowed developers to spur financially lucrative regentrification; at the same time, the city permitted a portion of the native residents to remain in what would become a contrived, mixed-income community. One developer was to construct 261 homes for rent and sale. Half would go at market price, about a third as public housing, and the rest discounted to bring in a working-class element.[8] Indeed, the long arm of regentrification is evident in the Cabrini community. A *Chicago Tribune* reporter noted that Holy Family Lutheran Church, once a church without spires or steeple and lodged amid grinding poverty, now is just steps away from $860,000 homes, fine dining, and a kayaking outfitter.[9] Residents of the original housing project were shuttled out of dilapidated buildings as the razing occurred. Thousands were forced out before even two hundred new homes were built, making it evident that there would never be enough room for all those who left. In one month, 350 families were given six months to move. Some were given housing vouchers as meager inducements.[10]

As for the mixed-income notion, such an economic contrivance, however well-meaning in part, is a form of sociological violence. There is a steady state of tension in such pseudocommunities. The locals resent the takeover of their community by the moneyed class. Market-rate residents become annoyed at the noise generated by the large family, low-income neighbors. The sorry state of the local public schools is of no concern to the well-to-do singles and childless couples. Although street crime can be controlled, it is not without the constant presence of police cars.[11]

Regentrificaton soon spreads out toward the perimeter, following the European model in which the rich live in the interior of the city and the poor on the outside. The attraction of the city in addition to combating the high-energy commuting costs has generated a movement toward buying affordable buildings elsewhere in the city and *rehabbing* them to new levels of luxury. The rehabbing itself has a spreading effect such that whole communities get turned over and regentrified into much more affluent neighborhoods. The net effect of regentrification, then, is not any sort of socioeconomic integration. If anything, economic segregation becomes more stark as affluent communities create walled subcities around themselves amid the hungry slum dwellers left behind.

The redeveloped, regentrified cities have taken on a decidedly international, European flavor, one that is global in nature. The Internet, ethnic restaurants, international films, the arts, the world stock markets, terrorism, twenty-four-hour international news cycles, cable networks, oil prices, international tourism, the governance system (World Bank, World Trade Organization, International Monetary Fund, North American Free Trade Agreement), inexpensive international phone calling, e-mail, and sports as international entertainment all point to the omnipresence of globalization. Globalization is so ubiquitous that over half of the one hundred top economies (organizations through which capital flows) are multinational. Amazingly, Walmart's Gross National Product exceeds that of Poland.

Moreover, major cities interact with the rest of the world through the cultures of their diverse populations in lifestyles, art, architecture and literature. Their academic institutions have powerful influence. The University of Chicago alone is home to over seventy Noble Peace Prize winners. Boston's Harvard University is an international force, as is the University of California in the Bay area, Georgetown University, and George Washington University in our nation's capital, among so many others.

This force of globalization represents perhaps the biggest change in the lives of Americans in the past two decades, particularly in the cities. Every urban community feels the impact of globalization. The resurgence of the downtown area with its multinational aura is where much of it begins. Cities then continue to invest in making themselves— beginning with their downtown areas—truly global cities. Rather than investing in neighborhoods, the municipalities pour revenues into things that will give them a global presence and global attraction.

Hence, the leaders in most cities are not concerned with the most vulnerable, but rather the best investments. Health care, education, housing, and job training are the losers as skyscrapers, world-class hotels, and new sports stadiums that are maximally convenient as tourist centers get the cash in a municipal attempt to build a world-class city. Cleveland's downtown area, Baltimore's Camden Yards area, and San Francisco's wharf area exemplify this.

Chicago is no longer the City of the Big Shoulders. The stockyards are gone, and along with it much of the city's blue-collar manufacturing base. Present is a magnificent lakefront boom with its attendant regentrification. Tourism, information technology, international corporate finance, and entertainment characterize its famous Loop area. One angry Cabrini-Green resident noted this global phenomenon as she watched her community being redeveloped. "Mayor Daley (of Chicago) is in Paris right now," she said, "trying to make this place like Paris."[12]

Key to globalization is finance and fun. The city is both an economic center and an entertainment machine. Every major city's downtown area is dotted with multinational financial institutions and entertainment centers—stadiums, arenas, tourist hotels, art centers, multiplex movie theaters, auditoriums, restaurants, and shopping extravaganzas. The goal seems to be to create not a manufacturing or minimal-service enterprise but a professional managerial city. (For an annotated globalization bibliography, see the chapter notes.)

EMERGENCE OF THE INNER CITY

Since the inner city is the major focus of this book, the concept requires definition. The inner city does not necessarily refer to the geographic center of the city. In fact, globalization and its attendant regentrification have brought a displacement of the poor. Some African American residents go back South, others to nearby racially segregated neighborhoods, and still others to economically declining suburbs, particularly those with a growing African American population, generating a curious new phenomenon: the suburbanization of poverty. As less-affluent suburban areas began emptying, due in part to regentrification, cheap housing stock became available for those displaced by the rich in the city. It is probably more accurate, then, when describing a given metropolitan area, to speak of its several inner cities. Other displaced people move in with relatives and friends, while still others become homeless.

An inner city can be defined as a poverty area in which there is much governmental activity and control but little activity by the private sector. Often, merchandisers, businesses, and churches have left the area. The usual urban amenities, such as dry cleaners, barbershop, camera store, appliance shop, and the like, are in limited supply. But governmental agencies, public housing, and social institutions are visible. Private institutions of this type—both for-profit and not-for-profit—are absent.[13]

Besides the term *poverty area*, there are a number of other synonyms for the inner city: low-income community, central city (if its near downtown), *ghetto*, or even *barrio*. Although technically referring only to a place of isolation, the term ghetto has come to suggest a predominantly African American community.

Inner cities are not always homogeneous, however they can be inhabited by almost any racial or ethnic group. African Americans are common because they have been the most urbanized of all ethnic groups and a sizable proportion (about one-third) are trapped in poverty.

In 1952 Ralph Ellison wrote his famous *The Invisible Man*, chronicling the neglected and overlooked status of African Americans in the United States. A half-century later we can say that inner cities are the *invisible communities*. Indeed, they are invisible. Middle-class people can drive around them and over them (on interstates and elevated, main city arterials) but do not have to drive though them, because there is nothing of interest to the larger city in these communities. In short, although inner-city neighborhoods may lie proximal to regentrified communities, the more-affluent citizens can carry on their lives as if those nearby communities do not exist, because these poverty areas are cut off. They are irrelevant to the rest of the city. There are many such communities, and they contain over half of the nation's poor. East Brooklyn, the Bronx, Newark, North Philadelphia, West Baltimore, major portions of Washington D.C. and Chicago, East St. Louis, Miami's Overtown, South Central Los Angeles, and large chunks of Detroit are essentially invisible communities.

With regentrified communities all but bumping against inner-city neighborhoods, major cities have taken on a Lazarus-Dives look. Luxury hotels, an ESPN Zone, Planet Hollywood, multiplex theaters, Starbucks, and shopping complexes dot downtown areas, while only a few blocks away, people live in the most blighted of neighborhoods. Often a single street separates a gated rehabbed community from one ridden with street crime, deteriorating housing, and joblessness.

Regardless of ethnic makeup, the inner city can often be characterized as "the other world." It is the other side of the American fence, opposite the side on which grass is green. An African American college student once wrote a term paper for one of my classes in which she described that other-world feeling she had had when she was younger. She wrote that as a young, black, inner-city child, she felt that she lived in the worst place in the entire world, for nothing that went on in school or her textbooks, from reading class to geography, was in any way related to life in the community in which she lived.

Almost invariably inner cities, by US standards, are crowded. The residential density (people per square mile) in a crowded inner city can be twenty times higher than for the larger metropolitan area as a whole. As many as twenty thousand residents can be packed into a five-by-eight-block boundary. New York's Harlem and Spanish Harlem are examples of areas teeming with people.

Overcrowdedness can have nerve-shattering consequences, especially for people with rural roots. Misery and degradation are packed together. Experiments with laboratory animals indicate that when rats are confined to an overpopulated space, they begin killing each other off until their numbers reach manageable size. Social scientists continue to debate the likely human implications of these types of findings.[14]

At any rate, building is lined up against building, or, in the case of high-rises, floor is stacked on floor, as the misery heads skyward. With exploding numbers come limited space, limited privacy, and the omnipresence of noise from voices, stereos, cars, and people themselves. Eight may live in a three-room apartment. "Go to your room" is a disciplinary statement that would be simply preposterous to an inner-city child.

Overcrowdedness, of course, points to as critical a physical characteristic of an inner city as any—inadequate housing. Quality housing in the inner city is in such small supply that the 1960s saw the emergence of a new cabinet department: Housing and Urban Development. The poor are, by virtue of their poverty, herded into central-city communities where land and, more particularly, housing are at an absolute premium. Where housing does exist, the buildings are old and crumbling. A ride through an inner-city area invariably reveals this phenomenon to the curious onlooker, who will see either ancient and deteriorated or gutted and burned-out buildings.

The only other housing available is often aging public housing such as the federally sponsored high-rises; limited space demands vertical rather than horizontal construction. One of the problems contributing to the decay of the inner city is that the poor do not own property. The welfare system allows recipients to rent dwellings but not buy them. To qualify for low-cost housing, a person must not earn in excess of a given, rather paltry amount, adjusted periodically for inflation. This works against the care of property because there is no pride of ownership.

While the rest of society laments the absence of moderately priced housing and reasonably sized lots on the urban fringes and in the more-affluent suburbs, the poor look for shelter of any kind.

Causes of Inner-City Conditions

A number of causes contribute to the conditions of over-crowdedness and inadequate housing in the inner city. The first cause is the transition from a stable neighborhood to a changing neighborhood. As people move away, vacant housing develops, followed by the entry of people socially different from the dominant residential group. The more different the incoming group is, the quicker the residents flee. Hence, stability is gone. No one is certain when the tipping point in any community will occur, but when it does, the community quickly turns over.

Although we live an age that gives public endorsement to diversity, xenophobia—fear of the unfamiliar—dominates. This xenophobia is not always based on racial differences. Linguistic or income disparities may also elicit a strong reaction. In previous decades, unscrupulous realtors would come in and prey on the fears and stereotypes of the anxious residents. They would plant fears of plunging real-estate values and imminent violence in order to buy resident housing cheaply, only to turn around and sell that same housing to incoming residents at a booming profit.

This practice is called *blockbusting*. Though politically incorrect and grossly unethical, it continues to be practiced in a less-blatant, more-covert fashion. Nonetheless, with perception becoming reality, whenever a group feels threatened by an incoming, different group, a rapid exodus can result, an exodus that land speculators can turn into big profits.

The second cause is fiscal dysfunction. Many neighborhood functions reflect personal income, which in part is turned into taxes to maintain semipublic enterprises such as schools, libraries, public offices, and hospitals. As income accumulates, the residents put it into banks. In turn, these financial institutions lend money in the form of credit to neighborhood residents to enable the community to grow and develop. If, however, the demand for housing decreases in the neighborhood, trouble ensues. Since the housing supply is fixed, this dip will drop prices, which will alarm financial institutions and cause them to cut back on loans. This cutback is called *redlining*.[15]

In the 1970s and '80s redlining referred to a practice in which bank officials outlined an area that they believed would decline over the next twenty to thirty years (the length of many mortgages). As a result of this prediction, the bank chose to limit the amount of mortgage money it lent to purchase land in the redlined area. Though illegal, this practice was used to protect the bank against high-risk lending. What happened, however, was that the bank, ostensibly a servant of the community, became its killer. People who desired to purchase in the inner city and then rehabilitate the dwelling found themselves ruled out of such an enterprise, while current owners became increasingly aware that they were literally stuck with difficult-to-sell property. This encouraged management toward demolition.

Redlining was (and continues to be) practiced by insurance companies who were either unwilling to insure inner-city dwellings at all or priced the premiums out of reach of the owner. In any case, the result of these redlining practices was that portions of the inner city took on the appearance of a ghost town as the area became dotted with burned-out, abandoned buildings, surrounded by open space. In spite of inadequate housing and this available land, there was no building going on. In every case the community and its residents lost because the bank, by virtue of its lending restrictions, had its prophecy of community doom fulfilled.

Though officially no longer practiced, a de facto, informal type of redlining—unwillingness to loan in inner-city, particularly African American, communities—continues unabated. Lending institutions carry it on in a variety of ways. First, with many smaller banks merged into larger conglomerates, lending institutions are even further away than ever from inner cities. Hence, there is little pressure to engage in inner-city community redevelopment, because the adjacent community is at least a regentrified one, not one struggling with the ravages of poverty. Lending institutions also redline simply by applying restrictive lending policies on individual grounds, all but ruling out applicants by virtue of individual credit histories or on other technical grounds.

A recent study of lending practices in Chattanooga, Tennessee, conducted by the Association of Community Organizations for Reform Now (ACORN), found that African Americans were rejected at a rate of 31.8 percent, Hispanics at 26.7 percent, and Caucasians at 18.9 percent. The ACORN study found that equal opportunity did not exist, even when incomes matched. African Americans who made the same as their Caucasian counterparts were rejected more than twice as often.[16] A veteran mortgage loan officer in the Midwest who has worked with myriad mortgages during her career, put it more succinctly. "Redlining is alive and well," she stated.

In a redlined area, however, the money flows steadily out. In the meantime, a community's fiscal health is largely determined by green flow—credit and capital funding. In stable communities, with deposits going into banks and with loans coming out, dollars continue to turn around within the community. When there is redlining and urban disinvestment—green flow moving in the wrong direction—a community becomes fiscally dysfunctional.

Nothing is built or developed, and the community deteriorates. The signs of negative green flow are obvious. Businesses, hospitals, banks, and other capital enterprises disappear only to resurrect in regentrified and suburban communities. A person can drive through an inner-city community and notice that literally hundreds of thousands of people live without a single financial institution to serve them.

Inner-city money flows to regentrified communities, affluent suburbs, and international enterprises. This fiscal hemorrhaging has a long, painful history. In the late 1970s, Chicago's South Shore residents had $31 million on deposit in two major Chicago banks but had received only $76,000 in loans. A careful, recent estimate revealed that the amount of capital necessary to turn that South Shore community around equaled almost exactly the total amount the residents had on deposit. All they needed was a recycling of their own money. This stood in sharp contrast to the $1 billion it would cost the government to tear down the community and rebuild it in the suburbs. Yet the government did exactly that. Approximately twenty-five thousand living units were built annually in the suburbs, and an equivalent number in the city were destroyed.[17] Today that money does not have to reach the suburbs. It can be poured into regentrified areas of the now-globalized city of which the inner-city community is a forgotten part.

In addition to the conditions created by blockbusting and redlining, another major problem occurred: *slum landlording.* Cities that wanted public housing to run down and be destroyed engage in this practice. One Cabrini-Green family discovered this quickly when they moved into their apartment in 1998. The father had to carry his bike up nine floors because the elevator was perpetually broken. When parts of the ceiling fell into his wife's frying pan, she burned her hand with the spattering hot grease. The family moved to another unit but had to boil water to take a bath. Other tenants had sludge backing up in their sinks and fungus on the bathroom walls. One family discovered that only two electrical outlets functioned, necessitating dragging extension cords across the floors to heat and illuminate rooms, all of which engendered a haunting fear of fire and electrocution.[18]

Privately owned buildings are commonly managed toward demolition. It begins by filling the building with as many tenants as possible, without any attempt to keep the building in repair. The aged nature of the building, coupled with its heavy usage by children and young adults, results in rapid deterioration. In the past, city inspectors, whose task it is to check the quality of urban structures and insure that they are "up to code," were easily bribed into not reporting housing-code violations. The inspectors' consciences were assuaged because they felt the city grossly underpaid them and that reporting building violations would simply set off lengthy legal procedures (sometimes as long as four years) that would likely end with either the landlords minimally repairing the buildings or abandoning them entirely and leaving the people shelterless. Though bribing is somewhat less common today, the court snarl is still an issue.

One of the reasons an owner does not make repairs is to keep overhead and real-estate taxes at a base level. Rents are picked up until the building is so badly worn that it either begins to collapse or the city demands repair. In previous decades, at that point the building was often torched—burned to the ground. Torchings marked the end of both the structures and the legal problems of the owners, who would probably collect fire insurance money since that is one premium they kept paid. Torchings often occurred with the inhabitants still in the building, destroying much of their goods as well as imperiling their safety. Such fires appear more accidental and raise less suspicion. They were extremely common, however. During 1974, for example, there were fourteen thousand fires in the South Bronx. In urban areas nationwide, literally thousands of such torchings of buildings occurred in old sections.

Although torching has given way to abandoning, razing, and simply selling delinquent buildings, slum landlording has changed little over the decades. Buildings are crammed with renters, and repairs are kept to a minimum. Most city court dockets continue to be jammed with cases such that an unscrupulous landlord, aided by a crafty lawyer, can stall the case for a long period of time. The only recourse left to the unhappy tenants is to refuse to pay rent. Beyond that, their absence of political clout and connectedness leaves them powerless.

In 2003 an incident reminiscent of the 1960s occurred in relatively tiny Benton Harbor, Michigan, a community of about twelve thousand residents located in semi-rural Southwestern Michigan. A twenty-eight-year-old African-American man named Terrance Shurn engaged in a high-speed police chase, lost control of his motorcycle, and fatally crashed into a building. About four hundred angry citizens in Benton Harbor began rioting for several days out of frustration with poverty and lack of municipal responsiveness. At least five buildings were torched. The disorder was intense enough to bring in police adorned in riot gear with help from the FBI. This was not Harlem, South Central Los Angeles, or the west side of Chicago. Nonetheless, Benton Harbor was overwhelmingly poor and littered with boarded-up buildings and vacant lots amid more crowded dwellings. The incident drew national attention, with Jesse Jackson and others standing in front of the cameras. A year later Jackson and the television cameras were gone, and free-standing houses were sold for as little as $10,000, while others continued to be neglected as tenants returned to their politically invisible status.

In addition to failure to repair buildings, slum landlords neglect utility needs of the renters. A not-uncommon practice is to fail to heat a building in the dead of winter. So prevalent is this problem that city television stations regularly flash the city hall telephone number where help can be obtained. Colds, influenza, pneumonia, and frostbite are common health problems in inner-city winters. From the standpoint of the slum landlord—who is aware that the court process is slow and that few poor city dwellers have any knowledge of it—ignoring the needs of a building is a low-risk, high-profit enterprise.

The landlords have grievances of their own. Rents in the inner city are limited by tenants' ability to pay. Many tenants have bad credit and simply do not pay, resulting in the need to evict them. Maintenance costs continue to escalate and tenants do not move. Vandalism, theft, and other damages are common in the inner city. Both landlord and tenant are trapped in the ugly Darwinian struggle.

Nonetheless, blockbusting, redlining, and slum landlording are outgrowths of greed and prejudice. This greed and prejudice will almost certainly be felt by the pastor who truly desires to minister to an urban neighborhood. As such, it is of utmost importance that pastors learn as much as possible about the institutional policies and processes attendant to high-density living.

THE RESPONSE OF THE CHURCH

For Christians the global concept must continue to gain attention if for no other reason than that it is biblical. Because creation is global, the cultural mandate is global, as our purpose is to redeem the world. Environmental concerns, human rights, and levels of international development are not only worthy issues of attention, they will continue to stare urban Christians in the face, owing to the global nature of our cities.

Churches in the city have to respond to both the globalization of the city and the emergence of inner-city areas. Some churches pass through several stages as they respond to their changing community, but many eventually relocate or close. Other churches, however, have sought ways to revitalize the community by dealing with conditions of inadequate housing, fiscal dysfunction, and governmental control.

The Church in Transition

Although churches and denominations like to affirm diversity and may even assert that a minority group would be welcome to take over a church if it becomes dominant in the neighborhood, according to Dudley, churches do not usually respond that way.[19]

Churches that are unable to effectively address the changes in their community pass through a series of stages strikingly similar to the stages through which terminally ill patients pass.

After initially adopting a fortress mentality within the changing neighborhood, the congregation realizes that some of its families have moved out of the area. The usual reaction to this is regionalism—redefining the church's identity by deemphasizing its neighborhood affiliation in favor of a more-metropolitan quality as it attempts to keep the relocated families in the church. The church attempts to weather what it chooses to see as a temporary crisis by holding fast to its initial ethnic, denominational, or doctrinal culture, all the while being in a psychological state of denial.

This is usually unsuccessful because those who have left tire of the commute to the original church and, at least subconsciously, realize that it is fighting a losing battle. As the church loses its vitality and its funds are drained, the pastor becomes exhausted and often leaves. This pseudoexpansion phase then gives way to contraction. The smaller church admits it is undergoing changes but stubbornly attempts to hang on. Key here is that the community outside, gurgling with change, is perceived negatively as a threat to the life and well-being of the church. A new vitality may emerge from this shared quest for survival, typified by increased giving and activity as the parishioners, rather than simply the pastor, become the church. Spiritual faith increases in this phase, and there is a sense of genuine zeal; however, it is one that operates as an adversary of the surrounding community rather than a part of it. Stresses build and, on occasion, people will explode for seemingly inexplicable reasons and leave the church. There is much suppressed anger in this response, and the church attempts to manage its way through the transition.

When the church runs out of money, the accommodation stage emerges. The church now needs the community and decides to expand its outlook, seeking to perform ministries in the changing community and being willing to share whatever resources they have with other groups in order to raise money. Church buildings will be rented out, grant monies sought, the pastor allowed to work in a secular job on the side, and so on. Bargaining characterizes this stage as the church lives in tension. It also renders the church vulnerable to being taken over by outside interests. Interestingly, the late Bill Leslie of Chicago's once-great LaSalle Street Church always maintained that a congregation should pay its own way for all conventional ministries, seeking outside dollars only for supplementary efforts such as legal aid or counseling.

The accommodation stage will bring congregations to lend their facility to other small, ethnic or minority churches. Koreans, Chinese, Hispanics, and other non-English-speaking groups in particular are accommodated. The accommodation phase, however, is not the answer. Younger, upwardly mobile families continue moving out, leaving usually the older parishioners behind. The resultant phase is one of grief. The grieving period gives way to death. The church may fade gradually by reducing its activity, or it may relocate. Regardless of the style, it is in its last phase.

On occasion, out of the contraction stage evolves a new type of church—one dominated by an ethnic or racial minority group with a faith expression congruent with its nationality. The Caucasians in these churches find it alien, however, because their formative experience with God is not rooted in a non-Anglo pattern.

Revitalizing the Community

In John 12:25 Jesus says that those who love their life will lose it, while those who invest it in spiritual activity will find it. The same is true for churches in changing communities. Those that attempt simply to perpetuate their own existence die, while those that invest their energies in serving and redeeming the community live. The church that chooses to be involved in revitalizing the community must seek creative answers to the problems of inadequate housing and fiscal dysfunction in the larger community, rather than turn inward in an effort to maintain its own survival. These answers may include such ideas as sponsoring rehabilitation organizations, offering courses in building maintenance and personal money management, using investment portfolios judiciously, and working with community and governmental agencies.

Before a church becomes involved in dealing with the issue of inadequate housing and the practices of redlining and slum landlording, it is wise to become acquainted with the dynamics of inner-city housing. The resources are plentiful. There is even an inner-city-housing simulation game.[20] Next it is necessary to do research into local community housing. Below are ten checkpoints.[21] Many of these issues can be investigated at a knowledgeable social agency. The social service agencies are available from the United Way, if not from the Internet.

1. Determine which way credit or money flows in community businesses and institutions. Does the money come from the residents, go into community enterprises, and then flow out of the community? Or do these institutions reinvest the money to develop a stronger community through expansion, community employment, and other procommunity activities? What about redlining by banks or insurance companies?

2. Check into institutions outside the community. Which ones, if any, are sensitive to inner-city needs and which are notorious for exploitation?

3. Find out who owns the community property. Is it privately owned? Slum landlorded? Government sponsored? How dense is the area? If there are vacancies, find out why.

4. What is the condition of the buildings? Why are they in that condition?

5. What kinds of aid are available in the public sector for housing development?

6. Have there been any redevelopment attempts that were aimed at providing housing for the community residents rather than driven by a regentrification motive? What aids for rehabbing are available?

7. What are the tax rates? Is there massive tax delinquency and corruption?

8. What community organizations are concerned about housing?

9. What is the future of housing in the community? Is the area becoming less residential or more so? Does the community have plans for the area?

10. Are there industrial and commercial job opportunities or do the businesses merely prey on the community's lack of shopping alternatives? If opportunities do exist, there is evidence of concern for the community; if they do not, the community has become more blighted.

Once armed with the answers to these questions, the church can proceed to the next step with greater confidence: discover the various ways that Christians and other groups are addressing the housing problem.[22] There are a variety of responses churches are making. One of the most aggressive occurred in the Sandtown Habitat for Humanity in Baltimore, a ministry of the New Song Community Church. Since 1989 over two hundred Habitat homes have been built in Baltimore's Sandtown neighborhood, a fifteen-square-block area. Habitat itself can be contacted for information and direction.[23]

The Inner City Christian Federation (ICCF) in Grand Rapids, Michigan, began in 1974 and now has three main programs that offer services across the entire housing spectrum. The programs include emergency housing, long-term affordable rental housing, and educational services on home ownership opportunities. ICCF meets families where they are and then moves forward in serving their housing needs and goals.[24]

Harambee Housing Services in Chattanooga, Tennessee, focuses on providing quality, affordable homeownership for low-income families living in the Glenwood neighborhood of the city. Over 10 percent of the neighborhood's housing is vacant or abandoned. Many have been taken over by the city or county. What remains are slum-landlorded and public housing. Harambee has designed a two-year program aimed at equipping residents with the skills requisite for homeownership. Harambee works with Chattanooga Neighborhood Enterprises to approve loans for residents. Harambee itself renovates homes and then sells them to graduates of their program at a below-market price.[25]

Churches that want to gain experience in dealing with inner-city housing needs are wise to volunteer with local housing groups like Habitat. After doing local research, finding out what others are doing, and involving itself in a local volunteer effort, the church can then start its own housing ministry.[26]

Much thought and care needs to go into such an ambitious project, but it can be done. It is important, however, for the church to acquaint itself with public housing policy in its city.[27] Moreover, a church should look first at what social agencies may be doing in the community before embarking on some costly, alienating, overlapping effort. Knowledge of such simple matters as key helping institutions in the community, city agency phone numbers, and other urban areas where housing can be obtained at low cost can be very helpful to confused residents who do not know which way to turn.

Some churches have done great things in addressing housing anguish. Bethel New Life, the development agency of the Bethel Lutheran Church in Chicago, has constructed a community economic development program. It has taken a turf stand on behalf of low-income residents of its west-side community, building over eight hundred housing units and offering employment opportunities to hundreds. Led by Mary Nelson, the program is based on Isaiah 58:9–12 in which God promises that if his people end oppression, feed the hungry, and aid the needy, he would dispel the darkness, guide them, and make them a well that never goes dry. In Chicago's Mexican-American community of Pilsen, The Resurrection Project (TRP) engages in home ownership, community organizing, asset management, and economic development. According Director Ray Raymundo, TRP is not about just building houses, but building community.[28]

Often to effect change in a community, particularly in the areas of justice like redlining and slum landlording, it is necessary to organize. Without organization there can be no coherent voice. It is important also to find indigenous leadership and build from that base. The revitalization of an inner city requires partnerships, alliances, and coalitions, rather than just money. Coalitions are important because of the interconnectedness of the community involved. Once there is a concerned and articulate community force, there can be effective negotiation with city hall. Moreover, it is crucial that positive relations are maintained with the government at all levels. Despite the fact that the government may sometimes be the adversary, without cordial relations little progress can be made.

Unfortunately, organization usually connotes an adversarial approach. It conjures up images of angry protests and marches, fist-waving confrontations, and other in-your-face tactics. That is not the way of the church. The church is to be a peace-maker, a reconciling force and, more practically, the church does not need more enemies.

Mary Gonzalez, a community organizer for the Gamaliel Foundation and the Metropolitan Alliance of Congregations in Chicago, says the organization is about agitation, not irritation. Churches should neither abdicate power nor run from power, but rather mobilize it responsibly to act on issues outside their doors.[29] Whenever possible, it is wise to involve those citizens in the church who are most affected by injustices in organizational efforts. This has an empowering effect and builds indigenous leadership.

Despite occasional agitation, a major goal of the urban church must be to be perceived as a friend of the community, a positive force for good for its residents. Urban pioneer William "Bud" Ipema offered some ingenious suggestions about how to work with, rather than against, social agencies.[30] First, it is important that they be approached in a positive way. A climate of cooperation is very helpful. To have maximum effect, however, it is important that the church know the mechanics of a given agency, that is, what services the agency offers, how application is made, and what procedures the organization follows.

Ipema suggests that those involved in urban ministry develop as strong a relationship as possible with social service officials. They are wise to be particularly on the alert for those who define themselves as Christians. In terms of hierarchy, it is helpful to connect with a middle-level official. Lower-level officials may provide unsatisfactory service, while upper-level officials may be enmeshed in the bureaucracy. In initiating a relationship, it is very helpful to begin by asking how the church may be able to help the agency. An enterprising pastor can identify needs and problems that the parishioners can help solve. Such a cooperative approach opens doors and builds relationships. Churches are also wise to surf the net for other aids. Consulting services, both secular and Christian, are sometimes available for research, resource definition, and plan development.

The urban-church worker is wise also to get involved in local community organizations. These alliances can be powerful forces in combating everything from pollution to prostitution, redlining to residential neglect. Such involvement is risky because the issues are controversial. However, community organizations by their nature are nonpartisan and people-oriented. Moreover, church workers may seek membership on a community organization's board of directors where they can have a real impact at the policy level.

If a church's research into housing conditions and community housing uncovers any de facto redlining practices, it would be helpful to join with other ministers in the neighborhood and approach the offending institutions on the matter. Often, Christians in these institutions are simply unaware of the damage these restrictive policies cause. In Chicago one church found a number of Christians at high levels of management in an urban bank and invited them to tour the community one morning to show them the results of redlining. Consciences were pricked and eyes opened, and the large bank turned its policy around. A church can invite bank officials to a breakfast at the church to discuss the issues. Area business leaders can be invited to a weekly Bible study and prayer group at the church. Even if nobody comes to the breakfast and no business leaders avail themselves of the Bible study, the offer itself is a witness to the spirit of cooperation on the part of the church.[31]

Financial institutions, of course, respond to money. As such, larger churches are wise to reassess their portfolios. If they are doing business with financial institutions that are insensitive and unconcerned about the community, pressure can and should be brought to bear on them. Larger churches can also be encouraged to invest in Christian, nonprofit housing efforts (as in the case of Harambee) or private lending institutions that will agree to extend low-interest housing loans. In addition, churches can organize neighborhood groups to confront lending institutions concerning their community responsibility. If credit is not being extended, the people can demand data justifying the nonlending policy. Often no such data exists; decisions are made on the basis of racial or socioeconomic bias.

There is no limit to what a visionary, stewardship-oriented church can do. A church can work effectively in its community by forming block clubs and organizing a community cleanup. A rehab business can be started that can both bring money to the church as well as spot below-market housing opportunities. In addition, churches can hold dinners and invite local city officials, local police, school personnel, garbage collectors, and public aid attorneys, in order to thank them for helping in the ministry to the neighborhood. After meeting local leaders, the church can confront them more effectively when accountability is low.

CONCLUSION

According to Mark Gornik, the current faith life in the inner city is characterized by three trends. First, there is a movement toward newer evangelical and Pentecostal churches and away from mainline and traditional churches. This is evident particularly in worship styles that are more emotive and celebrative with a heavier emphasis on energetic music. These churches evoke an intense spiritual energy in confronting the negative forces of the global city. Second, churches are becoming more focused on combining multiethnicity with community development. Third, coalitions among churches continue to develop as churches find their common commitment to the city is often more powerful than doctrinal differences.[32]

Whether alone or in conjunction with other churches, there are indeed many ways an enterprising congregation can be instrumental in revitalizing the community. As the church responds with creative approaches, the problems of inadequate housing, redlining, freezing conditions in winter, and the like, can be met. The church can have a part in encouraging financial institutions and private enterprises to invest in the community. Most of all, the church can weather the transitional stages and continue to minister in a changing city.

The effectiveness of these approaches is greatly enhanced when the pastor and as many members of the congregation as possible live in the community. Although such a residential commitment to turf is not always possible because of family, safety, or other important considerations, it is a powerful statement in the eyes of the community. It says we are one with you—your neighbors—expressing a communal rather than patronizing spirit.

ANNOTATED GLOBALIZATION BIBLIOGRAPHY

Prepared by Clinton E. Stockwell, Executive Director, Chicago Semester <www.chicagosemester.org>.

James Blaut, *Colonizers Model of the World.* Is neo Marxist/cultural pluralist, believes that the world is divided into the "core" and the "periphery." The Core culture is the developed world that is driving globalization and controlling the political and economic systems so that it benefits. The periphery (inner cities or less developed nations) are either exploited or are outside the system.

Manuel Castells, *Informatonal City; Network Society*. Believes that the "space of flows" (information) is more important than physical space. The early mythology was that information flows would render nation states and borders less releavant.

Benjamin Barber, *Jihad versus McWorld*. Believes that globalization is really a contest between forces that want to unify the world versus forces that want to maintain particularity and difference.

Thomas L. Friedman, *Lexus and Olive Tree*. Believes that globalization is a positive economic force and is probably inevitiable.

Barnett and Cavanaugh, *Global Dreams*. Believes that globalization is an American phenonmenon, as multinationals are based in U.S. and rest of developed world. Also Barber and RC Longworth, Global Squeeze.

Saskia Sassen, *The Global City; Cities in a World Economy*, etc. Globalization is about city building. Global cities are necessary in a global economy for reasons of management and technology. Globalization therefore has enhanced urbanization and centralization of "command and control" structures.

Tom Sine, *Mustard Seed versus McWorld*. Globalization is a lifestyle issue, consumerism versus those committed to a simple lifestyle, justice and preservation of economic system.

Walter Wink, *Engaging the Powers.; The Powers That Be*. Globalization is a domination system, powers are good, fallen and evil (Reformed paradigm), but globalization as a force is violent against third world nations, ecosystem, and those that resist. Terrorism as a reactive force is also violent. Faith communities should challenge the domination system in non violent ways.

David Ranney, *Global Decisions and Local Collisions*. Is neo-Marxist, believes that globalization is ascendancy of managerial class in the world, calls for organization of unions, peace groups, etc., for justice. Believes that the system is based on the overextension of credit-governments, corporations, and individuals. Politically, globalization is a new world order.

David C. Korten, *Globalizing Civil Society*. Believes globalization is a contest between the money world and the living world.

Jeremy Brecher and others, *Globalization from Below*. Believes that there are two competing globalizations, one that is corporate dominated and one that is a worldwide peoples movement. Is populist/union based in perspective.

URBAN STRATIFICATION AND THE NEIGHBORHOOD CHURCH **3**

Stratification refers to the arrangement of a society into a hierarchy of layers that are unequal in power, possessions, prestige, life opportunities, and satisfactions. More importantly, however, stratification provides unequal opportunities to accrue the most necessary and desirable commodities of earthly existence. It always generates differences in lifestyles, or living patterns. In short, stratification profoundly separates groups of people.

Stratification within cities is often related to regional boundaries. One of the more useful conceptualizations of this stratification involves a revised form of the concentric-zone model of urban areas.[1]

The central zone contains the business district in which civic, commercial (national and international), major entertainment, and governmental functions take place. Next is the transition zone that includes some slum neighborhoods and a growing regentrified district, mimicking European cities. The land in this zone is extremely valuable because of its proximity to the business district; therefore, there is ongoing pressure from moneyed interests to seize and redevelop the area. Because the buildings are aged and in decline, however, much work is necessary to make the area suitable for the expanding capital endeavors. The next zone contains working-class homes. In this area live people whose parents were able to escape what was once the transition zone. The fourth region is a residential zone containing single-family dwellings and apartment hotels. On the border is a commuter zone in which reside people seeking more desirable living spaces.

Once out of the regentrified district, the socioeconomic status of the residents generally rises further from the center of the city. Communities are more stable and organized, street crime is less frequent, and the quality of education and city services improves. Hence, upward social mobility means outward geographical mobility.

Understanding the larger or macro US stratification system, especially as it applies to the city, is of paramount importance in coming to terms with the dynamics of the more-immediate micro-system—the neighborhood. The bulk of this chapter is devoted to discussion of the larger system. This is then applied to the neighborhood and, more specifically, to the neighborhood church.

STRATIFICATION AND SOCIAL CLASS

Social stratification operates along a supply-and-demand equation to motivate individuals through the inducements of wealth, prestige, and power to assume positions that the society deems important and that require much talent.[2] An example of such a position is that of physician. Being a physician requires considerable talent, and because physicians deal with the critical issues of defining and treating health disorders, the position is of great import to the society. Hence, being a physician is lucrative. Entertainers and professional athletes are similarly rewarded because what they do requires a good deal of talent and the society, having more and more leisure time, demands to be entertained.

The Bases of Stratification

The primary bases of stratification are occupation, income, and education, with occupation being by far the most important.

When sociologists determine position in the social structure, they often use these three criteria for placement. Occupation is especially important because, as Robert Kennedy once noted, in America you are what you do. That is, social identity is largely determined by occupation. Moreover, occupations reveal a good deal about people's income, educational status, and the amount of prestige they enjoy. Among the consistently high-rated occupations in terms of prestige are physician, college professor, judge, lawyer, physicist, and dentist.[3]

Joseph Kahl presented a more expanded view of the bases of stratification, listing seven major dimensions that underlie the US stratification system.[4] If anything, these dimensions sketch the wide-ranging impact of a person's placement within the stratification system.

1. *Prestige.* Some members in the society are granted more respect and deference than others.

2. *Occupation.* Occupations differ in prestige, importance to the society, and rewards associated with them.

3. *Possessions.* This dimension refers to the varying amounts of property, wealth, and income.

4. *Social Interaction.* Different classes develop different patterns of interaction, and because people tend to associate with others at their same level, these patterns markedly separate the classes.

5. *Class Consciousness.* People are very aware of a social structure and their status in it, thus reinforcing its importance.

6. *Value Orientations.* There is evidence that different social classes have somewhat different value systems, which in turn motivate them to seek different lifestyles.

7. *Power.* Power is differentially distributed and those at the top of the social structure have greater leverage in controlling and directing the actions of others than those below them. Indeed, this power differential is as important as any criterion, for it not

only refers to the ability to control the flow of wealth and political advantage but also the ability to maintain an unequal status quo.

Stratification and Societal Dysfunctions

Sociologically, stratification has certain societal dysfunctions. Four in particular stand out. First, because people are born into a given stratum, they do not have equal opportunities at birth. As a result, *the full spectrum of society's talent is not discovered.* Where a person is slotted into the stratification system at birth impacts family size, the amount of parental interaction, and the amount and quality of education. If there were true equality of opportunity, it is altogether possible that more cures for cancer might have been discovered by now—or a host of other achievements might have occurred earlier. However, the poor are all but lost to society as a result of various factors: the poor quality of their education, their higher rates of infant mortality, and their deminished motivation due to the anguishes of poverty. A large sector is thus unable to contribute to the society.

Second, because of gross inequities in reward distribution, *there is a lack of unity in the society.* When some receive better health care, education, police and fire protection, and so on, there is bound to be discord and unhappiness over these inequities. The society disintegrates into interest groups, factions, and other divisions. These further divide the society and weaken it.

Third, with some in the society being granted greater deference and respect than others, *loyalty to the society is destroyed.* Who you are and who you know are very important in the United States. Having wealth and a powerful position guarantees no waiting in restaurants, better service on airlines, quicker contact with important officials, and greater expressions of social respect. The rich and powerful have the greatest ease in getting services of every kind—even free tickets to the major events. The result is that those who are not respected, who have to stand in line and be asked insulting questions when requesting public services, lose respect and allegiance for the system. It is little wonder that patriotism does not flourish in the inner city. It is difficult for people to become teary-eyed over the national anthem when it celebrates a society that does not really respect and value them.

Fourth, stratification affects self-image, which in turn is related to creative development. This issue is of special significance for children. Children who grow up well fed, respected, and loved, and who attend schools in which students are made to feel important and valued develop more positive self-concepts than children who realize that they are not deemed of much worth in the society. The result, more often than not, is that those who are made to feel positive are more likely to actualize their potential and develop their skills than those who feel they are not of much worth and who are discouraged from feeling they have anything to contribute. Where creativity and industriousness are depressed, *the society suffers from a loss in its collective reservoir of talent.*

These are but four of stratification's dysfunctions. It should be noted that they are societal; in other words, they hurt society as a whole. Some individuals may benefit from these societal dysfunctions, for they are advantaged by others' disadvantages; however, the society as a whole is still the victim.

Moreover, the very terms used to describe the US class system—upper, middle, and lower—convey subtle notions of superiority and inferiority that may also be dysfunctional to the well-being of the society as a whole.

The Social-Class System

The US social-class system can be analyzed in a variety of ways. Some simply posit an upper, middle, and lower class. Others add what is called a working, or blue-collar, class, sandwiched between the middle and lower classes. A more detailed approach cuts the social structure into seven sectors—upper-upper, lower-upper, upper-middle, middle, working, lower, and underclass. What follows is a rather brief outline of the seven social classes. For the urban pastor, who may be working primarily with the last two groups, knowledge of the structure as a whole can be valuable in understanding the social context in which parishioners live.

Upper-Upper Class. Often referred to as old money, these people are those who have possessed truly super riches over a number of generations. They are usually identified by family rather than as individuals. The Vanderbilts, Rockefellers, and Mellons would fall into this group. These people keep very much to themselves and associate within their own circles. Their elitism is protected and perpetuated by the tendency to marry within their own stratum.

Lower-Upper Class. Often called new money, this group differs from those in the higher status primarily in the length of time the wealth and prestige have been in the family.

In general, relatively little is known about the upper classes because they have a thirst for privacy and so escape the usual data-gathering efforts by sociologists. Moreover, most sociologists are middle class and so are not conversant with the lifestyle of the elite.

However, certain traits characterize the upper classes in general, and the upper-upper class in particular. Family reputation is very important. The upper classes are identified by families, and it is the family name that must be advanced and protected at all costs. Individual members of the upper class gain social standing by virtue of their family background and so are socialized to make family reputation a matter of high priority.

Expenditures are often made to magnify and elevate the family name. Many upper-class families, for example, have foundations bearing the family name, and upper-class individuals frequently lend themselves (and their names) as chairpersons of charity drives and socially respectable fund-raising efforts.

Women are very influential in social and style-related matters. Upper-class females are often pursued by the fashion media, are the subjects of newspaper features, and often become—whether engaged in a profession or not—social trendsetters. The upper-class people are often referred to as society, largely because of their social prestige.

Perhaps most important of all is that the upper class is truly super rich, controlling 40 to 45 percent of the nation's wealth. Their wealth is tied up in the major US industries and business enterprises, and hence, whenever the wheels of US commerce are turning, these people are making money. As long as capitalism survives, these people survive.

Upper-Middle Class. The upper classes constitute the elite of the society and comprise perhaps 2 percent of the society, while the upper-middle includes about 8 to 10 percent. The upper-middle class consists of the upper and middle levels of business and management, the major professions, high-ranking civil and military officials. Reputationally, they are viewed as highly respectable, not because they are actually more moral than other classes, but because their social values are the most dominant in the society and their thirst for respectability is probably the most intense among the strata.

It is the upper-middle class that takes the lead in civic affairs, including public education. In fact, it could be said that whereas the upper classes own and control the major corporations and institutions, the upper-middle class tends them on a day-to-day basis from administrative and executive posts. Because of this institutional dominance of the upper-middle class, it is imperative that those who wish to succeed in the US mainstream be able to communicate with members of this class. For that reason, it is the upper-middle-class clothing style and social demeanor that is taught as proper in most public schools.

Middle Class. These good, common people comprise about 30 percent of the US society. They come from the ranks of small-business people, semi-professionals, and other white-collar workers. Nurses, schoolteachers, police officers, and social workers are among this group. These people are often rather conservative politically out of a desire to hold on to their middle-class status.

They conduct their lives in a very ordered, patriotic, respectable, and self-improving fashion.

Working Class. The largest of the social classes at 40 percent, this group is often difficult to distinguish from the lower-middle class. Their values and lifestyle are very middle class out of a desire to be viewed as middle rather than lower class. Considered respectable, this sector includes skilled and semi-skilled (blue-collar) workers as well as tradesmen and farmhands. Working-class occupations usually do not require a college education. Their jobs are less secure and often tightly supervised. Moreover, work in the class, though less physically demanding than in the past, is tedious. As manufacturing jobs shrink and multinational companies outsource labor to other countries, this group is challenged by unemployment.

Economic status is not very important in identifying the working class, for in some cases their annual income will equal or exceed that of the middle and even upper-middle classes. The differences lie mainly in *how* they earn their money. They usually are paid by the hour and hence experience affluence through overtime and second jobs. Their economic status is rather tightly tied to the national economy; therefore, in boom times employment and money are plentiful, while during a period of recession, their lifestyle can become rather austere.

The upper-lower class is often rather unsympathetic toward the poor, in part because of their wish to be associated with the middle rather than the lower class. There is also a rather strong "I fight poverty, I work" doctrine operative in this group. Frequently, they will oppose public aid of almost any sort, as they feel its funding is coming from their hard-earned, blue-collar income. In short, although they are socioeconomically closest to the poor, attitudinally they are at a considerable distance.

Lower Class. This group—the poor, about 20 percent of the society—suffers from a negative reputation in the eyes of the rest of the society; they are often viewed as not having good, middle-class virtues. Probably the most painful aspect of being poor is the psychological assault it carries. The poor are considered the least worthy in a capitalistic system. They are viewed as takers rather than givers, burdens rather than blessings, contemptible and dirty rather than respectable and clean. The process of receiving public assistance is particularly humiliating.

The lower edge of this class includes unskilled laborers and poor farm workers. Members of this group rarely succeed in the educational system and are often targets of the legal system. This group usually exerts little political impact, other than in occasional civil disorders.

Underclass. The group includes the chronically unemployed, the unemployable, and those on public assistance and accounts for 1 to 2 percent of the society. Occupants of the underclass essentially do not or cannot participate in the larger cultural system. Many have profound personal disabilities or character disorders, while others are victims of extreme racism or some other injustice. They will be on public aid or simply drift in the undercurrents of the national economy.

CONTEMPORARY URBAN AND GLOBAL STRATIFICATION MODELS

When studied in the context of the global city, stratification is best viewed almost exclusively through an occupational lens.[5] This occupational model is rooted in the assumption that occupational status is the most predominating of the socioeconomic variables, inasmuch as it positions people in the global economic system and of course carries with it an associated level of education and prestige.

- Elites—This refers to the super-rich, entrepreneurial ownership class. These people own the buildings and substantial stock in the multinational corporations that dominate the urban marketplace.

- Professional and Creative Class—CEOs, lawyers, physicians, financial planners, administrators, and powerful figures in the major academic institutions populate the professional sector of this class. These include the occupational implementers, directing the corporate entities on a day-to-day basis and controlling job opportunities and life chances for many. In what has become a largely service economy, we may also include the creative class—those who develop the latest computer software, design in the graphic arts, and are technologically sophisticated.

- Service Class—Those employed in service occupations such as teaching, nursing, and customer relations form this group. This is a large and ever-growing sector of the class system, given the movement of the US economy from a manufacturing to service orientation.

- Working Class—Also referred to as blue collar, this includes skilled and semiskilled workers paid hourly. Those involved in the production end of manufacturing form the hub of the working class. This class, however, continues to shrink due to two forces: a decline in manufacturing and an increase in automation.

- Working Poor—These people take what's left of the US economy. Jobs include unskilled manufacturing positions, low-level clerical jobs, domestic labor, and other low-paying hourly slots.

- PublicAid and Disability—The term is rather self-explanatory. This group includes those receiving public assistance, owing to poverty or unemployment, as well as those who have mental or physical disabilities rendering them unable to be gainfully employed.

- Underclass—We could add this group, one for which the society has no place. This group consists of the permanently poor and unemployable. Due to being from second- and third-generation public aid recipients, having prison records, or being homeless, they will almost certainly never have a role of any significance in the larger national economy.

The inner city consists largely of the lower three categories.

Some collapse this six-level structure further into a two-tired service economy. The upper tier—the professional-managerial-creative stratum—includes the entrepreneurial, hi-tech, executive class. Creativity, ideas, and information are highly valued here.

The lower one, sometimes called pink collar, refers to those that are engaged in more basic, unskilled and semiskilled services—cleaning, food, low-level clerical, for example, along with part-time service employees. These involve routine service tasks, many of which serve the upper tier or the clients of the upper tier. It has been said that it requires roughly four pink collar workers to support a single upper-tier professional.

When the upper classes think of those at the bottom of the social-class system, there is a tendency to conjure up the image of an African American face. Such a notion is false; the largest number of those in these strata are Caucasian (although poverty strikes nonwhites harder by percentage). In fact, these classes are made up of many disparate groups. Every ethnic, age, and religious group has representatives in the lower and underclass.

Poverty is most apparent in the cities. As more and more affluent Caucasians leave the city neighborhoods for the suburbs or more economically segregated, regentrified areas, their place is taken by poor people, whether they be Mexican American migrants, Puerto Ricans in search of better job opportunities, African Americans from the South, South Americans, Middle Easterners, or European immigrants.

Some sociologists include among the poor all those in the lower fifth of the income distribution. Others use less arbitrary definitions and set the poverty population at forty to sixty million people. The official US government criteria for determining poverty are based on region of residence and family size and is adjusted for inflation. The figure, however, is set so low that an urban family of four would not be able to be fed, housed, and clothed adequately. The number one priority among the poor is obviously survival—little wonder, considering the economic deprivation in which they live.

Such tension and concern over survival issues tend to bring about a strong present, rather than future, orientation. The future is not something to look forward to if the economic and social horizon is not bright.

Life at society's bottom often has adverse effects on family life. Anxiety over acquiring the necessities eats away at intimacy and harmony within the family. Social life, especially in urban areas, is often not rooted in the home. While in the larger society, the home is a place of peace and surcease from the pressures of the workaday world, among those at the bottom of society, home is often a nerve-jangling, noisy, overcrowded place. Because homes are not owned by those who live in them and are often not kept up by slum landlords, there is little pride taken in the residence, and hence, little emotional attachment to it.

Pleasures and enjoyable leisure are in short supply in this sector. If an individual is unemployed, there may be a great deal of free time, but it is often not very relaxing or personally enriching. Pessimism and hopelessness corrode the spirit.

Despite all the problems of poverty and inner-city living, there are genuine strengths evident among the poor. Although family life is often under stress, there are many vital marriages in poverty communities. Moreover, many solid citizens and battle-tested, mature Christians emerge from single-parent and intact families in inner cities. Even in the areas of crime and drug abuse, the statistics can be read from two points of view. On one hand, rates do tend to be higher in inner cities and among the poor in general; on the other hand, they are not so high as to obscure the fact that amid all the deprivation, the majority of inhabitants of poor communities remain law-abiding.

Out of the crucible of poverty come impressive psychological strengths. The survival mentality gives rise to a resilient form of mental toughness, a courage bred of enduring a difficult existence. Coping skills are highly developed so that crises do not cause panic, and the insults of prejudice do not destroy character. More study needs to be made of the strengths among inner-city populations so that strategies can be developed that maximize these skills.

Conclusion. The social-class system is perpetuated by the unequal distribution of power. While the upper class tends to own the society, the middle class dominates and operates it. The result is that the system (whether it is economic, educational, or political) is governed by middle-class rules and styles of operation. For those at the lower end of the system, the middle-class method of operation imposes a dual burden. The poor not only have the usual worries about succeeding (a concern at all levels of society) but they also have to learn rules of the system in which the success game is played. This dual burden produces a great deal of tension among society's outsiders, tension which many insiders neither understand nor notice.

The consequence of this overall power disparity is conflict. It accounts for cleavages between labor and management, the poor and the rich, the government and those governed, and on and on. This is by no means an attack on the capitalistic system, for all political systems have their flaws. The point is that stratification produces winners and losers, and urban pastors are wise to understand the dynamics of the socioeconomic system as a whole, for it accounts for how the winners and losers are determined.

Perpetuation of Social Strata

The self-perpetuating nature of the stratification system is a critical element in understanding its inequitable aspects. Sociologists estimate (and this is a liberal estimate) that only about one in every four people moves up the social structure in the course of a lifetime. In other words, stratification is usually a womb-to-tomb phenomenon. Perhaps the best way to dramatize how self-perpetuating the system is, is to use an adaptation of Mayer and Buckley's Model for the Perpetuation of Social Strata (see Figure 1).[6]

Figure 1. Model for the Perpetuation of Social Strata

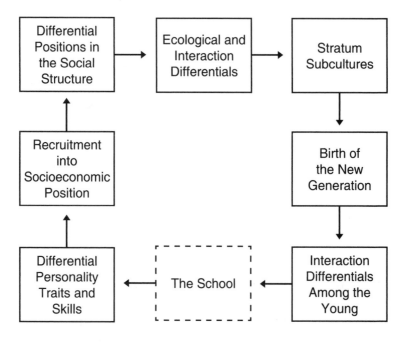

Differential Positions in the Social Structure. The model begins with the adult socioeconomic status. Beyond occupational position, income, and level of education, this status has implications for individual political power, community influence, access to the media, and personal satisfaction.

Ecological and Interaction Differentials. The adult socioeconomic status is related to the social and physical environment.

Depending on socioeconomic stratum, a person will be located in a community of the upper, middle, or lower class. Furthermore, the physical nature of this community—size of the lot, whether buildings are single- or multiple-family dwellings, recreational space, upkeep of the buildings and streets, age of the structures, residential density (people per square mile)—will also differ according to social class. These social and physical elements are powerful in shaping and socializing the individual. Spending time with a certain class of people shapes a person's thinking, and no matter how unpleasant the physical aspects, regularized contact brings a certain degree of acclimation.

Stratum Subcultures. This socialization gives rise to classes as subcultures. Each socioeconomic layer develops its own particular ways of thinking, feeling, and acting, distinguishable from the other classes. In short, each stratum constitutes a subculture—a way of life.

With regard to subcultures among the poor, there is a debate as to whether the poor hold poverty values. The prevailing position, the one this author is most comfortable with, is that although the poor are forced to make certain lifestyle adjustments as a result of their scarce means, these adjustments constitute adaptations rather than genuine value differences. People do not choose to be poor to enjoy a culture founded on deprivation.

Birth of the New Generation and Interaction Differentials among the Young. Within each stratum children are born and the differences in strata give rise to differences in socialization of these children. Lower-class children become accustomed to large families, limited space, poverty, and insecurity. Few of them will take vacations with their parents. Instead, they will develop local street savvy. Physical toughness and the ability to endure personal deprivation and hardship will likely be fostered. Upper-status youth will associate with other such young people, who have large homes and often big yards. They will have their own rooms, stereo equipment, and television. They may travel with their families across the country and perhaps around the world. Food will be in plenteous supply, and contact with adults within the nuclear family will be more frequent. They will lack few material possessions or creature comforts.

Differential Personality Traits and Skills. These socialization differences will, as already implied, have consequences for the development of personality traits and skills. What is crucial is that personality—that organized matrix of behaviors, attitudes, values, beliefs, and motives characteristic of an individual—is much determined by early socialization experience. Hence, poor youngsters are likely to develop a lifeview congruent with their social background. Street savvy, a job, a car, and freedom from the oppressive burden of poverty are likely to be more immediate goals than a first-rate education, a white-collar job, or travel.

Although lower-status youths may value the same things other children value, their sense of realism, coupled with their limited exposure to life in a more privileged setting, will likely cause them to act on a different set of values. Exposure to poverty, violence, drunkenness, and police harassment is likely to spawn political and social attitudes consistent with having viewed the effects of these problems. More-affluent youth, who have spent their time among people whose economic and occupational destiny are pretty much under their own control, are more likely to develop a set of attitudes that emphasize individual achievement along with economic and occupational security.

In terms of skills, the poor youngster is likely to develop abilities vital to surviving the physical and emotional traumas of life. Other children are likely to learn verbal skills, such as reading, writing, and speaking standard English, as well as how to present themselves favorably to the white-collar professionals who determine who will be employed. In short, although the skills learned by those at the bottom are valuable, if not absolutely critical, they will not aid the person in adjusting to or succeeding in the middle-class institutional network, beginning with school and leading to the job market.

Recruitment into Socioeconomic Position. Once preadult socialization is complete and personalities are shaped and skills developed, the individual is ready to assume a status in the adult structure. And, because of the markedly different set of influences and influencers, according to status at birth, the odds are overwhelming that the person's adult socioeconomic status will be the same as that of her childhood.

The School. The school is placed between the socialization differences and personality traits and skills because its entrance into the child's life occurs at that chronological point. Theoretically, the US school system is designed to equalize opportunity, that is, make certain that success or failure is a function of ability and effort. In short, it is intended to compensate for or eliminate the effect of socioeconomic status at birth. However, the overwhelming bulk of studies conducted by educators and sociologists indicates that, if anything, the school reinforces rather than removes status differences. In fact, the most powerful determinant and the best predictor of an individual's achievement in school is socioeconomic status. This should be no surprise when it is considered that the social and academic skills most rewarded and nurtured by the schools are those highly valued and almost religiously taught in the middle class.

Conclusion. An overall view of the whole, self-perpetuating system makes it obvious that instead of all people having equal access to the social classes, a person's status at birth largely determines the future. At birth, an individual is already set in motion—the train is on a track, on a route headed toward an identical adult status. Only a dramatic intervention en route somewhere will move the individual off the track and headed toward a different status.

Perhaps the most powerful of American myths is that people are what they are (socioeconomically) because of achievement rather than because they were born that way. It is this myth of self-congratulation and other-degradation that drains away empathy for those who find themselves at the bottom of the US socioeconomic system. It is this myth that makes it difficult for urban pastors to get help in the form of money or time from affluent congregations and denominations. People are thought to be poor because of their own deficiencies, not because of any inherent, self-perpetuating qualities of the socioeconomic system. This is not to say that individual effort and achievement are unimportant. It is to say that they are by no means the only dynamics involved. In the final analysis, if urban pastors can overcome this and related antipoverty biases, they will be more likely to gain support and involvement for urban parishes.

NEIGHBORHOODS AND THE NEIGHBORHOOD CHURCH

A knowledge of the societal stratification system provides insight into smaller systems such as neighborhoods. The importance of neighborhood is evident in the tendency of people often to think in terms of the neighborhood rather than the city in which they live.

In this work, the concept of the neighborhood, or at least community, necessitates expanded treatment because it is the direction urban ministry is going. Defining a neighborhood as a stewardship and service area provides the urban church with a manageable turf on which to do its work. This is extremely important. One of the Achilles heels of Lyndon Johnson's War on Poverty programs of the 1960's was that the service area was national. Lacking boundaries, these well-meaning programs got tangled up in myriad inefficiencies and wholesale lack of accountability. With the scope national, only national figures could serve as bases for evaluation. In short, the effort was unmanageable. Successful urban programs tend to be more micro- than macrocosmic. A geographical approach, based on church resources, increases effectiveness of programs, which can then be replicated elsewhere by others. Interestingly, virtually every urban ministry program with impact has a defined service area. Success is to be achieved with few before it can be spread to the many.

Types of Neighborhoods

An updated adaptation of Warren and Warren's excellent work in how to define, organize, and even change a neighborhood can be helpful in understanding a neighborhood. Warren and Warren used three basic principles in studying a neighborhood.[7] The first principle is *identity:* to what extent do the people feel they belong to a neighborhood, sharing a common destiny with their fellow residents? The second is *interaction:* how frequently and in what numbers do people visit their neighbors in the course of a year? The third principle is *linkages:* what and how effective are the channels people use to funnel information in and out of the neighborhood?

In a global era of increasing residential mobility and accelerated change within city communities, the identity and interaction principles become more diffuse. While old racial and ethnic residential barriers are breaking down in middle-class neighborhoods, paradoxically there is likely a lessening of neighbor-to-neighbor interaction within them because cultural differences remain. Less interaction leads also to a lowered sense of belongingness and unity. In that sense, the traditional meaning of neighborhood—one in which a person interacts closely with the person living next door—is largely a thing of the past. What does exist, particularly in middle-class and regentrified neighborhoods, is a growing concern about economic stability and physical safety. Urban neighborhoods do have names (Wicker Park, Fort Green, etc.) and the residents in these neighborhood communities are usually quite aware of these names and what they connote in terms of economic value and safety. Linkages, however, are more important than ever. The more upscale the neighborhood, the more will be its linkages to the global city of which it is a part.

In any case, these three principles are criteria for determining the social structure of a neighborhood. They cut across economic and racial lines and so can be used in any urban neighborhood. On the basis of these criteria—identity, interaction, and linkages—basic types of neighborhoods can be differentiated.

The first and strongest type is the *integral neighborhood.* Here identity, interaction, and linkages are all positive, with the people cohesive and active. They are involved both on the local turf and in the city at large. In a more global age, commitment to the integral neighborhood takes the form of identification with the community's status as a whole rather than a particular set of neighbors. The integral neighborhood is often one that is appreciating economically. There is physical safety, rising real estate values, and sound schools.

The *parochial neighborhood* is second. There is evidence of sound identity and interaction, but such a neighborhood receives a minus in linkages. These neighborhoods are an outgrowth of the cultural-pluralism era, with the ethnic village—Little Italy, Chinatown, Little San Juan—typifying it. As immigrants become more Americanized and the larger US mainstream becomes more homogenized due to more global influences such as the Internet and popular culture, these neighborhoods are disappearing.

The *diffuse neighborhood* has a sense of identity but little in the way of interaction or linkages. Such a neighborhood is homogeneous in the sense that it can be a new subdivision or inner-city housing project. However, the neighborhood lacks internal vitality and is not closely related to the larger region. There is little involvement with neighbors. This type of community is becoming more and more dominant in major cities.

The *transitory neighborhood* has little identity or interaction. It does have linkages to the outside, however. Here population change is evident and the neighborhood breaks into clusters. Often long-term residents are separated from newcomers. There is little joint activity or organization.

There is also the *anomic neighborhood.* This has little identity or interaction and few linkages. It is hardly a neighborhood at all because there is no cohesion, and there is great social distance between its members.

An urban pastor needs to identify the type of community within which the church resides. Moreover, having core church families visit sets of nearby families can develop friendships and build bridges. From these visits, neighborhood and community needs can be defined. After the information is gathered and discussed, needs can be identified and strategies for action developed. The church then can be renewed through prayer, reflection, and action, with bridges built within the church and between the church and the residents.

Neighborhood Empowerment

Analysis of the neighborhood is one of the precursors to effective ministry. In fact, such analyses lead to the real focus of contemporary urban ministry: empowerment.

Empowerment involves the transfer of control and neighborhood determination from outside forces to neighborhood residents. Neighborhood empowerment is an effort at the decentralization of power, enabling neighborhood residents to control their own situation. As certainly as individuals in therapy start improving once they realize they can do something about their problems, so also neighborhoods are revitalized when self-determination is in evidence.

Empowerment occurs when residents can move from a survival level in which there is dependence on public aid of some sort, to marginality in which they can barely make it on their own, to initial accumulation where there is down-payment money for a house or car, to moderate accumulation with savings accounts and planning for the future, and up to rapid accumulation in which money begins multiplying itself.

Unhooking a neighborhood from dependency on outside programming and resources is basic to empowerment. What is necessary is public investment in neighborhoods rather than public-aid maintenance dollars that assure barely a survival level. Too often public-aid monies earmarked for needy city dwellers never reach them. For example, over 50 percent of government monies targeted for the poor is funnelled through Medicaid and Medicare, so that much of it goes into the pockets of professional distributors. A bit of unpublished research in Chicago indicated there was enough dollar-flow into one low-income community to keep two suburban neighborhoods alive. Unfortunately, because those dollars were filtered through bureaucracies, most of the money wound up in the hands of white-collar personnel. Public schools and fire and police departments often receive special funding for work in inner-city neighborhoods, but they rarely make an effort to hire neighborhood residents who know their immediate needs and could use gainful employment.

Neighborhood empowerment requires organization and planning. It means addressing issues on a variety of fronts. Such issues include influencing institutions and businesses to hire neighborhood residents; gaining a voice in the administration and operation of schools; gaining control by means of property ownership; demanding proper and responsive political representation; improving health care, perhaps by developing an organization such as a health maintenance organization that yields benefits for staying healthy; and obtaining greater commitment and improved services from financial institutions. In addition, with the rise of modern government agencies, to gain an impact in urban political structures requires dealing with appointed bureaucrats rather than elected officials. Thus a key neighborhood empowerment issue is gaining bureaucratic accountability.

Below is a set of ten strategies for improving neighborhoods. They provide a jumping off point for a church's program aimed at neighborhood empowerment.[8]

1. Mobilize voters to clean out political figures who prey on neighborhood misery.

2. Work toward eliminating or reforming day-labor organizations through competition. Day-labor organizations hire unemployed residents on a day-by-day basis to do contracted

work. The workers are paid in cash at the end of the day. The profits are raked in by the organization, which, in some cases, encourages willing workers to bribe the officials in order to get a job for a day.

3. Work with the electorate to rid the area of undesirable liquor establishments and other trouble spots.

4. Deal head-on with the neighborhood's concern about street crime.

5. Provide escort service and other moral support for witnesses to appear in court cases dealing with street crime and intimidation.

6. Work at cutting through bureaucratic barriers in removing abandoned autos, vacant factories, and empty buildings.

7. Approach public officials to stop licensing additional public housing and sheltered-care facilities, such as nursing homes or half-way houses for the mentally disturbed, until the community has had time to deal with the ones already there.

8. Encourage local institutions to remain and adapt to changing populations and lifestyles.

9. Promote investment in older, multiple-family dwellings in order both to renovate neighborhood housing and to avoid the development of a slum.

10. Capitalize on the power of local institutions whose own futures are linked to the well-being of the community for support and strength.

A Stewardship Ministry

Working toward empowerment is a stewardship rather than a service ministry. The church must get beyond the old missionary model in which a missionary goes into an area with all the expenses and salary paid by outside sources and then performs a relief ministry. In the urban church, that kind of approach can be seen when the church is simply a clubhouse for activities and a dispenser of services to the needy. As important as relief ministries are, the church must go beyond being an ecclesiastical version of the welfare system.

Reform does call the church to deal with power. Power is, in itself, neither good nor bad. Power does not corrupt. The sinful human soul uses power for oppressive purposes. One of the most famous community organizers in the twentieth century, Saul Alinsky, spoke eloquently to the issue of power.

> Pascal . . . observed that . . . "justice without power is impotent; power without justice is tyranny." St. Ignatius . . . (said): "to do a thing well a man needs power and competence." We could call the roll of all who played out their parts in history and find the word power, not a substitute word, used in their speech and writings. It is impossible to conceive of a world devoid of power; the only choice of concepts is between organized and unorganized power. Mankind has progressed only though learning how to develop and organize instruments of power in order to achieve order, security, morality, and civilized life itself, instead of a sheer struggle for physical survival. Every organization known to man, from government on down, has had only one reason for being—that is organization for power in order to put into practice or promote its common purpose.[9]

For William Stringfellow, powers and principalities include all institutions, worldviews, traditions, policies, and national and multinational forces.

> Thus, the Pentagon or the Ford Motor Company or Harvard University or the Hudson Institute or Consolidated Edison, or the Diners Club or the Olympics or the Methodist Church or the Teamsters Union are all principalities. So are capitalism, Maoism, humanism, Mormonism, astrology, the Puritan Work Ethic, science, and scientism, white supremacy, patriotism, plus many,

many more—sports sex, may profession or discipline, technology, money, the family—beyond any respect of full enumeration. The principalities and powers are legion.[10]

Regrettably, the church at large and in its local form, often sees itself as impotent. In its own way, it adopts the same disability common among the urban poor: learned helplessness. Learned helplessness can also be corrupting. It has an immobilizing effect, leading to inaction, cynicism, fatalism, and a sense that events are unchangeable.[11] Particularly in an urban-driven, global era, things look so large, so unalterable, that people often feel a sense of inadequacy and resignation.

But the church is not powerless. It is one of the only institutions that has endured in the United States for the last two centuries. It has arguably stood more steadfastly and unchangeably than any other. More importantly, it is God's own institution, one that he has decreed that the very gates of hell will not prevail against. When courageous, the church has made a difference. The Gamaliel Foundation and the Metropolitan Alliance of Congregations in Chicago mobilize power to act on issues of temporal concern. The Civil Rights Movement of the 1960's was an almost entirely church-based form of organization. Prayer meetings led to marches and courageous, and usually non-violent, turn-the-other-cheek efforts at gaining social justice. Chicago's LaSalle Street Church organized itself in the form of the Cabrini Green Legal Aid Clinic, to provide legal protection and representation for its indigent neighbors. Churches have worked with gangs in Los Angeles and the homeless in Washington D.C.

Again, organizing is at its best when it involves those in the church community most affected by the issue at hand. Rev. Chuck Infelt of Holy Family Lutheran Church in Cabrini-Green understands that. He has urged community residents to remain in the community in the face of a lessening of housing stock, pressure from the city, and relocation vouchers.[12] Carol Steele remained. She became a part of an organization named Cabrini's

Local Advisory Council that threatened to sue the city over the destruction of its community and the forced displacement of its residents. For four years the council held off redevelopment efforts and then received a consent decree that until new homes were constructed, at least some of the buildings would stay up. Moreover, it guaranteed displaced residents a new home in the redeveloped community. With this legal decision, the tenants were empowered as never before. They were anointed codevelopers and entitled to a share in the rehab and the low-income housing construction profits.[13]

Indeed, new leaders emerge from community-based organizing efforts, and the church can become a voice for good in the community. More importantly, it becomes an instrument for the building of the kingdom of God on earth.

Key to the church's engaging power is that the acquisition of power is never the goal. The church is not interested in secular power. It is a spiritual entity, not ultimately of this world. Its interest in power must always be solely to confront evil forms of power and promote a socially just society. Furthermore, that power needs to be apolitical. The church is not a political organization. It is not a wing of the Republican or Democrat Party. Right-wing and left-wing Christianity are not forms of Christianity. They are the illegitimate offspring of an unholy spiritual and political union. The church's focus must be on issues not candidates, on justice not party loyalty.

Moreover, community organization is not a call for a local theocracy. Again, the church is not about political power, and its kingdom is not of this world. It is interested in justice, in the whole person—body, mind, and spirit—and sees its call to redeem the times spiritually and temporally.

The United States is a capitalistic society. Money is the driving force of its secular power. As such, reform often takes the form of Community Economic Development (CED). CEDs tend to focus on any or all of the following: housing, medical assistance and clinics, employment training and placement, and educational training. The Bethel New Life, a community development agency of Chicago's Bethel Lutheran Church, is one such example. Mary Nelson, of Bethel New Life, states that the goal of the organization is holistic, "to weave a healthy, sustainable community on Chicago's West Side."[14]

Other examples of CEDs are The Resurrection Project (TRP) in Chicago's Mexican American Pilsen community, Hope for Chattanooga, and others. These efforts at community economic development are Christlike in that they offer a form of unconditional love. Successful urban churches do not draw the line at helping only their members. They want Christ's love to be felt in the community among the unchurched. They have an evangelical impact by identifying the church with social justice.

Again, the temporal goal of community economic development is to create a sense of independence for members of the community. It is an effort to flee the client-recipient model typical of much relief effort and build healthy, functioning, empowered neighborhoods that can take responsible action for their own well-being.

Empowerment and community health efforts are aided by strength of unity. This is especially important because these efforts often mean dealing with institutions, the topic of the next chapter.

POVERTY FROM AN INSTITUTIONAL PERSPECTIVE 4

The truths of stratification and self-perpetuation of the socio-economic system are not widely known or accepted. As a result, negative attitudes toward the poor persist. The perpetuation of poverty by society results partly, as Harrington points out, from its invisibility.[1] It is very difficult for people to become concerned about problems with which they are not confronted. In cities the poor are so severely segregated that a person can live for years in an urban metropolis without ever driving to a poor neighborhood. When poverty is an abstraction, it is exceedingly difficult for many middle-class people to believe that there can be thirty to forty million people in the United States living below the poverty level. This invisibility is exacerbated by the immobility of the poor. Many are unable, because of physical illness or financial deprivation, to leave their neighborhoods. So just as the middle class do not go into poor neighborhoods, neither do the poor make their way into middle-class neighborhoods.

To argue that poverty is a self-perpetuating condition in a capitalistic society is to attack the nation's sacred civil doctrine of the self-made person. To suggest that a person is poor because of an unequal distribution of opportunities is to suggest that riches are as much a matter of good fortune as virtue.

Ironically, middle-class people have no feelings of inferiority about not being truly rich, for if asked why they are not more affluent, they will be quick to tell of their roots and how these precluded the opportunity for acquiring great riches. Yet these same individuals cannot accept a similar accounting for poverty. Humans are often rationalizing rather than rational entities. Never is that more in evidence than in our being critical of the poor while excusing our own failure to reach the economic heights to which we would aspire.

INSTITUTIONS AND THE POOR

In spite of the many poverty myths, poverty means much more than absence of money. It is powerlessness and alienation from the key institutions of society. The lack of integration of the poor in the major institutions of the society is heightened among the city poor who feel an overwhelming sense of powerlessness and confusion as they deal anonymously with massive, impersonal bureaucracies, in which size and officialdom have an intimidating effect.

In many communities, multistoried government buildings are filled with middle-class personnel whose main task is to orient aimless poverty victims to the prevailing system, referring them to employment centers, health clinics, neighborhood mental health offices, special school programs, city services pertaining to public aid and building maintenance, legal aid agencies, and so on. Probably no characteristic of urban poverty stands out more than this lack of experience and familiarity with basic urban services and agencies.

Sociologically, institutions are abstract collectivities that meet basic human needs. In the United States, six major institutions are often defined: politics, religion, economics, family, education, and recreation. The acronym for this institutional system (PREFER) clearly reflects the relationship of the inner-city poor to each of these institutions—the fundamental human needs of the people are barely met in any of them.

The urban poor are almost completely cut off from the wider society and yet are oppressively controlled by it. They are usually geographically separated from "polite society," but the power figures of the city hold tight control over what are euphemistically called poor neighborhoods. The police are ever present; the politicians regularly "ride herd" in the ghetto areas; the schools teach a main-stream lifestyle; large denominations constantly dictate policy to their urban missions; and the welfare system keeps tight rein on the lifestyle of public-aid recipients. The feeling of oppression—of a noose around a poor neck—often creates a volatile climate in the inner cities.

Politics

The real governing force in the global age is not that of the various nation-states, but rather international monetary governance. The World Bank, the International Monetary Fund, the World Trade Organization, and the various international stock exchanges now drive the national governments because of their stranglehold on the global economy. There is a sort of "econocentrism," one in which the closer a nation is to the center of the global economy, the more it benefits; conversely, the greater the participatory distance, the less a nation can experience through self-determination.

This global monetary force becomes visible as these larger financial sources link with local urban corporate interests and city governments in redevelopment ventures. A major—often multinational—corporation gains financial support from an international bank and then bargains with the mayor of a large city for a substantial tax break in return for locating in that mayor's city and contributing to that city's revenues by generating more business and expanding its tax base.

The poor in the United States, though citizens of a major global player, are nonparticipants in the global market. Moreover, this international monetary system is characterized by high-risk venturing. Therefore, whenever the global system suffers, there is negative trickle-down to the poor in the city. Less money at the top means less investment at the bottom.

Because of the impact of globalization, the inner city cannot be viewed in isolation, but rather as part of a larger global city, which in turn is very much a participant in a global economy and mindset. What happens in the world markets of Tokyo, London, and New York has consequences for life in the inner city of Cleveland.

At the national and too often at the local level as well, the poor are all but without representation politically. Not a single senator or congressman is noted primarily for championing the cause of the poor. Nearly fifty million people live without a voice. In fact, almost every well-known figure who is viewed as an advocate of the poor has been outside the prevailing system. Martin Luther King, Malcolm X, Jesse Jackson, and Cesar Chavez are examples. The poor are minimally represented because, in a capitalistic society, they produce little in the way of goods and services. What is more, with mass disorganization and estrangement, coupled with little stable community leadership, the poor vote in low numbers, making them almost irrelevant to well-healed, high-powered political candidates.

In poverty areas can be found the classic example of political reversal. Instead of the political system depending on the support of the people, the people depend on it and so become the pawns of the political system. A housing issue at a Chicago inner-city community during the days of knuckle-cracking machine politics illustrates this.

A mass meeting over a housing grievance was held in one of the neighborhood's churches. City officials, neighborhood residents, and community workers were present to hear the matter. The conflict was resolved with the city officials assuring the citizens that they would make good on their vows to provide and maintain adequate housing. A subsequent meeting was scheduled for a month later to check on the officials' progress toward honoring their promises.

A month passed and the day of accountability arrived. Much to the surprise of the community workers, neither the aggrieved neighborhood residents nor the city officials showed up. The church hall was nearly empty. A bit of investigation revealed a political coup. Apparently, an official from his downtown city office called the tenant council in one of the high-rise buildings and stated that he was privy to a rumor that if the meeting was held as scheduled, the welfare checks (due on the third of the month) would be late in arriving. Faced with a choice between improved housing or food, the residents quickly capitulated to the threat, and the meeting was boycotted. For the city it was the perfect squelch. They claimed publicly that they had obviously done their job well because the community, by virtue of their nonattendance at the meeting, showed that the matter required no further attention.

Intimidation among the poor is real. Statistics among African Americans are helpful poverty indicators because so many are trapped in inner cities. In any case, the long arm of the law reaches disproportionately in the direction of African Americans. For example, publicly available statistics indicate that in 1990 slightly over 500,000 African American males were incarcerated. By 2000 the number approached 800,000. More African American males are in jail than college. The US Justice Department projected that one in three African American males born in 2001 will spend some time incarcerated. Overall, about 70 percent of the total prison population is nonwhite.

Numbers like these, coupled with incidents like that in housing project, provide a stark explanation for why inner-city citizens who do vote often cast their ballots for the same oppressive big-city political regimes election after election. The voters are often intimidated. It used to be common for local political organizers to roam the streets and subtly but clearly warn the citizens that if candidate "X" did not receive adequate support at the polls, he would have little reason to serve the community well. Translated, that meant that fire protection might be even more lackadaisical than before, police service increasingly oppressive and decreasingly protective, project buildings ignored, slum landlords under even looser control, and garbage allowed to pile up, making the rat and roach epidemic even worse.

It is safe to say that veiled threats of various forms continue to exist, but less so. Today the inner city is simply disconnected, off the radar screen from the large global city. Voter registration is understandably low in the inner city. With the chaos and survival behavior going on in these crucibles, there is little time to consider voting. Besides, if a given city's political administration is reasonably secure, it is unlikely that a few votes in the inner city will turn the election; so, one vote will count for little. Should and individual decide to vote, however, it is probably safer to support the incumbents. Perhaps they will see that support and be more concerned about the city services on which the inner-city neighborhood depends.

In short, little political organization and savvy and a resulting lack of power account for the reason so few changes are made in the inner city. An urban church worker learns quickly that the people are not only beset with ineffective governmental programs and policies but, even worse, are without realistic grievance mechanisms to ameliorate these problems. In fact, many welfare-oriented government programs exist simply because of political powerlessness, and although they may be designed with the best of intentions, they are just substitutes for what is really needed: an equitable share of political power in a representative democracy.

Religion

Religion, as an institution, is also tainted by poverty. In many inner cities, the church is the only really caring agency of any enduring value. It is a meeting place, a fellowship center, and a source of support. However, these churches almost invariably exist on a hand-to-mouth basis.

Urban church staffs are small, with many positions filled by volunteers. There is a great need for professionalism and urban expertise, but there is simply no money to fund the programs that could use trained personnel effectively. If the church is nondenominational, it lives off the income garnered from the collection plate. Such a budget would provide only for the minister, if even that. In many cases, an indigenous pastor is only a part-time professional, spending most of available work time laboring in a factory or a store in the neighborhood. If the church belongs to a mainline denomination, it is most likely on that denomination's home-missionary budget, receiving a monthly pittance to carry on the awesome task. In short, another reversal is in operation. The churches that need the money for comprehensive and effective whole-person ministry receive the least support, while other congregations debate whether to purchase a new organ or better sanctuary carpeting.

In African American communities the larger churches serve as powerful social and political forces as well as a spiritual force. In fact, male pastoral selection in the more prominent black churches is wholly different from their white counterparts in the same denomination. An African American pastoral aspirant commonly serves under a mentor—a well-established senior pastor in the community—and only after he has completed this unofficial apprenticeship to the satisfaction of his mentor will he get his own church.[2] The apprenticeship, then, supersedes every other criterion for becoming senior pastor—academic degree, seminary attended, even personal gifts. This apprenticeship system serves a very valuable function in the African American community. It insures that pastors who have received on-the-job training in the local community will lead the churches. It is also establishes a clear hierarchy of community leadership among the various pastors serving the community. Nonetheless, money and power are problems in these churches as well. The numbers of well-educated, professional, and politically connected members are few, and the number of indigent many.

Economics

Nearly 10 percent of US evangelical Christians are in serious debt.[3] Moreover, 40 percent of the people surveyed randomly in

2000 stated that "in debt" was a proper way to describe their economic status.[4] For the poor, however, it is much worse. Poverty in economics connotes much more than simply a lack of money. High unemployment and underemployment mean a lack of access to acquiring money.

Much of the insensitivity of middle- and upper-class people toward the poor is an outgrowth of the Protestant work ethic. The Protestant work ethic, in its oversimplified form, suggests that if people work hard, they will attain success. It is a strongly procapitalistic-religious doctrine, emanating from the notion that God blesses those he favors and, therefore, if someone is living in God's favor and laboring faithfully, success will result. Much of the Protestant ethic is valid, for we would be hard-pressed to find many truly successful people who have not worked very hard at achieving that success. In that respect, its endorsement of hard work and attention to duty is sound. The problem comes with the Protestant ethic's unwritten corollary: If people are not successful, they have not worked hard. Once that corollary is accepted (and it is subtly taught throughout the nation's schools and churches), the seeds of prejudice toward the poor are well planted.

One aspect of this problem is that many people cannot understand why there is so much unemployment in the inner cities. A look at the daily papers reveals legions of job opportunities. This issue merits examination.

If we take a close look at those want ads, it becomes apparent that there really are not very many jobs for the poor. First, there continues to be a diminution of manufacturing jobs, once within reach of some of the poor. Second, those jobs that remain require a substantial amount of education or technical skill. Even those jobs that require less formal preparation still require well-developed literary skills. These requirements eliminate most of the poor. Third, many of the ever-shrinking supply of manufacturing jobs listed are not located close to poverty areas. Many industries, and hence jobs, have moved to the suburban industrial parks. Finally, the jobs in existence (this includes many pink-collar opportunities) pay at or near the minimum wage. At the minimum wage times forty hours, the vast majority of low-income families will remain below the federal poverty level. In addition, job-related expenses such as travel, perhaps baby-sitting, clothes, and other mundane items make it even less economical to accept such employment.

A large candy manufacturer once felt compelled to do something to relieve the pain of unemployment in Chicago's Cabrini-Green, an intense, inner-city public housing community. The company offered plant jobs to those who needed them. There were two problems. One was that they offered the minimum wage, and the second was that the jobs were fifteen miles away in a western suburb. What is especially poignant about this example is that it is typical of well-meaning attempts to redress poverty through employment opportunities.

Though less talked about, underemployment is also a problem. There are myriad poor who work, but less than full-time or at jobs well below their capabilities. For those who work part-time, there are sharp financial effects, making it doubtful whether it is economically wise to be working at all. For those who work at jobs below their abilities, there is a morale-deadening factor, one that robs labor of all sense of satisfaction and accomplishment. This widespread underemployment is not unemployment and is therefore not included in the monthly unemployment rates. It is obvious that work is not a guaranteed route out of poverty.

What has developed out of this is a huge, underground, cash-driven economy. Scores of poor Hispanics and African Americans find cash-only work. For many it is a matter of survival. For those on some form of public aid, working for cash will not show up on their record and so imperil their benefits. Moreover, with welfare reform tightening the noose on the poor, many others are ineligible for benefits and so look for tax-free income anywhere they can find it. This cash-employment system is particularly strong in restaurants, domestic work, and low- and mid-level construction.

In addition to employment problems, the poor also face exploitive consumer practices. The poor spend a greater proportion of their income for necessities in the form of food, shelter, and health care than do the middle class, although the quality of their investment return is much less.

The poor pay more for less. Inner cities are teeming with exploitive money hounds who prey on helpless residents. Because there are often no large grocery stores in the neighborhood and no transportation to stores outside the community, the people often buy their goods at small, neighborhood establishments. A walk through almost any such store will reveal inflated prices and inferior merchandise. The proprietor takes advantage of the patrons' lack of shopping alternatives. If the people do not do much looking elsewhere, they are often unaware of how badly they are being exploited.

However, the presence of a larger chain store is no guarantee of fairness either. In Chicago one such store "serving" an inner-city community was taking the spoiled fruits and vegetables from the suburban stores and selling them at increased prices. When confronted by a group of concerned citizens, the store simply closed down rather than rectify this or any other of its exploitive practices.

Moreover, with inadequate funds, the poor cannot take advantage of sales on food or other goods sold in volume. This means that poor shoppers invariably pay much higher prices for the staples of life.

Exploitation is most rampant in consumer fraud in the form of corrupt car dealers, furniture stores, and most importantly, finance companies. Usually the dealer will sell a gullible consumer an item for a very small downpayment and then sell the contract to a neighborhood finance company. The interest rates on the merchandise are exorbitant, but the purchaser, who lacks awareness about installment buying and is dazzled by the acquisition of a bit of luxury amid the squalor of poverty, eagerly signs on the dotted line. One Chicago-area auto dealer boasted in private of hitting African American car buyers with a 29 percent interest rate. Frequently, the purchaser simply defaults on the payments because of unexpected financial catastrophes, misunderstandings related to credit payments, or for some other reason. The result is the repossession and resale of the merchandise. The finance company is cut in on this bonanza through contracts laden with outrageous interest. These contracts prove extremely lucrative when fully paid, and even if the loan is in default, a good deal of interest money is usually pocketed. The victim is always the consumer. Such capers are successful again and again because the people are not aware of their rights, are lied to concerning them, or do not understand the legal channels open to them to redress these inequities.

There is exploitation even in financial transactions. The poor cannot turn to banks for their dealings. One reason is that few, if any, banks are located in inner cities. Moreover, because of their middle-class aura, banks are very threatening to many of the poor. Also, with little income, who can be concerned with opening a savings account or a trust fund? For many this means turning to payday-type loan stores for "juice loans" when money is short. These are short-term, high-interest loans to be paid off when the next paycheck comes in.

With few inner-city residents having bank accounts, either for checking or savings, almost all such transactions are done in cash. In order to do business, people must have checks cashed and obtain money orders. Such dealings are executed at a currency exchange, which is notorious for legally stealing from the poor. The currency exchange has a monopoly on cashing checks, supplying money orders, and paying utility bills (electricity, telephone, and gas bills are regularly handled at these places). The result is that the currency exchange demands ridiculous service charges for almost every conceivable activity. Thus the poor, who need to pinch literally every penny, watch dollars needlessly slip away.

On top of the problems of employment and consumer exploitation, there is little economic and consumer knowledge. Perhaps the most basic reason is lack of experience. Those who have been raised in poverty have never had much money to handle in the first place. Consequently, such middle-class childhood learning devices as allowances, toy purchases, and junior savings clubs are all but nonexistent, giving the people little or no conscious social-ization in money management. Adults do not have charge cards, checking accounts, tax accountants, and itemized deductions on which they sharpen their fiscal acumen and pass it along to their youth. There are simply no models. In female-headed families, the oldest child is often saddled with the shopping duties. Because such persons often have no knowledge of how to handle money shrewdly and have little cash to begin with, they are often the victims of economic exploitation.

Family

Sociologically, there is not a more critical institution than the family. It is the chief agent of socialization and the transmitter of basic values. Nowhere are families more frequently broken than among the poor. There is no shortage of reasons for this. Poverty itself is among the most important. The very economic system that operates in poverty communities breeds family destruction. For years, many states required that a family be broken before it could receive any public aid. As a result, many marriages broke up simply because the family could not survive with an intact marriage in which the male was jobless or perhaps unemployable.

Beyond governmental restrictions, the rigors of poverty eat away at the marriage bond. In the United States, a person's identity and worth are determined largely by occupation. If people are either terribly impoverished or, worse, unemployed, their identity and self-worth are under intense assault. Frustrated wives, exhausted by the ravages of poverty and slum living, are tempted to carp at their spouses about the squalor in which they and their children are forced to live. These forces wreak havoc on male egos and exert pressure on couples to separate.

As urban poverty worsens, the number of intact families decreases. Many of the inner-city statistics are focused on African Americans because they make up such a huge percentage of so many major inner-city communities. In terms of the African American family, in 1960 70 percent of them were intact; forty years later 60 percent were fatherless. As a result, in addition to the extremely high divorce rate in almost any inner-city community, often an equivalent number of marriages end in desertion or separation. In the case of desertion, the wife may never know the whereabouts of the departed husband. She is left with only the anguish of rejection. There is no contact, no resolution of the problems, and no visitation with the children. Nothing. For the departed male, this may seem the only sane option. Facing an alienated wife, hungry children, and a slum dwelling is only a reminder of personal failure.

Often in the case of desertion, divorces are obtained through legal-aid clinics. The process itself adds to the sense of humiliation. A notice of the divorce filing is published in the newspaper for a given length of time. If the deserting party does not respond to contest it, the divorce is granted. There is no alimony or child support of course, only a divorce, and perhaps the further indignities of welfare.

Poor families, then, are often female-headed. In a nation in which adult males are customarily the chief breadwinners, poor children are often robbed of models of how the ordinary familial system works. In such homes there are no flesh-and-blood examples of employed adult males who are succeeding in the occupational and economic market. This deficit of males can have real implications for the urban church, for it makes many become decidedly female dominated. Moreover, male children may be difficult to motivate along traditional educational lines as they see no real examples of successfully educated male adults living in their community. Beyond all this, children of both genders enter adolescent and adulthood with no family tradition of marital success.

Because many poor families are female headed and because even intact families are hassled with making ends meet, mothers seek employment outside the home. As a result, children lack adult supervision. Much of their socialization takes place in the street. For the poor child, there is an absence of constructive family conversation, family group activities, and even a sense of what an intact family unit is like. For many youth there simply is no adult to talk to, to listen to, or to learn from. The oldest daughter may raise her younger brothers and sisters while her mother is out working.

In some cases there is an extended family nearby, often consisting of grandparents, uncle, aunts, and cousins. Where the extended family is present, there can be real advantages. Aid in such practical matters as babysitting, changing residences, and even financial crises can be obtained at little or no cost.

In any case, the result of an absence of a healthy family tradition and effective supervision is often early and careless involvement in sex. For many disenfranchised youth, early sexual experience connotes a sense of mature masculinity and femininity. With little stigma associated with children born out of wedlock—for example, 70 percent of African American children are born out of wedlock—the young father or mother can feel like somebody in a larger culture that regards them as nobody.

For the poor the only security in old age may be their children, who will care for their parent until death. For most people old age is provided for by a pension, a savings account, and social security benefits. Poor families have few, if any, of these; so in the long run, children—in or out of wedlock—may actually aid the poor.

Education

Poverty is perhaps no more vividly reflected than in the institution of education. In major inner-city high schools, it is common for the average student to read at the third-grade level, with not a single student reading at a twelfth-grade level. This means that the valedictorian of such a school does not read at grade level. I recall working with a sixth-grade youngster (while I was teaching in an inner-city middle school early in my career) and discovering that the youth, by no means retarded, was unable to recite the alphabet. These are not exceptional cases.

There are many reasons for this educational outrage. One of them is a lack of models. In a poor urban community a youngster is likely to grow up without a single well-educated person with whom to identify. Virtually every middle-class child is surrounded with literate models. In fact, it is largely to avoid the criticism and scorn of these models that many middle-class youth learn to read and write. This is not so in the urban enclaves. The only well-educated inhabitants of the community are the social workers and teachers who labor in the community by day and then quickly exit to the suburbs by late afternoon. The role models of the poor are from the ranks of the unemployed, unskilled, alcoholic, disabled, and criminal. Ironically, the criminal group includes the most affluent of the lot: the three Ps—prostitutes, pimps, and pushers. In any case, time is spent on the street and watching television. Reading is obsolete.

A second reason for poor education is the limited formal education of the parent(s), coupled with a lack of opportunity in general, so that the youth usually has little contact with books and newspapers. This limited involvement with print is a powerful factor in accounting for reading and writing difficulties among inner-city students. In short, there is a lack of preparedness in the form of experience and motivation for learning to read and write. Moreover, many children, because of large families and overcrowded surroundings, do not enjoy the common and delightful experience of millions of other children—having their parents read to them. It is widely known that reading to youngsters can be a powerful motivating factor in stimulating them to reading by themselves.

Yet another reason is lack of space. A child's room may be the room for four or five brothers and sisters. There is no solitude. Whereas most children have sufficient privacy and proper facilities for cogitation, the lower-class youngster must try to study in noise, heat, and overcrowdedness.

Overcrowdedness does not afflict home life only. Urban schools are almost universally characterized by high density. Bulging classes, filled to the brim with academically needy youngsters, are the rule rather than the exception. For a teacher to salvage even a paltry percentage of this teeming group is a considerable accomplishment, considering the magnitude of the task.

A fourth reason is the condition of the schools and academic materials. Although some cities boast of their high per-pupil expenditure in the inner-city schools, they rarely mention the amount of this outlay that goes to the upkeep of ancient and collapsing buildings and the purchase of often sadly irrelevant textbooks.

Finally, poor education is the result of teacher transience and lack of accountability. Most urban school systems abide by the seniority rule, which means that any teaching vacancy in the district is open to application and granted to the teacher with the largest amount of seniority. Hence, as openings occur in the city's fringes, an exhausted urban warrior fills it, leaving almost all openings for first-year teachers in the most trying and needy schools.

This transience is particularly harmful at the administrative level. A key to inner-city education is the principal. However, functioning effectively in an inner-city position is energy sapping and not very overtly rewarding. Therefore, many administrators, like teachers, move up and out. The stability of models who are responsible and committed to educational growth—day in and day out, week in and week out, year in and year out—is removed. The only people of any permanence are the repeatedly truant students.

There is also the matter of accountability. Urban educational bureaucracies are infamous for their lack of accountability. Teachers come and go; administrators are shuffled like cards in the inner city; policies are ever changing; funding is no more stable than the stock market; and programs seldom last for more than a year. As a result, no one is really in charge. The bureaucratic web is so intermeshed that it is difficult to determine personal or institutional responsibility. The result is that everyone is accountable, and therefore no one is accountable. More importantly, with politics at the center, no one wants to stand up and be counted. All that is known is that the casualties of such a monstrous system are the children.

Out of all this emerges a rather ambivalent attitude toward education. As the children "progress" through the school system, they develop a vague awareness that the really good jobs necessitate a sound education. However, with no models and a biography of negative experiences with traditional forms of learning already built up, little of a concrete nature is done to actualize their academic potential.

The consequences these conditions have for aspiring inner-city students are devastating. It is not uncommon for diligent inner-city scholars, who have attained a near-perfect grade point average and ranked in the upper divisions of their class, barely to make a C-average in college. This is because the quality of the education these youths received was so markedly different from that which is necessary to prepare students adequately for a liberal arts college. With few of even the finest successful, it is only realistic that other students merely endure, rather than enjoy and profit from, the whole educational experience.

Recreation

Recreation is yet another institution that reflects poverty. Chicago's Cabrini-Green, at its height, had one swimming pool for ten thousand children and young people. Even that pool had limitations, however. It was only three feet deep at its deepest point, and it contained no water. Moreover, there were fewer than ten basketball courts. Certainly, no coach need worry about players fouling out with so large a collection of potential participants. There are no tennis courts, golf courses, baseball diamonds, football fields, or handball courts in most inner-city communities. The result is idleness. Idleness breeds drug usage, sexual mischief, vandalism, and petty crime. If there is anything from which inner-city residents in general and juveniles in particular suffer, it is the lack of life options. Nowhere is this more obvious than in the recreational dimension.

It comes as no surprise that so many of the finest baseball, basketball, and football players in the United States come out of poverty environments, for particularly African American and Hispanic inner-city youth are of aware of sports superstars from their subcultures. Moreover, these are sports that, with a bit of ingenuity, can be played in most inner cities. A hoop and a round ball provide countless hours of entertainment for thousands of urban youth, although even a hoop can be hard to come by. Baseball is often played with the building as the backstop and the street as the outfield, while football is squeezed into any noncement space. Dawn-to-dusk involvement in these sports, played under the most menial of conditions, creates excellence; and such excellence is a badge of status in these communities. Conversely, suburban youth dominate championships in swimming, golf, and tennis. In fact, it is not uncommon for the best of inner-city athletes to be unable to swim, hit a golf ball, or use a tennis racket at all.

All of this serves to reemphasize the fact that being poor means having less of everything, including the much-needed psychological relief that constructive leisure and recreation have to offer. Poor communities are blighted communities, and included in the blight is the lack of recreational facilities of all types—from big-league stadiums to city parks. The poor turn to destructive alternatives such as alcohol and drugs.

SUGGESTIONS AND GUIDELINES
FOR MINISTRY

What can be done in terms of service, and especially stewardship, in the institutional arena? Below are suggestions in each of the six major institutions discussed in this chapter. Following that are some overall guidelines for developing programs or ministries.

Politics

In the area of politics, it is helpful for those involved in an urban ministry to gain a comprehensive understanding in order to see the political situation as a full system with all its attendant interconnections. Urban workers can learn from the community residents and local neighborhood organizations. In addition, they should become acquainted with political representatives and government workers. Understanding and knowledge will then enable urban workers to give more effective counsel to various people in the community who have difficulties with the political forces. Their advice may often be sought because they may be among the few figures in the community who are both well educated and caring.

One important aspect of the urban pastor's political education is to determine the reputation of the various political officials working in the community in order to find which ones are sensitive to the needs of the area. Because a great deal of activity is accomplished at the grassroots level, a pastor can convey certain concerns to caring local officials and see that the concerns are acted on.

A note of caution is in order regarding political involvement. As mentioned previously, it is vitally important that neither the church nor the pastor be aligned with any particular party or candidate. Parties, regimes, and candidates come and go, but the church's mission lives on. If the church should tie itself to any organization, it will be acquiring short-term gain at the expense of potential long-term loss. For if the political entity loses its base, the church will lose a great deal of its leverage; and, worse, if the political candidate or organization turns corrupt, the church will be in the embarrassing position of either having to renege on the political tie or be found furthering the cause of exploitation. The optimal position is one of aligning with issues rather than organizations or candidates. Opening the church for political discussions and debates can be beneficial, for its makes public the church's concern for justice and the New Testament's call for faithful citizenship. However, an open forum for interaction and debate should not degenerate into endorsement and support.

One specific idea for the church's involvement in the political arena on behalf of the poor is the formation of a church justice committee. This group can examine community problems and seek solutions. Such a group can assess everything from the quality of merchandise in the neighborhood stores to the accountability of political candidates.

Finally, contact with other churches and pastors in the community can be of great value both in learning about the political scene and in garnering advice concerning what posture to take when faced with dilemmas.

Religion

There are a number of avenues open for bolstering the religion-as-an-institution aspect of the ministry. If the church is a part of a mainline denomination, it is helpful to make contact with pastors from some of the more affluent churches in the metropolitan area and make specific requests for help. A receptive pastor might be willing to identify several couples in the congregation who would be willing to make a one-year commitment to an inner-city church. This would include regular attendance, at least on Sunday morning, as well as tithing and voluntary involvement in at least one church ministry. The enlistment of a number of such couples can do wonders for the budget, moral support, and leadership, in addition to spreading the word about the inner-city church more widely.

The urban pastor might also request opportunities to educate Christians as to what poverty is, how it is perpetuated, and what its consequences are. This can be done by speaking in other churches, writing articles for denominational publications, working with seminary interns, meeting with students on field trips, and so on.

No matter how the pastor develops an audience, it is of considerable import that the myths of poverty be exploded. For unless they are dissolved, urban churches will continue to operate on an economic shoestring as the second-class citizens of large, wealthy denominations. That crucial second chapter of James will be violated at every annual denominational meeting, as rank-and-file church members will continue to believe that poverty is the result of personal inadequacy and, therefore, does not merit much in the way of action and concern.

Christians usually can be divided into three categories with reference to urban concern: those who do not care and must be disregarded, those who are open but lack knowledge and confidence, and those who have a genuine interest in and knowledge of urban dynamics. The second group is not small in number and is salvageable if the pastor can get the message to them in their suburban or regentrified ecclesiastical enclaves.

Reeducation is a difficult task. Yet reeducation efforts can lead to greater interest and extended opportunities to proselytize middle-class parishioners into a passion for urban ministry. Opportunities to speak to adult-education groups, college clubs, and home-missionary committees are valuable. Joint worship services held both in the inner city and in the outlying areas can also serve to recruit support for the inner-city effort. The point of all this is rather obvious: if a network of churches can become involved in even the most ancillary fashion in the inner city, the isolation of such a pastorate is reduced, and aid can be obtained in efforts ranging from food drives to prayer chains.

Opportunities to address seminary classes and students are also valuable. The urban location of the church is likely to place the pastor near such educational institutions. Seminaries are aware of their urban-ministry deficits. Many realize they are short on street experience. The result is often an openness for articulate urban workers; who can both spread the call for greater concern for urban ministry and recruit interns and volunteers for their particular parish. Educational institutions may also supply interns who can both serve the church and gain a hands-on education in urban issues.

As mentioned previously, forming alliances with other churches in the community is also expedient. Even where there are deep theological differences, there can still be common ground on temporal concerns. Coalitions formed on an issue-by-issue basis is a good way to make progress in the community.

Alliances with other pastors in the community can serve the dual function of presenting a united front when dealing with unaccountable secular institutions and being a base of fellowship and support to buttress the urban pastor against the forces of loneliness, isolation, and pessimism.

Economics

In the economic realm, much can be done without handing out any money. A critical economic front is always employment. There are several avenues the church can take.

If the church has some effective suburban and fringe connections, the pastor could determine what potential job opportunities exist there. Then, consulting with colleagues, the pastor can get the names of business people in these areas, requesting one job a year for an able-bodied, energetic member in the inner city. In the immediate neighborhood, job openings can be posted on the church bulletin board. The church bulletin board, by the way, can be of inestimable value and is often underused or nonexistent. These boards convey vital information and bring area residents into the church.

A survey of the industries and businesses in the community should reveal any discriminative employment practices extant there. Where they exist, the justice task force, an alliance with other neighborhood pastors or some other entity, can bring pressure to bear on the perpetrators.

At every opportunity the church would do well to employ neighborhood residents in paid positions. Often there will be less than top-quality labor because of limited education and underpreparation in handling institutional responsibilities. It is a prime example, however, of practicing what is preached. If community residents are employed, they should be carefully selected and have clearly defined job descriptions, so that if they do not work out, they will realize it even before the church has to inform them.

Hope For Chattanooga has a job-training and partnership program. One of its graduates was an indigent woman who had undergone a kidney transplant. She completed the Christian-based, twelve-week training program and was referred to a local business committed to employing program graduates. The Hope program has twenty-seven job partnership chapters around the nation, with 83 percent of its graduates remaining employed at least a year after completing the training.[5]

There is also education. The Chalmers Center for Economic Development notes the importance of the poor learning the basic rules of economics. Dr. Jim Sutherland states, "One-on-one financial counseling for personal debt and fiscal chaos consistently produces more impact than any other ministry I've had, hour-for-hour."[6] He goes on to say that churches of one hundred or more need to have a trained financial counselor who has excellent teaching and training resources.[7]

According to Steve Nash, one of the leaders of Advance Memphis, an inner-city ministry, the national median net wealth for African Americans (once one excludes a house and car) is zero. This means parents and grandparents have nothing to pass on to their children. Advance Memphis has developed an Individual Development Account (IDA) program in which each dollar saved by a program participant (up to a thousand dollars) is matched by two dollars, provided the participant completes a biblically-based financial stewardship class and the savings are used for an approved asset.[8]

Finally, a benevolence fund, coupled with a well-stocked and sharply supervised pantry can be very positive. Some churches more aptly call such a fund a sharing fund. This and the other ministries witness to the church's concern over hunger and poverty.

Family

To deal with the family, the church may have to take an indirect tack. Sermonettes regarding fidelity, intact marriages, and responsible child rearing are usually not very well received. They tend to have a judgmental ring, as they are based on some naive assumptions. This is not to say that fidelity and family concern is only a middle-class ethic, but rather that it is too easy to treat such concerns without proper awareness of the pressures attendant to inner-city life.

If the church succeeds in attracting community members, there can be church educational programs on family enrichment, child rearing, hygiene, and other family-related issues. If such programs are offered, every attempt should be made to insure that the leadership includes community residents—whether formally connected with the church or not. This will avoid investing such programs with a heavily paternalistic quality.

Day-care programs can also be valuable. They can be pay-for-themselves efforts by employing neighborhood mothers and paying them with monies garnered from working mothers who need good baby-sitting services. Such a ministry can have far-reaching effects. It brings the community residents into the church, demonstrates the church's concern for temporal needs, provides more adequate community child care (freeing older children from the responsibility of being part-time mothers), and is a breakthrough in the area of family concerns. Church events that have a family focus, ranging from potluck suppers to retreats, also witness to the church's commitment to family life.

Beyond this, the pastor may find it helpful to consult with neighborhood social workers and family agencies. These people can provide valuable insight into major family needs in the area as well as suggest realistic ministries that can address these needs.

Education

It is difficult to change educational institutions; however, there are a number of educational options available. One is to start a church ministry that addresses the peculiar problems afflicting community students, primarily illiteracy. A good start may be a well-planned, seriously aimed tutoring program.

A tutoring program will require good tutors. These may be obtained from among educated members of the congregation, concerned citizens in the community, nearby seminaries, other churches, and students from local Christian and public colleges and universities. Colleges and universities are often extremely valuable but untapped talent resources. A few well-placed calls to departments of sociology, psychology, and education may yield a number of people who can aid in urban ministry. Many colleges have internship programs, independent studies, or community-field experiences designed to allow interested students to grapple firsthand with the realities of the city. Often these experiential programs lack strategic placement options and would welcome an urban-church opportunity in tutoring, provided the experience is well planned and the student is effectively supervised. In addition, individual professors may grant classroom credit to students who are willing to immerse themselves in the life of the inner city.

Good, serious students in the tutoring program should be recognized early and, in turn, promoted to become teaching assistants. This gives the tutoring effort a healthy indigenous quality and facilitates peer learning, a method that seems always to outstrip traditional methods in effectiveness. It also develops models for other learners.

To motivate students in the tutoring program, commercial enterprises such as department stores and banks can be asked to contribute. Many large organizations pride themselves on any and all civic improvement activities. I recall requesting assistance in motivating youngsters to read in a program in Michigan. A department store chain sent a large quantity of coupons redeemable at their stores for merchandise, such as records, pop, ice cream, and candy.

The Lifting Hands Education Development (LHED) program of Hope For Chattanooga offers year-round resources for city youth. Their K-5 basic literacy program is aimed at keeping 100 percent of its students performing at or above their respective grade levels. LHED has additional opportunities for older students including a GED course.[9]

If an effective tutoring program can be designed, it is helpful to inform the local schools of its existence. The purpose is not to suggest deficiencies on their part, but rather to alert them to the church's interest in assisting their academic efforts and to invite their suggestions. This is honorable, and it is good politics.

The political aspect is noteworthy, because it is important that the school not become the church's adversary. If the schools see the church as an ally, they are more likely to be responsive to those issues raised by the church that fall within the schools' sphere of responsibility. One church has done so well at both tutoring and school relations that some of the tutoring now takes place right in the school. Ultimately, the goal is better education and greater accountability.

A church task force on education may also bring fruitful results. Such a group could oversee the tutoring program and develop relations with the neighborhood schools. A primary objective of the task force would be to develop skill and motivation in students.

Educational concern can carry far beyond tutoring and church-school relations. Students who show particular academic skill and motivation can be steered toward Christian colleges or state universities that will give them maximal educational benefit.

Recreation

There are a plethora of possibilities in the recreational area. One is to develop church softball, basketball, and even touch-football teams and enter them in leagues. Such teams should be well supervised with clearly articulated expectations for team members. Lacking these guidelines, members can become careless participants who may "grandstand," fail to attend, quit during the season, or engage in other counterproductive activities. If playing is a privilege, with certain, easy-to-abide-by expectations, these teams can be wonderful vehicles for ministry.

In addition to the teams, there can be group outings to professional events. A call to the office of a professional baseball or basketball team, explaining the community's needs and the church's interest in meeting them, may bring reduced prices or even free tickets.

Another possibility is to develop a recreation center in the church itself or a nearby building. A pool table or Ping Pong table makes a good start. The specter of making the church building vulnerable to the wear and tear of city youth is repugnant to many beginning pastors. However, if any ground is to be gained in urban ministry, people's needs must always supersede consideration for buildings. Beyond this immediate step, it might be wise to investigate various local and national Christian youth organizations, to determine whether they have a ministry nearby. If they do not, it may be possible to invite them in to work spiritually and recreationally with the neighborhood teens. A number of such organizations have become increasingly sophisticated in urban concerns over the past years.

If talent and interest exist, a church youth program that zeroes in on developing relationships with neighborhood kids can be inaugurated. The "relationship first" concept is critical, for any attempt to evangelize or change attitudes will be met with incredible resistance if the youth feel they are simply scalps for the kingdom rather than persons who are cared about. Again, national youth organizations can be helpful in developing such a program.

Guidelines

These suggestions are only a beginning. The larger and more energetic the church, the more that can be done. However, it may be helpful for the urban pastor in the storefront church simply to begin by getting to know the community and then developing manageable ministries one at a time. Inaugurating a mélange of uncoordinated ministries will bring nothing but frustration.

Assessment. At the outset, the turf and its needs must be defined. Then, a sober assessment of the church's resources, actual and potential, must be made. After this step, the development of ministries is in order.

Goals and Procedures. Ministries should have clearly defined goals and procedures. Inner-city communities are often characterized by minimal organization. With morbidity (illness) and mortality rates high, constant fear of fire and police brutality, the ever-present threat of urban renewal and forced removal, the inability to meet next month's rent, and so on, the focus is so heavily on getting by and surviving that there is little time to develop community roots and unity. Residential mobility, chief among the producers of community disorganization, can be a consequence of death, illness, financial catastrophes, fire, or urban renewal. The Michigan school in which I taught saw fully 1,100 of its 1,200 students change residences within a calendar year. Disorganized ministries play into this chaos.

Moreover, if goals and procedures are clearly laid out, certain expectations can be made of those to whom the ministry will be directed. There need be nothing high-handed about this, for to require certain very basic things of the community participants is to convey respect for their autonomy and independence.

Regular Evaluation. Defined ministries can and should be regularly evaluated. Inner-city neighborhoods are unceasing targets of governmental programs of every sort. However, these programs are almost invariably long on money and short on hard-nosed accountability and self-evaluation. The result is that they fail, and the people become accustomed to their failure. Simply to replicate governmental failures is to waste God's time. Ministries that work should be continued, and those that do not should be scrapped or renovated. Failures will occur and are not to be mourned over; what is unforgivable is to give up trying when failures do happen. Evaluations should be periodic so that ministries run long enough to take effect, but not so long that they do not receive proper attention. Finally, and most importantly, evaluation processes should include assessments on the part of those served by them.

Knowledge of Resources. There is no substitute for simple knowledge of the community and its resources. There are social-services directories available that list thousands of agencies. If the church simply gained an intimate knowledge of such services in the community and took the time to make phone calls to the appropriate ones for confused and needy community residents or, even better, taught community residents how to help each other, they could perform a major ministry and quickly be defined as friends of the community. Though such a service lacks a spiritual emphasis, until the church can develop its own more tightly focused ministries, knowing where people can go for help and assisting them in getting there can be a major ministry.

For larger and highly motivated urban churches, it can be helpful to assess what federal monies may be available for ministry. The notion of receiving government funding is anathema to many orthodox Christians who feel the mission of the church has to be totally separate from governmental interference. Nonetheless, when earmarked for social ministries and requested in the context of very clearly presented, open-faced statements of goals, seed money from federal or state sources can be a real boon.

Closely allied with this is money from various foundations. There are many potential sources in this area. However, it is important to realize that foundations tend to contribute almost exclusively to new ministries and programs and rarely to support and maintain existing efforts. Hence, if foundation money is sought, it is wise to think of ways in which the newly inaugurated program, once off the ground, can generate its own revenue to keep it afloat.

Conclusion. Whatever ministries are begun, every ministry should make the safeguarding of the dignity of those served a high priority. Any ministry that smacks of white, liberal do-goodism, in the form of "Here, let me show you how to live better, like me," however well-intentioned, is utterly doomed and has no place in the church. There is level ground at the cross of Christ; status differences do not exist. Every effort should be extended to remove them in church ministry as well. James 2:1–13 emphasizes the doing away with preferential regard. The key is servanthood and concern. Those who minister can learn much from those to whom they minister. Optimally, the ministry will be two-way, with the inner-city residents teaching the church representatives much.

Finally, if not a single program ever begun, successful urban ministry must begin on the street. The church building is only a resource, and often a rather minor one. The church is wherever the people representing it are ministering to others. In that respect, the pastor must be prepared to wear out shoe leather. The pastor's study will have to include the streets of the community, taking the gospel of eternal and temporal love to the people right where they are. The number of worshipers in the sanctuary on Sunday may be proportional to the time spent there by the pastor during the week. It is ironic that some of the largest inner-city sanctuaries are the emptiest on Sunday morning while storefronts are bulging.

With this institutional perspective in mind, we turn now to a closer examination of psychological aspects of poverty.

INSECURITY AS A WAY OF LIFE 5

Perhaps the most pervasive psychological quality of life in the inner city is insecurity. Most sociological analyses of poverty life omit this characteristic; however, living in insecurity is a realistic fact of life in the inner city.

It has been said that any minority who is not at least a little paranoid is indeed crazy. This, of course, is based on centuries of racism, exploitation, and oppression visited against minorities. For inner-city residents, regardless of ethnic affiliation, paranoia is hardly a sign of pathology. On two separate consulting projects, I have encountered this understandable paranoia. In one case, a Cuban American who was a committed Christian nearly lost his job, not because he did not work hard or was not a man of integrity, but because he repeatedly told the Caucasians in positions above him what he believed they wanted to hear rather than the truth. When confronted, he acknowledged that he had learned not to trust Anglo-American authority figures (in this case even when they encouraged him to be candid) but to placate them.

This paranoia or insecurity grows out of a life experience characterized by a lack of what is called "fate control." The poor simply are not in control of what happens to them. They are respondents rather than initiators, reactors rather than actors, passive recipients rather than active participants. It could be no other way because they are powerless in the educational, economic, and occupational realms of this capitalistic nation.

Whenever social programs are constructed, they almost never have adequate representation from the ranks of the indigent they are supposed to serve. The poor are simply on the receiving end of these often well-intentioned governmental efforts. However, while the economic quality of the recipients' lives may occasionally be affected positively, such programs underscore the lack of fate control; for the poor had nothing to do with developing the program and have no recourse if it is suddenly taken from them.

This issue of representation from among those served deserves repeated emphasis in urban ministry. For many church social programs have failed simply because the poor were discouraged by the fact that they were not even consulted by those who designed the programs. The efforts had a paternalistic, "we know what's best for you" quality.

A plethora of programs for the poor—ranging from welfare to model cities, from Head Start to the Great Society—have suffered, at least in part, from this lack of representation and consultation. Again and again, compensatory programs are developed as a substitute for changing the distribution of power and opportunity. Often these programs are not optional but are foisted on the target population. That is, the programs are not done *for,* but *to,* the poor. Powerlessness and insecurity are reaffirmed.

SOURCES OF INSECURITY

Inner-city residents are dependent, in the most literal sense of the term, on the political establishment. As a result, any change in municipal policy is extremely threatening. This is especially true because city services are in greater demand in slum communities than anywhere else. Such services include protection of property and life by the fire and police departments, legal aid, housing assistance, education, welfare, health care, and sanitation. There is also the problem in a global age of city ties to the high-risk international economy, in which any major downturn—whether due to terrorism, energy costs, natural disasters, or whatever—evaporates the revenues of a global city and hence the municipal funding available for critical services.

Life-Threatening Forces

Life is always in danger in the inner city. One of the city services on which inner-city residents are dependent is the fire department. Though likely less prevalent with torchings being less common, there remains a substantial fear of fire in the inner city. Poorly constructed project buildings, nonmaintained slum housing, and overcrowdedness, along with carelessness, a top-heavy youth population, and delinquency, contribute to a vulnerability to fire. If city officials become disenchanted with the community, they can retaliate by reducing the responsiveness of the fire fighters. The people are never able to control their own destiny with regard to fire safety. With the plethora of gangs and drugs, violence is ever present. Guns and bullets are everywhere, with often the innocent dying from an errant bullet or a drive-by shooting. The impact of this life-imperiling environment exacts a huge psychological toll. A Johns Hopkins researcher determined that the adverse effects among Baltimore's inner-city children exceeded that of children in war-wracked Bosnia.[1]

Property over Life

This issue of safety and protection leads directly to one of the greatest sources of insecurity for the poor: the tendency to value property over life. Dating back to the genocide of the American Indians, we can find striking examples of property superseding life in importance. People will firebomb homes into which minorities have moved if members of the resident population feel land values are in jeopardy. During the riot-torn 1960s, mayors in major cities sent out a shoot-to-kill edict with regard to looters. One Chicago policeman tells the story of a squad car racing to the scene of a discount shoe store during a riot. The shoe store was one of those poor-quality, deep-discount establishments. As the car screeched to a stop, one of the officers observed a very small child inside, reaching for a probably much-needed pair of shoes. Quickly, in obedience to the shoot-to-kill order, he drew his gun, aimed it at the unsuspecting child, and pulled the trigger. The speeding bullet tore into the head of the child, killing her instantly. Only one example, to be sure. But when we consider all such edicts and other examples of property protection such as the well-armed legions of security personnel who watch over condominiums and businesses and the quick response of the police to any burglary call in a more stable neighborhood, the property-over-life picture becomes rather clear.

Inner-city residents, however, have essentially no property, just life. Without property their lives are not worth much in the US economy. The result is a less-than-vigorous response by the police and other protective agencies to their needs. What is more likely to occur is that what little property they have will be taken from them.

Urban Redevelopment

There is always the ever-present fear of urban redevelopment (once called urban renewal) in its various forms, even where housing is adequate. Urban renewal was sardonically viewed as a euphemism for poor-people removal. Redevelopment is no different. What occurs is that a city marks off an area (much the way a bank redlines) and decides to refurbish the neighborhood. However, this refurbishment does not benefit the present inhabitants of the community, as many people believe; rather, the area is "cleaned out," meaning that the existing buildings are leveled and new construction occurs. This new construction is often in the form of structures that cater to the residential and economic interests of upper-middle-class entrepreneurs. Housing developments, shopping malls, and other commercial entities are erected, signaling radical change.

It is no accident that urban redevelopment almost invariably is embarked on in highly desirable locations. As affluence moves closer to the border of an inner-city community, insecurity increases, because it reminds the residents that they are sitting on coveted property that may soon become urban-renewal land as a justification to seize it. The federal government, though not always in the absence of political pressure from local land barons and business tycoons, becomes more mindful of choice property on which the poverty community rests.

Sometimes these redevelopment programs have been termed, curiously, *land reclamation*. This is a most interesting term. When broken down, it simply states that the land is being reclaimed—of course without any consultation with those who presently have squatter's claim to it. It amounts to much the same as a one-time property owner, who has long since sold a house, coming back to the former dwelling, walking in, and reclaiming the dwelling. A seemingly outrageous analogy perhaps, but not so outrageous when we consider how cities, under political pressure from land barons, simply move in and take residential property from those who desperately need it.

The more recent term, *community* or *neighborhood redevelopment*, has a benign, even positive, ring. Nonetheless, this redevelopment is not for the benefit of the indigenous residents, but rather a regentrification venture aimed at bringing more revenues to the city.

Once underway, urban redevelopment—whether a bold-face form of regentrification or an attempt at a mixed-income contrivance—simply means the mass exodus of poor people, who are given minimal help in finding housing elsewhere. Never mind that they may be further separated from their families, neighbors, churches, and perhaps even jobs; because they are renters, they simply have to move—with little or no recourse or control in the matter.

Chicago provides several excellent examples of land reclamation. In the late 1990s, land was reclaimed on its near west side to build the United Center, site of the Chicago Bulls basketball team. More recently the city has allowed the near-loop Cabrini-Green housing project to dwindle to but a few buildings, razing the others as the rich land grab from the regentrified downtown lakefront spreads west.

A recent twist to regentification has arisen called Tax Increment Financing districts (TIFs). A TIF is usually a several-square-block area that a city marks out as a target for redevelopment. A major step is that all the taxes garnered within the district are pooled for future economic redevelopment. In other words, taxes are not used to fund education, hospitals, the fire and police departments, and other city services, but rather to fund reconstruction, streets and sanitation, and other ventures that enhance the tax base. The TIF cycle often runs in excess of twenty years. When the redevelopment begins, eminent domain is established—meaning the city claims the district as its own fiefdom—and work begins. Buildings are razed; streets are changed and created; parks are installed. Every alteration is aimed at attracting a more affluent residential and commercial clientele. In cases in which poor residents are displaced, no more than 25 percent of the original residents are permitted to remain, and these people are carefully screened for credit, police records, and the like, so that only the most "sanitized" poor are allowed to remain.

School Desegregation

Almost the entire school desegregation problem is actually a real estate issue. The life chances of inner-city children are being swapped for continued residential segregation in the city, whether that segregation is racial or economic. Parents from a variety of ethnic backgrounds held some very justifiable objections to busing and other forms of transporting students during the 1970s, but there remained citizens who clung to rationales based on illusory "neighborhood school doctrine" (illusory because no legal provision anywhere affirms this notion) in order to keep certain nonwhites in particular and the poor in general from invading *their* turf. If desegregation occurs in education, according to that domino-theory reasoning of many, it will soon become a residential and perhaps even a marital reality.

Realizing that their children are unwelcome pawns in the desegregation tug-of-war increases the sense of lack of fate control among the poor. It is interesting that those most victimized by segregated education were rarely consulted or made a part of any official desegregation power front. They simply waited to see if the powers-that-be would act in accordance with the Supreme Court doctrine of equal and desegregated education for all.

In the 1970s, much of the educational desegregation that did occur involved busing; more often than not, it was largely one-way busing. The children of the inner city got up an hour or so earlier to get on what they derisively referred to as the "cattle wagon" and be bused across the city into an alien community, knowing all along that they were not welcome there. Tension and defensiveness ran high in forcibly desegregated schools. There was a constant fear of disorder. The resident community feared angry outbursts by the minority students, while minority students, ever aware they were on alien ground, were in continuous fear of arbitrary discrimination in the form of low grades, unwarranted suspensions, or violence.

This is the educational tradition out of which the poor come. Cities differ in how they now address the issue of segregation. Many, however, have given up on addressing racial segregation simply because there are too few Caucasian children available to balance out the numbers. So many of the urban affluent are single, childless marrieds, or able to place their children in private settings. Some cities have put together magnet schools, locating at least some of them in or near poorer neighborhoods. These are special schools for the more gifted learners in specific areas such as literary skills, science, and the arts. By providing these accelerated-learning institutes, the cities hope to keep the best and the brightest of their children in the public school system. The problem of the others, however, remains without adequate solution.

Sanitation and Health Care

City inspection and code enforcement is another arm inner-city residents must lean on. There are often more rats than people in poverty areas. Rat-bite fever, illnesses resulting from bites by rabies-infected dogs, and disease emanating from unsanitary living conditions are daily occurrences among the city poor. The best way to combat these illnesses is with improved sanitation, rather than with more health clinics. In fact one ministry demonstrated this when it embarked on a preventive program on Chicago's poor west side, aimed at rounding up stray dogs and performing other clean-up activities instead of inaugurating additional treatment centers.

The poor, however, do not have authority over the vigor of city inspectors and other officials who can make certain that living conditions are sanitary. They can only hope that people who occupy these important posts are people of good will.

Nothing seems to produce instant anxiety among people more than a threat to their health. Yet in the inner city, where living conditions are optimally ripe for disease, health care is the poorest, both quantitatively and qualitatively. The poor do not have nearby hospitals, family doctors, or health insurance to prevent financial devastation when facing a serious illness. Rather, they join the lines at the neighborhood health clinic to see the overworked and under-assisted physician who is on duty; or if the crisis is particularly severe, they enter the hospital emergency room, where they are likely to receive quick and less-than-comprehensive diagnoses and treatments.

In the mental healthcare field millions of people spend large sums of money receiving psychiatric treatment for sometimes even the mildest of behavior disorders. But in the inner city, where basic day-to-day living conditions assault the psyche, competent mental healthcare practitioners are in short supply. So again, where problems in living are the most severe and help is the most necessary, it is the least available.

Public Aid

The public aid system is among the most insidious of the insecurity bacteria. A trip to any public aid office will quickly display the indignity and humiliation to which the recipients are subjected. Long lines of gloomy, pessimistic, and depressed poor wait like sheep as harried and overworked middle-class personnel cryptically dictate to them the rules of the system and what aid, if any, for which they qualify in an era in which public aid allocations have been cut back.

Once on public aid, the poor receive visits from caseworkers; these visits are thinly disguised attempts at checking up on the recipients to insure that they do not spend their money foolishly or violate the public aid code in some fashion. Personal autonomy and fate control are again destroyed as the poor take on a dependent and childlike status before the all-powerful social welfare system. The entire process, from application to reception, is seemingly designed to remind the recipients that they are unilaterally dependent on the welfare system because they are noncontributors to the society on whose dollars they depend. The upshot of this methodical degradation is to drain out of them what little optimism and positive self-concept they may have had. It is little wonder that the poor shuffle along aimlessly from office to office of social service bureaucracies, with a look of desperation and defeat etched on their faces.

Moreover, any change in the nature of public aid—whether in the form of disability benefits, welfare, or unemployment compensation—is totally outside the control of those who are most dependent on it.

Inflation

Whether a person is on welfare or not, there is insecurity with every increase in inflation. One of the main afflictions of the poor today, as opposed to those of decades past, is that in earlier days the price structure was geared to the poor, since few people were affluent. Now prices are standardized at middle-class incomes.

The result is that a bargain is a bargain only if a person can afford it. For the poor, there are no bargains. If even the middle class is revolting over sudden jumps in the cost of living, how much more are the urban poor affected. They fear sudden price jumps in food, rent, energy costs, and other essentials. There is no protection against such increases, because the jobs the poor hold do not carry with them wage increases commensurate with the rising costs of living.

Employment Problems

Employment problems are also a source of insecurity. If a poor person has work, the job is most certainly one that is devoid of power, authority, and security. That means there is no pension, seniority, or protection against a capricious dismissal or lay-off. Once a job is lost, things get worse. Rising unemployment and inflation rates make getting another job more and more difficult. If a job is obtained, it will be an unskilled job that will also be subject to the vagaries of the national economic cycle. If inflation thickens, the minimum wage rises; however, if the company experiences a fiscal downturn, the job will be among the very first to dry up.

Police Brutality

Another city service on which residents depend is the police department. And yet police brutality is a routine occurrence in US cities. This practice is not only written about by sociologists but is acknowledged by the police themselves. The report of the National Advisory Commission on Civil Disorders placed this, along with housing deficiencies and employment problems, among the top three factors involved in bringing about riotous behavior in the infamous 1960s.[2] Moreover, almost every major urban riot, including the one in Benton Harbor, Michigan, in 2003 is set off by an incident with the police.

Legal aid clinics are besieged with complaints about police harassment. The Cabrini-Green Legal Aid Clinic in Chicago, founded by LaSalle Street Church, actually grew out of problems the community was having with the police. Some of the cases handled there illustrate sharply why the residents often quake in fear at the sight of the big blue police car. In one case, documented by court records, an angry group of police officers were set on incriminating Roy Harris for a murder. They needed witnesses to sign statements that Harris had done the killing. They found a very effective method. A neighborhood youth, who had witnessed the killing and knew Harris was not involved, was confronted with a typed statement indicating Harris and to which the police wanted him to sign his name. After he steadfastly refused to sign, an officer went to the closet in the already-intimidating interrogation room and pulled out a shotgun. The shotgun was then held near the youth's head while the shells were ejected, caroming off the skull of the already-traumatized youth. He screamed, became hysterical, and signed the statement. Fortunately for Harris, the coercion came out in a dramatic court scene. This contributed to his being exonerated.

In another incident a man named Arthur Scott was riding with a friend through the community. The driver was pulled over by the police for a minor traffic violation. The police did not, however, stop with the motorist, but did something they never do in middle-class communities. They demanded to know who the passenger was. Hearing the name, one of the officers exclaimed: "Arthur Scott! We have several warrants at the station instructing us to find and arrest Arthur Scott!" Scott was then unceremoniously carted away to jail. Being indigent, he was unable to get a lawyer and was simply left to vegetate in jail for weeks, awaiting the disposition of his case. It was very apparent, once his case was investigated, that he was not the Arthur Scott in question. He did not even remotely resemble the description of Scott in the station files. This was of no consequence to the police, who could have easily checked this matter at the time of arrest. Why? Arthur Scott was poor and powerless and apparently did not merit first-class justice.

The principal reason why inner-city residents are so often victims of police brutality and insensitivity is that they have little status or importance in the prevailing social structure. And, what's more, they have no real power to redress their grievances. They pose absolutely no legal threat to the police. It is little wonder that so often poverty communities redress their grievances with an assassin's bullet. Unfortunately, that bullet may kill a caring policeman, one who genuinely sought to serve the community. Assassins, however, do not see policemen as individuals, but simply react to the uniform, just as insensitive officers react to the poor simply as worthless slum dwellers.

Bill Leslie, former pastor of LaSalle Street Church, received a slum dweller's treatment firsthand. One evening, attired in a sweatshirt and old pants, Leslie was carrying some chairs out of the church. Suddenly a squad car pulled up, blocking his car. The officers leaped out, grabbed Leslie, and flung him spread-eagle on the hood of his car. "Who are you and what are you doing?" they demanded angrily. "I am the pastor of that church," responded Leslie, pointing to the church sign. With immediate apologies, the police discontinued their rough-house tactics. "The altercation would never have occurred if I were wearing a suit and tie," explained the street-wise Leslie. "I could have carried anything out of that church I wanted."

I have spent some time with police officers and have found among them those who are crude and bestial as well as those who are serious and sensitive. No single stereotype accurately describes police personalities or behavior. One thing is certain, however: there is a bent toward aggressiveness and intimidation in low-income communities. Police will use verbal or physical strong-arm tactics to intimidate the inner-city resident. Many officers openly acknowledge this fact. Such intimidation breeds insecurity.

The police side of the picture is that inner-city communities are long on street crime and short on cooperation. Open disrespect for officers and even violence are key concerns. The cleavage or alienation between the police and the urban poor is deep. It becomes a chicken or egg dilemma: Are the police abusive, producing this lack of cooperation? Or are inner-city communities hostile, giving rise to police aggression? It is perhaps a bit of both. However, the police are enjoined to "serve and protect," and in poor communities, where there is the greatest need, there is the least service and protection. Many sensitive officers abhor the overaggressive behavior of some of their colleagues, for brutality incites assassins and stimulates community bitterness. That bitterness is often not so much aimed at the police as at the entire society that has left the community powerless and insecure.

Justice System Inequities

Contact with the police is only the beginning of the insecurity-producing urban justice process. No matter how important or trivial the offense, inner-city residents almost never have a legal defense. This almost certainly leaves them with the public defender system. Public defenders are usually hard-working, inexperienced, very competent, and hopelessly overworked lawyers. A public defender may handle as many as fifty cases in a single day. This allows absolutely no time for interviewing, research, investigation, and careful preparation of a defense. It usually results in plea bargaining.

Plea bargaining involves pleading guilty to a lesser crime contained within the charge against the individual. The US criminal justice system could not operate without it. It is a trade off. When defendants plea bargain, they get a lesser sentence, while the prosecutor gets a conviction with minimum effort. Whether guilty of the initial charge or not, defendants will often eagerly accept a plea bargain simply because it means that things will go easier than if they are found guilty. In addition, the public defender will often urge a plea bargain simply because going through the whole trial process is time consuming, and it is very risky if not enough time is taken to investigate the case and prepare an adequate defense. What inner-city residents are not always aware of, however, is that by plea bargaining, they have pleaded guilty to a crime of some sort and have acquired a record.

In the case of a felony charge, such as murder or armed robbery, for example, the situation is much more serious. Without an adequate defense, a person is likely to be found guilty. Public defenders do have some assistants to aid in the preparation of felony defenses, but again, plea bargaining often is the accepted route, as it is the safest. Even if the person is guilty, however, there still has been a denial of an adequate defense, something theoretically guaranteed all defendants in the US justice system. And if not guilty, the person is still officially identified as a criminal.

The contrast between this procedure and justice for the rest of society is scandalous. First, middle-class crimes are often white-collar rather than street crime. White-collar crime is almost never aggressively investigated. Hence, the likelihood of a white-collar person being charged with an offense is remote. However, when charged, the more well-to-do defendants immediately contact their lawyers—just as they call their physicians when ill. These lawyers will most certainly be in private practice and will present formidable defenses. No plea bargaining here, unless the client is obviously guilty and the conviction is sure.

In the cases of misdemeanors and drug charges, especially among teenagers, there is always the pay-off route. It is not at all uncommon for a poor woman, working as a domestic in a suburban home, to hear a father chuckle about how he beat a legal charge or protected his wild-oat-sowing teenager, while she worries about what will happen to her son if he is apprehended for a curfew violation. More-affluent juveniles may be objects of tremendous concern to their parents, but they are almost invariably protected from legal proceedings if only to guard the family name.

The police are occasionally involved at this level too. Many an aware urban pastor knows of the ghastly practice of policemen demanding sex with welfare mothers in exchange for not pursuing the prosecution of an arrested teenager.[3]

If a defendant is found guilty, the socioeconomic background of the individual is again critical in determining the severity of the sentence. Called discretionary justice, there is the tendency for the judge to sentence on a case-by-case basis. Often it means that a middle-class person will be allowed to return to the community with a probationary sentence, while the inner-city convict is incarcerated because, in the judge's opinion, the domestic environment is not conducive to rehabilitation. Whether this assessment of recidivism is accurate or not, it means preferential treatment based on social status.

This is not even an adequate introduction to the inequities endemic in the US justice system. With continued cutbacks in funding of legal aid assistance for the poor in even civil areas, things appear to be getting worse. In any case, it is a brief glimpse into one of the greatest sources of insecurity in inner-city life.

Add to these the powerlessness of the poor in education, government, institutionalized religion, recreation, and the other spheres discussed in the previous chapter, and the insecurities and paranoia experienced by the urban poor are easily understood. In short, they emanate from the fact that the system was not designed for them and does not work for them.

RESPONSES AND ATTITUDES

The poor respond to this insecurity in a variety of ways. That response is seen both in lifestyle and in overall attitudes. Nearly a half-century ago poverty scholar Lee Rainwater offered a still relevant, rather simple typology of lifestyle strategies common among the urban poor.[4] The first is an expressive lifestyle. This is a flashy style. It may include gaudy dress, a financed car, and other material props to support the joking, impulsivity, and spontaneity at the core of this mode. Often this expressiveness gives rise to drunkenness, drug addiction, and sexual promiscuity in an effort to appear cool and stylish. This maverick air is aimed at either denying or masking economic vulnerability. While in some instances, it may be truly expressive of the financial state, the street affluence in question is often ill-gotten through trafficking in drugs or prostitution.

Second, a failure to sustain this mode can bring on a strategy of violence. This unpopular, fear-producing activity, in which others are forced to meet the needs of the poor person, is adopted out of desperation and out of rage with the hopelessness and degradation of poverty. The inhabitants of the inner city, though not pleased about it, accept violence as an inevitable ingredient in urban poverty existence. Murder, muggings, teacher and student assault, and gang conflicts are regular occurrences. For urban church workers, coping with violence is often the most difficult psychological adjustment.

Finally, there is the depressive strategy, which involves scaling down goals to the level of necessities and adopting a "live and let live, don't bother me and I won't bother you" attitude. Essentially a defeatist strategy, it insures against further disappointment and heartache. This strategy is common among older poor whose spirit has been pretty well broken under the yoke of poverty.

As Rainwater suggests, some adjust passively to the messages of inferiority emanating out of poverty, low educational attainment, and joblessness, while others will challenge any bearer of the putdown.

In either case, however, what develops is a psychologically deadly *learned powerlessness* in relationship to the larger system. Most people believe that they simply cannot succeed through the accepted channels of the system. Education, honest employment, and good citizenship are not avenues through which they can reap rewards. Instead, the system is viewed as keeping them down. Moreover, it seems mammoth and overwhelming, and therefore a sense of powerlessness develops.

Regardless of response or lifestyle strategy, coping in order to survive is the main issue. Survival may be achieved creatively. Youngsters learn how to survive summer heat by cracking open fire hydrants, and winter cold by starting small fires. They use every conceivable method to get by in school. They are ingenious in petty theft of candy and material things. They try to dupe the police at every opportunity, and they verbally put down authority with smart remarks as a necessary weapon in their arsenal for psychological survival.

Responses to insecurity are found not only in a lifestyle strategy and creative coping but also in attitudes. Poverty conditions, personality, and certain attitudes are likely to be particularly common among the poor.

Localism. There is often a sense of localism—an apprehensiveness concerning the unfamiliar. Many urban youth have never been more than twenty-five blocks from their homes by the time they are in the sixth grade. Adults do not take vacations or go on business trips. So the urban turf is the only familiar element. Suggestions for change and new experiences are often rejected, partly because of this localism. From a pastoral standpoint, it is important that ministries be rooted in the urban enclave to minimize responses issuing out of uncertainty.

Little Respect for Authority. There is often little respect for authority figures. Societal authority is peculiarly heavy-handed in low-income areas and almost never works to benefit the poor. In essence, middle-class authority tends to hold the poor "in their place" to insure that the status quo—favorable to the middle class—is protected. Experiences with the police are commonly so bad that the alienation emanating from police-public interaction permeates relationships with virtually every other authority figure.

It is almost impossible to overestimate the degree of hostility that issues out of the experience of the urban poor with the police. In short, they view the police as a militia commissioned to patrol their areas to keep them under surveillance—and under control. While cases of police brutality are legion and well documented, the police realize that the highest rates of street crime occur in low-income communities, and so they are pressured to maintain order. This mandate to maintain order—as opposed simply to enforce the law—generates rather aggressive activities on the part of the police. The psychology of fear and force predominates, particularly in a Lazarus and Dives era in which the poor often live on the border of, or at least near, regentrified communities. Fear and force produce insecurity and therefore hostility and retaliation—as the number of policemen murdered in poor neighborhoods testifies. The result is often more intimidation and an even greater devotion to maintaining control.

The emergent attitude is alienation, and this alienation and distrust soon invade attitudes toward any authority figures, whether they are policemen, firemen, teachers, social workers, or pastors.

Hatred. There is often a heavy dose of hate in the hearts of many poor. Martin Luther King is said to have spent the first few hours of the many times he was imprisoned praying for deliverance from the bitterness he felt. If a person of King's character required divine intervention to overcome resentment, it is little wonder that many of those who live at society's bottom are filled with vengefulness. With every shred of institutional life reminding them of what they do not have, it cannot be any different.

Moreover, this hate is fed by fear. It is often a defensive hatred, growing out of the fear of not surviving, of receiving the ultimate putdown in the form of academic failure, unemployment, psychological devastation, or a policeman's bullet. Because it is invariably an authority figure who delivers this knockout punch, there is a great potential for an overflowing of hatred expressed in a street uprising.

Pessimism. Above and beyond everything else, the poor bear a heavy strain of hopelessness and pessimism—variations of the learned powerlessness discussed above. This is to be expected, for nothing in their lives has worked. The American Dream has been just that—a dream. Politicians give out promises but rarely deliver on them; and the community has remained poor as long as any of its inhabitants can remember. As a result, even when opportunities do present themselves, the people may be held back by pessimism. There is every desire to avoid yet another disappointment—an additional letdown.

Urban workers quickly discover these fundamental psychological responses and have to develop a great deal of patience and empathy if these barriers are ever to be penetrated and the people ministered to.

SENSITIVE MINISTRY

Ministering in the midst of this insecurity is a delicate task. It requires, above all, *awareness.* Any change must be presented with the people's background, both social and psychological, in mind. Tragically, so many well-intended programs and ministries have failed for lack of this awareness. They are presented from an alien worldview.

A theoretical example might be helpful. Suppose you were a reading expert and were able to teach anyone of reasonable intelligence how to read in the space of four weeks. Because you realize that literacy is closely tied to occupational success, you decide to open a reading clinic in a nearby poverty area. You rent out a room and offer reading instruction each Monday night for an hour, assuring the populace through your advertising that within four weeks they will be able to read. The first Monday night finally arrives, and you are poised to deliver on your promise. No one shows up. Not a single soul comes to this free reading clinic, put together entirely at your expense to teach this absolutely necessary literacy skill. You have two alternatives: either you can go home angry and embittered, or you can analyze why there were no takers. A bit of thought should reveal quite easily a variety of reasons why no one has come.

If your advertising was in print, it was probably useless, since the people cannot read the signs anyway. For those who are aware of your clinic, a number of deterrents confront them. At night some may fear walking the streets to your location. For those who work full-time during the day, there is inevitable evening fatigue. Those with children are held back either because there are no babysitters or simply because they feel they should spend this time with their children.

But what of those not encumbered by any of these problems? For many of them, there is skepticism. How can anyone teach them to read in four weeks when they did not learn after ten or twelve years of formal education? The idea seems even more preposterous than many undelivered political promises. There is also the embarrassment and self-consciousness many feel of going into a clinic like this and admitting to a strange middle-class person that they are ignorant and need to be taught something so basic as the ability to read. This process of self-abasement is for some the most difficult barrier of all.

In addition, the whole literacy issue is an abstraction for many in the inner city. What these unemployed, would-be students need is a job, not reading skills. Although reading and employment are closely related, knowledge of this relationship is middle-class knowledge; the inhabitants of the poverty community lack any firsthand examples or models of people who were able to parlay reading skills into occupational success. If the reading expert could guarantee a job for every graduate, the rented room would likely be too small to accommodate the throng. However, simply offering the skill of reading is not enough—people see themselves struggling with bread-and-butter rather than reading-and-writing issues.

The foregoing example is not intended to discourage ministry creation or program development. Its purpose is to underscore the importance of serious reflection and careful planning in offering innovations.

An urban pastor will likely confront less than an accepting response from many poor parishioners. The skepticism of the poor, who have been promised to, preached at, and experimented on without significant improvement in their quality of life, is very understandable. Many will view a new urban pastor as a temporary prop who will soon be gone. Few urban workers—ministers, social workers, teachers, or whoever—last long. After spending a frustrating year or two, they pack their bags and head for less stressful environments, taking their ideals with them. All that is left behind is the suffering population they attempted to serve. After witnessing untold numbers of well-intentioned middle-class professionals come and go, the poor are not likely to get very excited at the outset over new programs or goals.

Knowledge of the sources of insecurity and awareness of the attitudes of poor parishioners will provide a basis for the urban pastor's ministry. What other ingredients are necessary for a sensitive, effective ministry?

Listening. It is important that each individual be accepted as a person. Operationally, this means that instead of stereotyping the poor or handling them bureaucratically, the urban worker will care about an individual's feelings and will listen attentively to the needs. Listening and caring of any genuine sort is in short supply in an urban poverty community. All too many urban workers, besieged with seemingly endless multitudes of problem-ridden clients, feel forced to find quick solutions for any one individual's problems. A pastor has a calling to minister to whole persons, and therefore listening and resonating with the feelings of groups and individuals becomes a vital aspect of urban ministry. It is the difference between dealing with clients and ministering to persons.

Identifying and Suffering. Listening and caring develops the ability to identify with the people's needs and experiences. Empathy in the form of walking mentally in the shoes of those served is vital. Once workers do this, they know how to care, how to act, and even how to avoid being manipulated. Identification entails the ability to see the situation through the eyes of the other. This requires reading, reflecting, and listening. Identifying is a process rather than an event, and so it will not come quickly. Almost any urban worker who has been reared in the middle class will find this difficult at first. But it is a necessary skill. Moreover, once the worker can identify with the poor, they quickly notice it, and the worker becomes one of them—a person they trust.

What is often the bottom line of effective ministry is the willingness not only to identify with but to suffer with a victimized community. This suffering is also a process rather than an event. Simply rushing in with the gospel of Christ, where other pastors have feared to tread, often leaves the impression that the pastor is more interested in proselytizing than serving, in winning followers than ministering.

Active Caring. Care must be active. In their epistles both James and John point to the ludicrousness of inactive caring, upbraiding those Christians who do not shelter those who are cold but simply wish them God's blessing (James 2:14–17; 1 John 3:17–18). Doing something is of the utmost importance. Therefore, when the urban pastor is confronted with a need, the desire to act on it should become an almost reflexive response.

Facilitating. Active caring does not necessarily mean *doing* for the person; rather, it usually means *thinking* of problem-solving ways that can be effective for the person in need. In many cases individuals can enact these by themselves, but they have not done so, simply because they are not aware of their options.

This engages the issue of facilitation, returning to the theme that wherever possible, it is helpful to devise strategies that enable people to be active in solving their own problems. This develops a sense of fate control and self-responsibility on the part of those who are able. If pastors only *do* for others, they risk both burning themselves out and also creating unhealthy dependencies on the part of their parishioners. Realistic expectations for parishioner action are always appropriate. It is important, however, that they be realistic in the context of the inner city, rather than the middle-class milieu from which pastor may have come.

It is also wise to develop participatory programs, that is, ministries in which the parishioners have a direct stake and responsibility. This should not be overdone, such that unrealistic expectations are made or genuine expertise sacrificed; but whenever reasonable, it is valuable to have people gain self-determination.

It is important, in this regard, that any and all church programs take into account the reactions and feelings likely to be elicited in the community by them. This can be done preferably by bringing inner-city residents in at the planning stage.

Star Parker is a controversial and confrontational activist. His organization, Coalition on Urban Renewal & Education (CURE), attempts to inject a sense of empowerment and responsibility into low-income communities. A fierce opponent of the welfare system, CURE seeks to inject self-government and free enterprise into inner-city communities. In addition, CURE goes into poor communities and holds empowerment conferences, training clinics, inner-city town hall meetings, and church lectures.[5]

Reciprocity. In addition to helping parishioners, it is important that a pastor ask parishioners for help as well, even in such practical ways as babysitting or car repairs. Openness to being helped is often every bit as much a ministry in the inner city as openness to helping others. Mutuality builds relationships, trust, and respect. Kindness, openness, and appropriate vulnerability can go a long way in developing a sound relationship with the community. Being open and vulnerable humanizes pastors, removes them from an ecclesiastical pedestal, and makes them part of the community. Praying for others is important, and asking for their prayers is equally important. A major enemy of pastors everywhere is social and psychological isolation. A major deterrent to such isolation is personal openness with the individuals being served.

Community Involvement. Showing respect for and encouraging involvement in neighborhood and community organizations is a way of combating the sense of victimization felt in inner-city communities. Often there are organizations that lack only a large, active membership to be effective. Attending meetings and encouraging others to attend may eventually bring about greater organizational stability and, ultimately, effectiveness.

Although the use of the church facilities for civic meetings, discussions, and other public activities may cause some to see the church as endorsing a given point of view, it is important to model involvement and response in the community. The church does not have to compromise its spiritual mission to do this. Rather, it witnesses to the church's belief that organizing and planning strategies in a community are constructive ways to confront institutional problems. However, if the pastor in the church does not show *active* concern for the obvious afflictions of the community and the need for addressing them, it will be extraordinarily difficult to minister to people's souls with the gospel.

Again, there need be no compromising with ministering to spiritual needs and bringing lives to Christ by opening up on the other fronts. If the church's objectives and priorities are clear, other activities need not interfere with spiritual ministry. Instead, they are examples of a whole-person ministry that, of course, can augment receptiveness to spiritual concerns.

Showing Respect. Of greatest import of all in dealing with this reality-based insecurity is to evince respect for the human worth of each person. It is important that the dignity of each parishioner be carefully guarded. At the root of most oppression of the poor is a form of psychological assault and degradation—the insensitive, "who cares because you are nothing anyway" treatment they receive from bureaucrats. Even sensitive and caring pastors may convey a patronizing notion that superior education and experience make them and their perceptions most valuable. If perceptions are better, they should be so by their very own worth rather than on the basis of whose they are.

The reader may notice the absence of concrete examples of ministries to deal with the insecurity syndrome. That ought not to be surprising, for insecurity is a psychological, rather than a concrete or structural, phenomenon. It does, however, arise from institutional injustices. Therefore, on the surface, insecurity may be best dealt with through respectful and affirmative human relations. But, at a deeper level, modeling involvement and organizational activity, in addition to confronting the real problems of powerlessness discussed in earlier chapters, must occur in fighting the battle on larger turf.

YOUTH 6

By percentage, youth constitute a major sector of almost any inner-city community because of the plethora of single-parent families with large numbers of children. Because youth are in such great numbers in the inner city, the topic merits special attention.

Almost every church has some sort of youth program. An awareness of the dynamics of the youth subculture in the inner city can be of value in developing effective programs.

ATTITUDES AND BEHAVIORS

At least partly because of limited parental supervision and an absence of constructive recreational alternatives, the youth in most poverty areas take on certain common attitudes and behaviors. These include a limited amount of time spent in the home; lack of appreciation for time-oriented routines; involvement in gangs, drugs, and sex; and lack of future orientation.

An instructive experience for the uninitiated is to drive through an inner-city neighborhood relatively late in the evening. What will amaze many is the number of children—even small children—playing out on the street well after dark. Some of this street-centeredness can be accounted for by a vacuum in parental attention, but much of it results from a lack of recreational outlets and an overcrowded apartment.

When youngsters are not on the street, they may stay up late watching television and sleep well into the morning. This late-to-bed, late-to-rise syndrome desensitizes them to the notion of a time-oriented routine. Lacking adult work models (over 40 percent of some cities' public school children are from public aid families), youth find it difficult to develop an appreciation for dependability in work and time. This is not to suggest that many parents do not work in their domestic roles, but rather that this type of work is not congruent with the kind of demand expected in the employment market at large.

As a consequence of this limited contact with parents and other adults, along with the absence of success models, a peer culture develops. The peer group—greatly influenced by the usual youth-oriented appeals of thrills, excitement, and new experiences—develops its own code of conduct. Often this code places great emphasis on group loyalty and camaraderie; lone wolves become rather unpopular and even objects of harassment.

Gangs

In many urban neighborhoods, youth organize themselves into gangs.[1] Gangs provide the adolescents with a sense of identity and belonging as well as a network through which opportunities and excitement can be shared. The majority of gang members are *homeboys*, youths with no legitimate alternatives for success in the straight world. Many of these gangs are not violent to any appreciable extent, but they will become so if a member of a rival gang picks on one of their own members. Others are led by hard core, *New Jacks*, hardened leaders willing to kill anyone for any reason.

One feature of gangs is the establishing of turf boundaries. This turf boundary phenomenon is fascinating. Some years ago in a Chicago poverty community in which gang-consciousness was heavy, one of the neighborhood high school students was developing a very peculiar academic record. In all but one of his courses, he excelled and received superior grades. However, in the remaining course he was obviously failing partly through excessive absences. There seemed to be no academic accounting for this anomaly. However, on closer examination it was determined that he was a member of one of several gangs in the high school and that gang awareness and competition were so acute that different areas within the high school were considered the property or turf of certain gangs. Unfortunately, one of the student's classes happened to meet on the turf of a rival gang, and rather than incur violence, he felt it wiser to accept academic failure.

Admittedly, this is an extreme example, and in many cities aggressive gang activity has lessened. However, in any inner-city community, these alliances in the form of gangs and their structures, whether violent or not, do keep the allegiance of their members. Thus, this gang orientation is extremely important for church workers to understand, for it explains why one youth simply will not cooperate with another in a recreational activity or why some youth avoid "trespassing" on other areas in the community.

A second feature of gang involvement is the tendency to elevate collective gang values and depress the more individual, competitive values. For many youngsters, the gang or clique is the primary source of acceptance, attention, and identity, so a youth's stature in the group and integration into its activities and interests are vital. The notion of the nonconformist or individual is not very prevalent in the inner city.

Third, the gang structure itself militates against educational excellence. Whenever adolescents run up against a challenge too formidable for them, they tend to reject and belittle that challenge as not meaningful for them. In that vein, school in general and academics in particular are disparaged in the streets. The compensatory behavior often takes the form of gang activity, in which turf is ruled and others are manipulated. School can be a frightening experience for many youngsters, as often school gangs extract protection money from those who are not members of a gang in exchange for not being attacked or harassed on the way to school.

There is power in knowledge. However, if a youth does not possess book knowledge—the type that can be translated into success in occupational pursuits—gaining power on the streets through fear and intimidation is an appealing alternative. Power and influence are very attractive to inner-city youth. Thus the fourth feature of the gang is that it provides a mode through which to obtain power and influence.

Among the most cherished forms of power is gang leadership. In some gangs this is still determined through physical prowess, aggressiveness, combativeness, and toughness; in others the leader is simply the most persuasive or perhaps the oldest or most affluent member. In any case, with leadership come power and a sense of autonomy. Most members aspire to leadership for its power and influence. Other members will frequently seek power in other ways, for example, by excelling in activities approved by the gang.

As leaders gain power through fear and intimidation, they nonetheless shows a careful awareness of how the judicial system operates. In many gangs the fifteen- and sixteen-year-olds do the crimes because the gang leaders realize that seventeen-year-olds can be tried as adults if apprehended by the police. The victims of these crimes can be anyone, from children going to school, to shopkeepers who are ordered to come up with cash to ward off arson and vandalism, to senior citizens whose money may be taken as they leave a currency exchange after cashing their social security checks.

This careful awareness of the operation of the judicial system illustrates once more the highly developed survival orientation operating among urban youth. For a middle-class youngster, survival consists of succeeding in school, going to college, and then landing an economically rewarding job. In fact, if middle-class youth do not do well in school and at least go to college, they are often regarded as failures. This can be very oppressive; a student once pointed out that whereas the poor are often denied opportunity for success, the more affluent youth do not have the right to fail. In any case, survival is equated in the suburbs with educational and occupational success, but in the inner city survival has a much different, close-to-the-bone quality.

Once in a gang, however, it is very difficult to get out, because it becomes part of a youth's identity. It is how a youth is viewed in the community and by the police. Beyond that there is the power and often easy money associated with gang activities. Mary Schmich of the *Chicago Tribune* tells of a young man who tried to get out.[2] He tried pumping gas, shoveling snow, even moving from Chicago to Milwaukee. He ran out of money. "Rent was kicking my hair out," he explained. Moving back home, he pressed on. He took a job as a janitor and volunteered at the YMCA. Then, with his hours reduced, and his paycheck evaporating, he thought of all the family members who relied on him for money and of the lucrative income he had received from selling drugs. Soon he was back in the old lifestyle.

Eventually, he was arrested for stealing a car, making him yet another inner-city youth with a police record and hence unlikely to land a decent job. Asked if he would like to start over once more, his answer was telling. "Like to? I'd love to," he said, "I'm getting nowhere." He then raised his hand above his head and made a tugging motion. "Got a string around my neck." On probation, living in a community of quicksand, and unwilling to leave his family behind, the young man's future is grim.

Drugs

In the absence of other recreational outlets, there is a tendency among inner-city adolescents to become involved with drugs. Marijuana is as common as cigarettes in many inner cities, and, of course, a large number of adolescents look for something more powerful. The inner city is a haven for drug pushers, many of whom get their supply from someone outside the area and then sell to youth ranging in age from thirteen to twenty-five. Addiction rates are high because the power of the peer culture and its favorable view of drug involvement provides an optimum psychological setting for getting hooked. Younger students can be started by a pusher who simply laces candy with a powerful drug and gives it to the youngsters in the washrooms of the schools.

The whole process can be seen as a cycle of victimization. The pushers are often those who are themselves addicts and are unable to get or hold a job. They rationalize their pushing with the belief that if they weren't doing it, someone else would. The intense desire of the restless, excitement-starved youth draws other community youngsters into drug experimentation. At first the drug experience provides an exciting, boredom-breaking alternative to the usual forms of entertainment. Often beginning with mild drugs, youth are pressured by the peer group for higher-level experimentation, and some become addicted to the "biggie"—heroin. Drugs are expensive, and their costliness makes them all the more attractive. As a result, mugging, stealing, prostitution, lower-level drug pushing, and various forms of petty crime are engaged in to raise the necessary funds.

The police, with a mandate from both within and outside the community, become the chief adversaries as they work to break up the drug rings and kill the drug supply. Whenever there is a giant drug bust, non-drug-using veterans of inner-city life are ambivalent. On one hand, they rejoice over the cleansing effect such a bust might have; on the other hand, they realize street crime is likely to escalate because the bust will place drugs in short supply and raise the price necessary for purchase.

This is not to say that all inner-city adolescents are drug involved. Nor is drug involvement limited to the inner city—it is a national trend. What is important is that drug activity is apparent, and whether a youth or a gang is involved or not, inner-city youngsters are products of an environment in which the devastating effects of drug addiction and pushing are a significant part.

Sex

As it is elsewhere in the society, sex is free and cheap in the inner city. Ever aware of adult street realities, urban young people thirst for adult pleasures, especially in the absence of the usual middle-class recreational outlets. For males, sexual conquests are measures of achievement and fathering a child is a sign of manhood. For females, sex and especially giving birth—in or out of wedlock—affirms desirability and maturity in an atmosphere in which there is little positive reinforcement. For females, who do not have the gang opportunities available to males, there is particular pressure. They tend to be regarded as sex objects to be used for physical pleasures. Although they long for more genuine forms of love, sexual attention provides some compensatory value.

Despite high levels of sexual activity, there is often an appalling lack of knowledge about biological and reproductive systems. It is not uncommon for a poor teenager to believe that pregnancy occurs only when true love is involved.

The illegitimacy rate among teenage girls is alarming. The rate in the United States is almost twice that of England and four times that of France. This stems not only from a lack of knowledge about reproduction but also in part from the absence of birth-control information and practice. Because of the high value placed on children among many poor, abortion is not a popular alternative. This is an important point, for abortion is common among youth elsewhere in the society. The higher rate of illegitimate births creates the illusion that premarital sexual activity is much more prevalent among the poor than among other classes. Though there may be a difference, the difference is probably not as great as it appears.

The high rate of illegitimacy is also related to a desire for companionship, love, and a feeling of importance. For many poor girls, having a child is a sign of womanhood, and a child may provide needed intimacy as well as relief from the loneliness and isolation that poverty brings.

Lack of Future Orientation

One effect of having children is the limiting of life options, especially for the unwed mother. However, poor youth place no greater value on future orientation than their elders do. The reasons for this are obvious. If the past is any indicator, the future holds little promise. The intense focus on present-day survival makes looking to the future a luxury only the more affluent can afford. And, again, inner-city youth just do not have contact with adults who have successfully practiced deferred gratification. Some inner-city residents have used future-focusing for advancement; the problem, however, is that their success has taken them out of the community and removed them as models for the next generation. For many the issue is nitty-gritty physical survival—today, not tomorrow or next year.

This lack of future orientation is illustrated in the case of a fifteen-year-old girl who was truant on a regular basis. On examination it was determined that she was making a very lucrative living as a prostitute, bringing in substantial sums of money every week. When confronted with her truancy by the high school principal, the girl pointed out that school didn't pay; after all, she was making money comparable to that of the principal who was administrating the school. The principal's response was in the form of a question: "What will happen in ten years, when your flesh will no longer be fresh and salable?" The young prostitute had never projected ahead that far. Ministry to inner-city youth must take into account these attitudes and behaviors when planning programs: limited contact with parents or any successful adult models; absence of constructive, recreational alternatives to gang involvement, drugs, and sex; and lack of time-oriented routines and of future orientation. The urban worker must be sensitive to the youths' needs for positive reinforcement and genuine caring and love.

GUIDELINES FOR MINISTRY

For those developing urban youth ministries there are a number of guidelines. These include focusing on groups, developing attractive programs, establishing expectations and accountability, and showing personal care for the individual.

Group and Family Focus

Formally educated people tend to prefer working with individuals—one-on-one. Counseling and many evangelistic efforts take that form. Although this may be effective with many youth, it is less effective with lower-income African Americans, Appalachian whites, and Hispanics. Youth in these ethnic groups live in a clan culture and hence do not respond favorably to isolation. Thus, working with a group, preferably in a family context, is much more fruitful. There is scriptural precedent for this group approach. In John 4, Christ offered a spiritual decision for the woman at the well along with her family.

It is important to emphasize that all phases of a youth-ministry program should be conducted within the context of the family situation. This is consistent with the clan culture of the inner city. The vast majority of parents at least verbally subscribe to the goals and Christian values of the program; so their aid in encouraging their children, working with them, and assisting in the program is invaluable. If the mother is opposed, the effort will be quickly harpooned. The mother is one of the few constants, one of the few sources of care and love to the urban adolescent, and so she becomes central to the carrying out of the ministry. When adherence to a program's goals and roles is supported by the parent(s) and other family members present, there is a powerful added impetus toward opening the mind and heart of the youth to the ministry.

Some urban youth programs focus on working with entire gangs, as Young Life began doing as far back as the 1970s. In addition, children who show interest in a program are often interviewed with their parent(s) so that the home can reinforce what the program is seeking to develop. Where individual attention is desirable, it is offered. But because the program has a group focus, the youths are not surrounded by outsiders attempting to change them. They are instead given acceptance and affirmation as a base from which to explore other spiritual and social realities.

Attractive Programs

Whether the program is as individualized as tutoring or becomes more broad based, it is important that it be attractive. Without attractive aspects of the program, there is absolutely no point in going any further. There is no inner-city tradition of going to church for abstract ventures into catechism and church doctrine. As important as this type of learning is, it has to be packaged in ways that appeal to the youngsters. Therefore, the urban youth worker must ask: What do I have to offer that will attract and appeal to youth at their level? Such programs may need to include tickets to major (especially sporting) events, campouts, and other excursions.

Reasonable Expectations

After an attractive program has been designed, the next step concerns the price the youth is willing to pay to be a part of it. This is a vital step, for if there is no responsibility incurred in involvement, the program loses its appeal. Moreover, a clear expectation for the youth not only enhances the look of the ministry but also builds a sense of accountability and reinforces an "I can" self-concept—matters of significant import to inner-city youth. It is especially helpful if this expectation is in the form of a contract signed by the youths and their parent(s), for this gives it a sense of seriousness and dignity and will reduce the likelihood of conning and reneging on a verbal agreement.

The contract must have reasonable provisions that can be lived up to. In addition, it must be adhered to by each party. This again supports a fate-control orientation and makes the youth a responsible participant in the program. Dave Mack and Steve Pedigo, two veteran Chicago Young Life leaders, used the contract method with inner-city youth. One example from their experience involved an out-of-state camping trip. In order to be a part of the expedition, all members were required to attend a Monday night meeting. At the meeting they were told they must have a physical along with a permission form signed by their parent(s). Failure to comply with any of the foregoing automatically removed the youth from being eligible to participate in the camping trip. To be sure, some youngsters tested the limits by failing to comply. The rules, much to their surprise and chagrin, were enforced. The youth were not tossed out of the youth program as a whole, nor were they scolded, harassed, or preached at for not complying; they were simply and courteously informed that they could not go along with the rest of the group on the camping trip—maybe next year.

The expectations must be attainable so that no one has to fail. The youth can choose to drop out by not complying, but the program itself drops no one. It simply adheres to its rules. If the youth think that the program has failed them rather than that they have opted to fail by not discharging their responsibilities, they will sense a strain of arbitrariness about it and become skeptical or even rebel against it. Nevertheless, this gentle, no-nonsense approach is highly effective for use in any attractive program.

Personal Care and Communication

Although the larger focus is on the group, there must be room for quality time with individuals. Listening to, conversing with, and caring for individual youngsters who respond to the ministry is essential. This can be done on an informal basis or in a very flexibly scheduled format. Important focal points in dealing on the individual level include finding out what youths' lives are like; how they feel about school; what their family life is like; how they resonate with the youth program; what, if any, life goals they may have; what recreational interests they have; and who their friends are. It must be remembered that inner-city adolescents often have few, if any, adults who show a genuine interest in their lives. A serious, nonpatronizing approach to them by concerned adults is potentially very effective.

It is likely that many will attempt to con adults who evince such interest in order to test their sincerity. An urban church worker's character and commitment will most surely be tested, because adolescents have a tremendous desire to determine whether a person "is for real." The tests may be frequent and repetitious. But, once the test is passed, there is real potential for growth and relationship.

If there has been an effective demonstration of individual caring and interest, a relationship of some quality and permanence is likely to result. It is through this communication and relationship that everything from evangelism to educational aid can be carried out. Without total, personal care and involvement, evangelism smacks of notches on a gunbelt. However, once youths feel they are genuinely associated with caring adults, all facets of their being will open. When this openness occurs, it is critical that no exploitation take place. Such abuse will be quickly spotted and cut off further ministry. At all points dignity must be protected. The youths must respond to the church's love just as the individual Christian responds to God's love.

In this atmosphere of personal care and communication, a youth's values can be challenged. In the earlier example of the high school principal's dealing with a young prostitute, the principal opted against lecturing the girl but instead used questions to challenge her values. Questions are almost invariably more successful with inner-city youth than declarative statements, for they carry a sense of respect for the dignity and worth of the other; whereas, sermons tend to make objects out of their intended audience. It is often the difference between an expression of authoritarianism and a genuine demonstration of interest in the youth's perceptions.

The key to inner-city youth ministry is unconditional love. This no-strings-attached love, however, must be both gentle and tough. If it is not gentle, it is not loving and caring in an environment devoid of much love and care. If it has no tough side, it becomes patronizing and can easily be undercut by con artists who will only scorn their gullible targets. Too soft an approach may also create unhealthy dependency and a lack of growth. Quality, caring love and involvement is time-consuming but enormously effective, for any real self-giving, agape love exists only in the abstract for many inner-city youth.

MODELS OF MINISTRY

This final section cites the kinds of attractive programs that have been effectively used in urban youth ministries. Two national groups have long been active in various cities: Youth for Christ and Young Life.[3] Both of these organizations have decades of experience in working with urban youth. In some cases there may be a Youth for Christ or Young Life ministry near an urban church. If not, gaining readily obtainable information on their ministries can serves as a guide for a local youth ministry. The final program is one developed by an individual church—the LaSalle Street Church in Chicago—in conjunction with Young Life. That time-tested program is explained in greater detail and offers some principles basic to successful urban youth ministry.

Youth for Christ

Youth for Christ offers some realistic programs for urban youth. The City Life ministry is aimed at helping young people to function constructively in society. It teaches basic life skills, connects the youth with a caring adult, promotes a positive self-image though Christ, and offers opportunities for positive peer group experiences among other things.

The Teen Parents program connects trained adults with pregnant girls and teenage parents designed to help the participants make healthy life choices in their own lives and the lives of their children. Not only is the rate of teenage pregnancy high, in the majority of cases teens will go through with their pregnancy and be the primary caregiver. Young Life assists them to become the best mothers and fathers they can be.

The Youth Guidance ministry also connects youth with caring adults who can aid them in making positive life decisions through contacts in institutions, juvenile justice, or service agencies. It is estimated that 25 percent of US young people can be deemed at-risk youth. Youth for Christ defines an at-risk youth as one who has incurred significant damage and is likely to damage the lives of others. A significantly damaged life is characterized as one containing negative life influences that increase the probability of unhealthy life choices.

Young Life

Multicultural and urban Young Life ministries are carried on in 176 cities. Successful urban ministries have also been carried on by Young Life in various cities. As mentioned earlier, the focus is on working with groups as well as individuals. The Young Life ministry addresses the negative value-systems that are taught in the culture of the streets, as well as the low self-worth present among so many urban youth. Young Life has long worked in high-density, inner-city communities using adult-friend role models and basic life-skills training. Young Life is well known for offering interesting recreational opportunities for youngsters, such as winter ski retreats, trips to summer resorts, basketball leagues in the communities, appealing social functions, and a host of other attractive options. There is also evangelistic activity, but it is often of a low-key variety. It seeks values clarification and confrontation with certain spiritual realities that point to the meaning of Christ in an individual's life.

LaSalle Street Church

The low-income neighborhood once surrounding LaSalle Street Church in Chicago has become largely regentrified. Nonetheless, at its height, LaSalle had a rather successful youth-ministry program. Its effectiveness was the result of much experience in the Cabrini-Green public housing community, a great deal of work, much trial-and-error effort, and plenty of failure. Associated with the Young Life program in Chicago, it had a staff of paid workers as well as volunteers. Some of the staff were graduates of the program and lived in Cabrini-Green. Indigenous leadership is extraordinarily valuable, for these people not only develop powerful lines of communication with youngsters in the program but also function as models for them right in the neighborhood.

The LaSalle program had four major goals: to develop disciples of Christ who could function as Christians in any environment, to help youth develop a positive and accurate self-image, to cultivate skills and abilities, and to enlarge the vision of the youth and supply motivation. The ministry did not simply seek quick, shallow Christian commitments in the absence of growth. Rather, it built whole-person relationships with the youth in order to enable them to live out Christian values no matter what their immediate life context.

Discipling inner-city youth is a very challenging task and must be undertaken with tremendous patience. At LaSalle the youth did not have to make a Christian commitment to be a part of the group. They merely had to abide by the contract and attend regularly.

The ministry consisted of recreational activity and personal and group involvement. One night a week there was an evangelistic activity, taking the form of values clarification, Bible study, and sharing who Christ was in the lives of the leaders and how Christ was a motivation for the entire program. Augmented by frequent trips, basketball leagues, and camping opportunities, this low-key evangelistic approach had brought about a large number of Christian commitments from the youth.

Not all the youth made a genuine Christian commitment, but those who did were carefully and caringly discipled in the Bible studies and by personal contact, so that they could grow to spiritual maturity. The Bible studies emphasized application to daily life. They were practical and life focused. Urban youth, living from crisis to crisis, are best equipped spiritually when the Scriptures help them evaluate and act on each crisis.

The discipling process was carried on through dialogue and interaction. Preaching and other didactic techniques were discarded in favor of relating and discussing. The aim was to aid the youth in seeing alternatives to the street values—to open minds and enlarge perspectives. This is best accomplished by encouraging open expression of thoughts and ideas orally or in writing. Every effort was made at establishing candid exchanges and overt reflecting in order to bring about the greatest interpersonal impact. This relational method is a mutually beneficial activity, one that enhances the ministry as leaders learn more fully what is going on in the minds and hearts of those with whom and to whom they minister. The gospel must have credibility, and such credibility is best attained if the methods of communicating it are honorable and open—and above all, nonmanipulative.[4]

The second major goal was to help youth develop a positive and accurate self-image. Despite the bravado and rebellion so common among inner-city youth, there is often a sense of inferiority underneath. They live in a society in which they are disliked and degraded. And they know it. They can attempt to reject that society's values, but it is very difficult to do when that society controls everything from the labor market to the media, and ultimately controls a person's economic and social destiny. Although, as Malcolm Muggeridge pointed out, we meet very few rich people who are happy, we never meet a poor person who does not wish to be rich. This is true largely because wealth translates as significance. Hence, any inner-city child, regardless of ethnic background, has a high risk of developing a less than positive self-concept. And without a positive self-concept, a cornerstone of motivation and drive is absent.

A part of developing a stable and positive self-image involves the third goal: cultivating skills and abilities. Some of these skills are physical. Each year at Young Life summer camps, the recreational deficits experienced by inner-city youth were apparent. Many of the urban youngsters were unable to swim, play tennis, or even play basketball and baseball as well as their more recreation-saturated suburban counterparts. Although many great professional athletes have emerged from the concrete playgrounds of the cities, there remain thousands who are left out of playground competition because of the lack of space on which to play. As one inner-city veteran stated, "You can mouth unceasingly that Black is beautiful, but if you can't do anything of a skilled nature, it is not internalized." There must be a sense of achievement and accomplishment, and that requires appropriate skill development.

The youth program offered opportunities to develop recreational skills by conducting basketball leagues as well as other sporting ventures. Achieving a bit of success in an amateur basketball tournament can go a long way in building self-confidence and a feeling of significance. However, excellence is not easy to come by in the academic domain. As discussed earlier, inner-city youth come from a nonacademic tradition and lack contact in the home and community with people who are accomplished educationally.

A fourth goal, then, was to enlarge the vision of the youth and supply motivation. The Young Life workers discovered the need for this very early. At the outset of one of their programs, they inquired of the youth what they would like to be when they were adults. A sizable percentage of the youth openly expressed a desire to be a pimp, prostitute, or drug pusher. This is really not surprising, as these types are often the only community residents who do well economically and have a bit of social influence. The pimp drives the shiny new automobile, sits around and drinks wine all day, has attractive women at his beck and call, and above all, has a rather lucrative income. This is very appealing when set off against the dirt-poor unemployed or the overworked but underpaid laborers. For girls, the prostitute lives a rather charmed life. She has an attractive apartment, makes very good money, is protected by a pimp, and has men constantly desiring her favors. There is a sort of celebrity status in all this. The pusher, of course, is really into the big bucks. He has great power on the streets and carries a rather awesome profile. It is interesting that each of these is a type of self-employed businessperson. The note of free enterprise takes a delinquent turn, because of the lack of legitimate opportunities.

As a counter to this kind of worldview, the Young Life program developed what was called "Black Achievers" in Cabrini-Green. They realized that matching the achiever ethnically with the youth was very important. The youth were taken around various offices, factories, and other establishments to meet African American adults well respected for their work. Some were executives; some were professionals in medicine, publishing, and teaching; others worked in industrial plants. What they all had in common was success at what they did. These models told the youngsters about their lives, how they got into their present occupation, and what it required to succeed in it. The experience astounded many of the kids. Most had never seen anyone like themselves, from their own roots, who held these kinds of jobs. At the end of the several months, when the youth were asked about their future goals, almost all had abandoned their desires to be a pimp, prostitute, or pusher and had set their sights on a more conventional occupational pursuit.

The altered outlook indicated an elevated "I can" self-concept. Reminded of what the various models had said about success, some of the kids approached their school work with renewed vigor, attended the church tutoring program with a more serious outlook, and in general began making constructive progress toward what they now viewed as attainable goals. In short, enlarged vision and improved motivation paved the way for skills to be developed.

Worthy of note is the role of accountability and contracts here. Once youngsters had made a commitment to some achievement goal, the Young Life program had the students and parents sign a waiver allowing the staff to go into the youngsters' school to check their attendance and academic records. The purpose of this was to impress on the youth the importance of making commitments and keeping them, while not being able to con anyone along the way. Again, this school checking was not done in any punitive or manipulative fashion. It was only appropriate in aiding the youths in becoming accountable to themselves and the program, once they had decided to embark on something that would require that sort of diligence.

Commitment to self is a key. Youths were not asked to commit themselves to the program or its leader. They were told that they were really making a commitment to themselves—their own goals and desires; and making good on that commitment required a certain accountability, which the program leadership would help the youngsters to achieve.

In this chapter guidelines for and examples of ministry have been presented in the light of the attitudes and behaviors of urban youth. But a fuller understanding of urban youth necessitates studying minority experiences. Not only are US cities becoming more and more nonwhite, but those nonwhite populations are, on the average, much younger than the Caucasian groups. Higher birth rates among minorities, coupled with the large number of children among some immigrant groups, mean increasingly that the face of an urban youth is likely a minority face. We turn now from our focus on youth to an investigation of racial and ethnic minorities.

MINORITIES 7

Any white urban workers who underestimate the virulence and all-pervasiveness of prejudice and racism in US society are setting themselves up for a tremendous amount of frustration and failure. The white pastor who works with minorities is working in a sociological tension, for any society with a number of distinguishable cultural or ethnic groups is a society in tension. Its members, especially the minority members, are constantly aware, at least subliminally, of that tension. They live in a "we-they" society in which they are the "they." White pastors represent the "we" and have to demonstrate very clearly that they do not want to be aligned with the "we."

The US social system is in a continually conflicted state. On one hand, there is what the Swedish social scientist Gunnar Myrdal called the public ideology, holding that each person is equal in worth before God and in the eyes of the law. This public ideology is celebrated, alluded to, and very nearly worshiped as part of democratic dogma. On the other hand, the United States continues to be a racialized society, one in which "race matters profoundly for the differences in life experiences, life opportunities, and social relationships."[1] Moreover, it is one that "allocates differential economic, political, social, and even psychological rewards to groups along racial lines; lines that are socially constructed."[2] We say that race is socially constructed because people are classified socially by physical characteristics, yet only selected racial characteristics (skin color, for example) have social meaning.

Out of the racialized society comes a private norm of prejudice and discrimination that very clearly accords differential degrees of respect and deference to individuals based on group affiliation. This private norm is an operational or practiced norm, while the public norm is the doctrine that assuages the troubled collective conscience.[3]

White urban workers have grown up in a society that daily socializes its members according to the private norm. In fact, it can be argued that all white urban workers or pastors are to some extent affected by prejudice or racism simply because they live in a heavily racist society. This is not meant to be an indictment, for to be white and somewhat racist is normal. For just as those who regularly breathe polluted city air should not be the least bit defensive about having some pollution in their lungs, so those who are regularly exposed to a racist and prejudice-laden society could hardly be expected not to be somewhat prejudiced. The point is that most people start out as racists and then must make active and ongoing efforts to eradicate this racism.

If white racism is defined as having notions of white supremacy, it becomes rather easy to see how these tendencies become subconsciously internalized at a very early age. If a small child is taken to visit a number of major institutions such as a hospital, university, bank, or large corporation, that child would not have to be very astute to notice that the group in positions of power and respect is overwhelmingly white, while people of color are concentrated in such menial positions as dietary and cafeteria work, scrubbing, and cleaning. Unless someone sits down with that child and explains the nature and history of prejudice and inequality of opportunity, this child is certainly going to assume that there is something supreme about whites. As children grow up they may live in largely white neighborhoods, go to predominantly white schools, and attend white churches. Thus these racist notions calcify. All the well-meaning, patronizing statements they may hear about prejudice and disadvantage in society are counter-balanced by the epithets, racial slurs, and attitudes they encounter even among Christians.

Then as children reach adulthood and plan, perhaps, to go into Christian ministry, they attend Christian colleges with a largely white faculty, staff, and student body, finally to finish in white middle-class seminaries that tries to prepare them for working with all kinds of people. If by then they are not to some extent a purveyors of racism and prejudice, it would be rather surprising, for all agree that a person's environment is a major influence on attitudes, values, beliefs, and behaviors.

Thus a white pastor or urban worker is by conditioning and environment at least partly racist. One step in eradicating this racism in order to have an effective urban ministry is to understand the history of US prejudice and discrimination. Such knowledge should encompass the historical and sociological factors in racism and majority-minority relations as well as the present-day issues affecting minority groups in the United States.

HISTORICAL AND SOCIOLOGICAL FACTORS

Academically speaking, prejudice or racism can be accounted for in terms of four related and interacting historical and sociological factors.[4] The first is *historical conditioning*. This refers to majoritarianism (or majority rights, discussed below) as well as the sheer inertia of history. From the near extermination of the Native Americans to the enslavement of African Americans, the heritage of the United States is heavy with prejudice and oppression.

A closely related factor is *cultural conditioning*. Prejudice, once it has endured over decades and even centuries, becomes institutionalized—sewn into the very life of the culture. A good example can be found in language. Such ancient colloquial expressions, burned in US folklore, as "eenie, meenie, minie, mo . . ." and "shinier than a nigger's heel," "Indian giver," and "Jewing him down" illustrate this. Interestingly, no one ever

163

"Catholics" anyone down or "Lutherans" others into economic submission. People become so accustomed to subtle forms of Caucasian supremacy that they go unnoticed and are simply accepted as the natural course of things. That minorities are more often arrested, constitute the majority of prison inmates, and receive humiliating treatment in stores and other public settings not only goes unquestioned but is hardly noticed. Even minorities eventually become habituated to such shabby treatment, viewing it as the American way of life.

A third factor concerns the *social structure.* The earlier example of the small child making its way through major institutions illustrates how the social structure communicates prejudice. People in the United States become conditioned to seeing whites giving orders and nonwhites carrying them out, whites coolly directing and nonwhites sweating in toil, and whites in business suits and nonwhites in overalls. Although there is a growing number of exceptions to this role, they remain exceptions and suggest a sense of white supremacy.

The fourth factor is *psychological need.* Prejudice can be explained by a desire to feel superior to or significant in comparison with someone else. In a culture driven by strivings for status and prestige, it is only natural that scapegoats are created. "Free, white, and twenty-one," "Well, at least I am not black," and other verbal toss-offs are pregnant with this psychological factor. Lust for power and advantage gives rise to competition. When victory cannot be gained within the system economically, educationally, or occupationally, it will often be seized through forms of prejudice and oppression. To have advantage, even on illicit and immoral grounds, is preferred to risking a possible setback in status. While whites cringe at notions of black power, they have casually accepted white power as a way of life.

Two of these factors—historical conditioning and cultural, or institutional, racism—will be looked at more closely.

Historical Conditioning

Historically, there are two major trends that have been factors in forming the US brand of prejudice. These include, first, the discrepancy between public ideology and private practice in administering rights. This discrepancy can be traced to the difference between European group rights and US individual rights. And second is the rapid urbanization of the United States, which brought a conflict between urbanism and ruralism.

European Group Rights versus US Individual Rights. Not surprisingly, the US brand of prejudice can be traced back to Europe when the Peace of Westphalia in 1648 divided the continent in such a way that Protestants held dominance in the northern and eastern regions and the Roman Catholics in the southern and western areas.[5] As a result of this settlement, the religious group in the minority incurred rather distinct political, economic, and social disadvantages. For a Catholic living in the Protestant sector, it was very difficult to succeed in business; any hopes of political power were completely unrealistic; and social acceptance was provisional at best. The same was true for a Protestant residing in a Catholic region. The alternative was very simple: if you were unhappy with the disadvantages you incurred, you had only to move to a sector in which your religion held sway. In short, this majoritarianism was accepted as unquestioned reality.

The writers of the US Constitution, realizing this rather oppressive state of affairs, decided to insure that the United States would not have this majoritarian flavor, especially since most immigrants were among the losers in Europe. For that reason it was made clear that religion would not be a test for political office or legal acceptance in the new land.

Despite their noble intentions, however, this constitutional safeguard was not adequate to prevent the activation of prejudice and discrimination. As certainly as the Europeans who came to

America were Americanized, so also America was Europeanized by their presence. The immigrants took more than their physical necessities on the ship to America; they also took their political notions, prejudices, and other distorted attitudes. Hence, on the issue of human rights there can be seen a European and American dichotomy.

The European concept of rights was group-based; that is, rights were related to religious affiliation. A member of the "right" religious group could expect greater and more advantageous rights than one who was not. Rights were viewed as deferrable in that minorities had to earn their rights—showing by diligence and dependability that they could rightfully be treated with human dignity and respect. Finally, there was obvious inequality in the possession of rights.

The constitutional notion of rights suggests that they are individual. Each citizen has individual rights. Before the law there is no group-affiliation test that delineates differences in rights. Rights are not earned—they are present at birth. Rights are just that—rightful guarantees of proper treatment and human dignity. Lastly, all rights are equal. Not even a president should be treated in a different way from any other citizen.

On paper the US concept is nearly ideal. It is what Myrdal would call the public ideology. However, at the private level, there is still the application of a European approach. Such statements as "This country used to be for Americans (whites), now I guess its for the Puerto Ricans (Mexican Americans, African Americans, Jordanians, Pakistanis, etc.)," or more directly, "People should remain with their own kind; let them live over there and we'll stay here—that way there will be no trouble" are evidences of the group-based aspect.

The expression "They shouldn't get their rights until they act like (white) Americans" is a rather brazen example of the deferrable component. All forms of provisional social and occupational acceptance are also examples of this aspect.

Finally, any discrepancies in rights indicate the inequality component. Whenever groups are locked into depressed areas, have difficulty buying homes, are left with public defenders for a less-than-adequate legal defense, receive longer and more arbitrary prison sentences, are given lower-quality education, or are under undue disadvantage in seeking political office, inequality in rights is being observed. In sum, the United States lives in a tension, straddling these two concepts of rights, and this tension has lasted for three centuries.

Urbanism versus Ruralism. The second major historical trend that has been a factor in US prejudice is rapid urbanization. Urbanization is not urbanism. The former refers simply to the physical movement of populations into urban regions. The latter means discarding or reducing a rural outlook and adopting a frame of mind, a social perspective, appropriate to urban life.[6]

Ruralism is characterized by smallness, simplism, homogeneity, independence, changelessness, and xenophobia. Ruralism can be found in tribal cultures and even in rural America where populations are small in number. In the rural outlook there is a lack of complexity and sophistication; the people are very much alike socially and ethnically; individuals are usually self-sufficient in that they hunt or farm and therefore do not have to rely much on others for their livelihood; life seems very static; and there is a clannishness that views outsiders with distrust and a sense of we-theyness. This perspective, of course, works very well in rural settings. And since humankind has been rural in character throughout history worldwide, ruralism has been an effective mode of living.

However, when people reside in cities, this ruralism is counterproductive. It breeds distrust, prejudice, discrimination, bitterness, crime, and violence. What is needed to cope with urbanization is a healthy urbanism—a way of thinking that values (and is comfortable with) large numbers of people; that is cosmopolitan, diverse and heterogeneous, complex and sophisticated, interdependent and reliant on others in all phases of social existence; that accepts constant change and development; and that is at ease in interacting with those who are culturally different.

What has happened is that in the space of one century, the forces of urbanization have driven humankind into city living, while doggedly retaining a ruralistic outlook. Prejudice and racism thrive on this problem. For not only does the ruralistic outlook feed clannishness and rejection on the basis of extrinsic factors such as skin color and national origin but also the diversity of the urban population provides millions of victims on which to visit this prejudice.

Institutional Racism

Even more devastating than individual forms of racism and prejudice bred by historical and social conditioning is institutional racism. Whereas individual racism refers to a conscious or subconscious belief in white supremacy, institutional racism is prejudice and discrimination practiced in the day-to-day workings of large institutions.

There are a host of examples of institutional racism (or prejudice) at hand. The push for affirmative-action guidelines, set down by the federal government, is proof of the presence of institutionalized racism, for they would not exist if such racism were not being practiced. That no major political party in the United States has felt safe in nominating an African American even for the vice-presidency is additional testimony to the existence of deep-seated individual and institutional racism. Standardized tests—whether for entrance to college or graduate school or for eligibility to serve as a policeman or fireman in a major city—have been demonstrated to be biased in favor of Caucasian, middle-class respondents and are also examples of institutional racism. The disinvestment by cities in minority communities while regentrified districts thrive is a stark instance of institutional racism. Any and all unwritten but widely practiced quotas that limit the hiring of minorities or limit the hiring of nonminorities because the quotas are not filled, are further illustrations of it. Still another more recent phenomenon involves "environmental racism." With the economic abandonment of the inner city comes empty factory sites. Called "brown fields," these often are rife with toxins. In Chicago the federal government identified over sixty "superfund sites," locations targeted for environmental cleanup, many located in inner-city communities. There is also redlining and blockbusting, discussed in an earlier chapter.

What is vital here is that once these institutional policies are put into force, they can be carried out by well-meaning, good citizens. In fact, often executors of institutional racism are wholly unaware of their deleterious actions. Urban pastors themselves may be involved if they serve a denomination that has racist policies with regard to funding, location, and personnel. This subtle racism has been practiced by many Christian colleges, institutions well known for their Anglo outlook, unaggressive recruitment of minorities (other than as attempts to indicate diversity in the student body), Caucasian faculties, and, hence, lack of sensitivity to cultural differences among the student population.

The matter of institutionalized racism is so critical and pervasive that it merits detailed attention.

Businesses. Businesses and corporations are tainted by institutional racism. The hiring record of major businesses on the fringe of a minority neighborhood may provide evidence. A disproportionate number of white faces is a symptom of institutional racism. If minorities are visible in a business, a closer look may reveal a more common phenomenon: a swelling of the lower echelons with minorities, with the ranks getting whiter and whiter toward the top of the ladder. Moreover, the blacks who have moved up an organization's hierarchy, on merit, reach a certain level and then find themselves held there permanently, simply because the door to the very top executive suite often has an invisible sign on it: Whites Only.

Labor Unions. Labor unions have long been notorious for discrimination. Although many of the nationwide unions devoutly affirm openness at the national level, their local affiliates are commonly operated by community hacks who have a vested interest in keeping minorities out in favor of the many blue-collar whites who are hungering for union work. Trade and craft unions are regularly taken to court where they lose civil rights cases.

Education. There is wholesale institutional racism in education. This can be seen in the culturally biased IQ and achievement tests, the low priorities given the needs of inner-city schools, the biased textbooks—especially in history, and the tendency to place the least experienced and often least committed teachers in the most needy schools.

Again, it is important to realize that much racism is carried on by very well-intentioned people, including politically liberal pastors. Overt feelings of prejudice or racism may be absent; however, feelings of white supremacy linger on for all the reasons discussed. Unless people stay consistently vigilant in dealing with such feelings through reading, discussing, and self-examination, they have no business dealing with nonwhites in an urban church.

Majority-Minority Relations

In addition to understanding the historical, cultural, social, and psychological factors underlying personal and institutional racism, it is helpful for an urban worker to have knowledge of the various ways majority and minority groups relate and the strategies each group uses to establish normalized relations.

The state of majority-minority relations in the United States can be seen quite vividly when we consider the various forms majority-minority interactions can take. As with any group encounter, whenever a majority and a minority come into frequent contact, they develop a regularized, normalized set of relations. Matters will not remain precarious for long. Sometimes relations will be marked by fairness and mutual respect, but more often by oppression.

There are essentially three major stages of majority-minority relations: accommodation, assimilation, and amalgamation.[7] These reflect a movement from rather strained, one-sided interactions to full equality.

Accommodation, the first major stage, suggests a minimal cultural exchange, sufficient to avoid open conflict and disruption. This accommodation usually necessitates that the minority divest itself of its most objectionable (in the eyes of the majority) traits in order to facilitate interaction. The minority is expected, primarily, to adopt the dominant language and economic system. Failure to do this will bring about serious conflict. Native Americans suffered genocide as a result of clinging to their own culture when they were confronted with Caucasian culture.

There are four subtypes of accommodation. The first of these is *conquest.* This, as the term indicates, is the most brutal form. Here the majority simply conquers the minority and brings the minority under its control. There are a number of regretable examples of conquest in US history. Forcing Native Americans onto reservations and making them learn Anglo culture in Bureau of Indian Affairs schools is one example. The institution of slavery is another grisly example.

A second subtype is *toleration.* Less repulsive to the minority, toleration involves an acceptance (on the part of the majority) of a number of culturally different minority traits. Rather than forcibly moving the minority in the majority's cultural direction, the minority is allowed to adjust more at its own speed. In any case, the power differential remains, and this tolerance has very real limits. Almost every nonwhite minority has experienced this type of toleration during its American tenure—a condition in which the minority is aware that it can retain some of its own customs, provided these are neither offensive to the majority nor too overtly displayed.

Compromise, the third subtype, is the result of a bit more power equality. Although the majority still holds the edge, the minority is significant enough either in number or institutional position to necessitate less-repressive treatment. Here a more peaceful relationship exists, one that is characterized by negotiation rather than coercion. Currently, the United States contains many examples of this. Such features as protection of minorities by law, increasing numbers of minorities, and the establishment of nonwhites in the US labor market make it less advantageous for racist whites to discriminate openly. Therefore, many grievances are bargained out, with minorities getting something (though perhaps less than an equal share) out of the bargain.

In *conversion,* the fourth subtype of accommodation, the minority willingly divests itself of its cultural distinctiveness in an effort to join in with and be accepted by the majority. What makes conversion different from conquest is that the minority converts voluntarily. This subtype is practiced more on an individual level than on a group level. That is, some minority persons will seek acceptance by Caucasians and so blend in as much as possible with them. Many Asian Americans, light-skinned Puerto Ricans, and Mexican Americans have done this. However, conversion is only successful if the would-be convert is accepted by the majority. As a group, most minorities have been rejected, regardless of any conversion strategy, and so conversion has its limits. Also of import here is that the price is high. Conversion means a denial of a person's cultural identity, that is, what a person or a group really is, historically. Such a denial has psychological consequences, for it means rejecting one's heritage in quest of economic or social advancement—a form of selling out, repugnant to peoples of any ancestry.

The next major stage in majority-minority interaction is *assimilation.* Much could be said about this stage, but in short, it suggests maximal cultural interchange. A relationship develops that is characterized by open, unselfconscious interaction between cultures. These cultures eventually become blended to the extent that they are fully united into one larger culture. The emerging culture will, in all likelihood, resemble the original majority culture more than the minority system; nonetheless, there is a unified mixture. Assimilation usually takes a long time if the minority culture is highly developed and quite diverse from that of the majority. What is especially important here is the sense of harmony and oneness in this stage. Clearly there is little white-nonwhite assimilation as yet in the United States.

The final stage is *amalgamation,* and it comes on the heels of whole assimilation. Amalgamation refers to complete cultural and biological mixing. Here majority-minority differences disappear through cultural unity and intermarriage, such that there is ultimately no trace of the previously existing separate groups. There is amalgamation in Hawaii, where various civic organizations once boasted of the new "golden man"—a mixture of a variety of different ancestries.

Both the majority and the minority have favored strategies for how they would prefer to establish normalized relations. Understanding these strategies can be very helpful at the parish level, for once an urban worker comes to grips with them in theory, it becomes easier to see how the minority and the majority are relating in the immediate community. These strategies are not openly enunciated, but are operationally demonstrated in majority-minority interactions.

Majority Strategies. For the majority, there are six strategies.[8] The first, but by no means the most desirable in the eyes of the majority, is *pluralism.* Here there is unity with diversity; that is, the minority is allowed to retain its cultural identity, provided it conforms to certain larger demands affecting the national interest. Such demands may include the payment of taxes and the observance of the laws. The advantage of this policy for the majority is that it minimizes open conflict. However, it means the minority can retain many of its aggravating (from the majority perspective) and threatening differences and thus demonstrate the divided nature of the society. Multiethnic churches that celebrate cultural diversity through carefully planned worship services, activities, and programs exemplify pluralism.

Assimilation is the second and more preferred strategy. This assimilation is not of the type described earlier, in which there is open and easy interchange. Rather, it has a coercive quality, expecting, perhaps even demanding, that the minority waive its cultural distinctiveness in exchange for at least provisional acceptance by the majority. It is unity with uniformity, with the bulk of the change being carried on by the minority. Many non-English-speaking European groups have willingly taken this option (a sort of conversion), while nonwhite groups have experienced more forceful treatment from the majority in bringing them into accordance with Anglo culture. Of import is that, especially in the case of nonwhites, this assimilation is often not full assimilation. For if they are brought into congruity with Anglo styles, they may still not be fully accepted into the Anglo world, although they will be treated much more humanely. Predominantly white churches that welcome nonwhites to join them but that make no real attempt to adapt to the cultures these minorities represent are advancing an assimilationist policy.

Legal protection involves the protection of the minorities from outside, vicious attacks while keeping them in subordination to the majority. US history is filled with examples of this policy. Keeping African Americans safe from Ku Klux Klan attacks while stopping far short of insuring equal justice is one illustration. The protection of various Indian tribes from violence and the holding of the Japanese in relocation centers are two other examples. Here the majority can congratulate itself for its paternalism, while making certain that the minority will not threaten them by being able to compete with them on a fully equal basis. Whenever a church takes minority children into its Sunday school program but, whether intentionally or not, shows little interest in bringing their parents into the fellowship, it is operating in a legal protection-like style.

Population transfer is self-explanatory. It simply refers to the movement of a minority from one region to another for its own good or, more likely, for the majority's good. The forced move-

174

ment of the Cherokee Indians along the famous Trail of Tears is a prime example. The herding of the Japanese into the relocation centers is another. The placement of various Indian tribes on reservation land is probably the best-known illustration. In any case, this transfer may be done with or without the minority's approval.

Continued subjugation is a condition in which the minority is unceasingly oppressed and accorded less-than-equitable treatment. All cases in which discrimination and humiliation have endured are examples of this policy. Continued subjugation was the state of almost every nonwhite minority prior to the passage of the civil-rights legislation in the 1960s. Any church that affirms segregation through intentional denial of minority membership is using segregationist tactics.

The final policy is *extermination* or *genocide.* US history texts have done a skillful job of disguising this policy, making it seem as if it never took place on this continent. Nothing could be further from the truth. The original, nonwhite minority—the American Indian—was the object of genocide. If indeed "the only good Indian is a dead Indian," as the cliche says, then there were many "good" Indians prior to the 1850s. It is estimated that there were about one million Native Americans on the continent at the time of the arrival of the first Europeans. That number shrank to about 240,000 by 1900. Native Americans are the only ethnic group to decrease in absolute numbers in US history, and they decreased by three-fourths. Only recently have their numbers climbed above the original one million.

Minority Strategies. Minorities have four policies of their own.[9] One is *assimilation,* much like conversion. Interestingly, almost every nonwhite minority has at one time or another attempted this policy. Sadly, lack of acceptance by Caucasians made it disadvantageous and forced these groups to opt for other strategies. As discussed earlier, assimilation is costly, meaning loss of identity. Nonetheless, even in the face of continuing disadvantage and possibly extinction, assimilation can appear very inviting. All-out attempts by minorities to join and blend in with a Caucasian church evince assimilationism.

The most favored of the minority policies is *pluralism,* also described earlier. This guarantees full societal participation along with the retention of favored cultural traits. This policy is often more ideal than real. Involvement in multiethnic churches that value their diversity reflects pluralism.

When attempts at pluralism and assimilation are thwarted by majority resistance and rejection, *secessionism* may result. Here the minority withdraws from the culture and even from interaction with the majority, in an effort to develop its own culture in isolation from majority interference. The attempt to form a confederacy among the Southern states is the best-known example of this policy. However, black separatists in the late 1960s also espoused a form of secessionism. Their argument was that after 350 years of submitting to the dictates of white America, only to experience continued subjugation and oppression, it was time to separate, to develop their own cultural identity and strength, so that future encounters would take place on more-equal footing. Totally African American, Hispanic, and Asian churches suggest a secessionist policy, sometimes brought on by necessity rather than choice.

Militance is a strategy that means more than radical rhetoric, large Afros of 1960s, or vivid Indian regalia. Militance refers to the minority's often violent attempt to overthrow a society's institutions to gain majority power and dominance. Militance can be a last-resort tactic when survival is threatened. Native Americans were forced to practice it when faced with the extermination efforts of the pioneers. In the church, majority-minority battles over power positions within major denominations can smack of militance.

If urban workers are reasonably observant, they are likely to be able to observe one or more of these strategies as they analyze almost any majority-minority encounter. As they come to grips with this analysis, at the here-and-now parish level, they will find it much easier to predict majority and minority behavior and to know what action to take.

Overall, it is important to stress that knowledge of the majority's policy is usually the more valuable; because of its greater power, the majority is usually better able to carry out its policy than can the minority. Also it is necessary to recognize that these policies are almost never entirely clear-cut. That is, they overlap to some extent. Finally, not all members of a majority or a minority will be in full accord on a given strategy. Nevertheless, the leaders of both groups need to be watched and their actions will indicate the direction the groups will go. Being able to discern this direction can be a valuable cue in knowing how to manage the role of peacemaker and minister of justice and reconciliation.

If an urban pastor is blessed with a multiracial ministry, special efforts need to be made to keep a balance of power. There are transitional areas in major cities in which several distinct language-group congregations—English, Spanish, Chinese, and Korean—may share a single facility. When these disparate groups are part of one larger church identity, the structure needs to be relational rather than hierarchical so as to avoid any one group dominating. The church-at-large also needs to affirm this cultural pluralism and the dignity of each culture, as well as provide for the addition of new groups or the phasing out of a declining population.

Uptown Baptist Church in Chicago once had five different language-group congregations in one church. Like the Los Angeles model, no group was permitted to dominate, because church board representation was designed to prevent any power bloc from gaining an edge. While all were members of the larger congregation and met occasionally in a mass worship service, each group had its separate worship and fellowship opportunities as well.

Knowledge of the historical and sociological factors, then, is vital. Although it is beyond the scope of this book to provide a comprehensive treatment of the experience of every nonwhite minority group (particularly because of the many Hispanic, Asian, and Middle Eastern peoples), what follows is a more condensed presentation of the US journey of five traditional minority groups. These five different yet overlapping experiences offer a basic perspective on minority experience for those who are interested in effective ministry with various nonwhite groups.

TRADITIONAL MINORITY GROUPS

Native Americans

Native Americans are the only US ethnic group that has never really desired assimilation. Much of this hesitancy is traced to the multiplicity of tribes. In fact, it is incorrect to speak of an all-inclusive minority group called American Indians or Native Americans.[10] Although Native Ameircans constitute less than one percent of the US population, it can be argued that they represent as many as half the languages and subcultures in the nation. It is more accurate then to speak of Navaho, Sioux, Blackfoot, Hopi, and so forth, for each tribe has a unique culture of its own. Urban Native Americans are often separated from their tribes; hence a certain area in a large city may consist of a conglomerate of tribal traditions. However, it is helpful not to assume this in ministering to them, as a neighborhood may be dominated by the ancestry of a particular tribe and so be resonate with that tribal tradition.

Anthropologically, Native Americans are a mixture of many peoples. Some are from China and Southeast Asia, but most are from the inner recesses of the Asian mainland—from Siberia to points west. It is assumed that many entered the New World across what is now the Bering Strait and headed east, and then south, all the way to Mexico and even South America.

In contrast to television portrayals, many of the tribes had very highly developed cultures, reflected in the architecture of temples and religious centers, as well as complex agricultural systems. In order to minister to and among these people it is necessary to understand their religious and cultural heritage.

The religious culture of Native Americans is permeated with respect for and even worship of nature in general and the earth in particular. The notions of private ownership and capitalism, with the accompanying land rape and air pollution, are repugnant to the very heart of Native American culture and are considered sacrilegious. Today many Indians, especially those on reservations, still cling to native faiths, or at least aspects of them, while others embrace some form of Christianity. Effective Christian ministry obviously has to accommodate some of the essentials of Native American religious culture—essentials that can be argued to be more in harmony with Christ's teaching and life than much of our contemporary industrial exploitation.

Indian culture is very nonconfrontive, very accepting of others' freedom and dignity. As such, Native Americans have considerable difficulty understanding or certainly appreciating contemporary US competitive and adversary notions—such as labor versus management, plaintiff versus defendant, and team versus team. In that sense, a patient, low-key, and respectful tone is most effective in dealing with Indians truly steeped in their culture. The aggressive, intense way of the white man is brutish and discourteous to these people. Developing sound relations, then, necessitates sensitivity, respect, and understanding.

In addition to understanding the culture, it is important that an urban minister have an accurate view of the history of the relations between the Indians and the white settlers. The history of white-Native American interaction is best written in blood. The Native American stood in the way of the white settlers' desire to push west. That the Indians did not immediately convert to European notions of Christianity was a primary enzyme in the justification whites felt to destroy them. Indians were regarded by the whites as the Philistines were by the Israelites. The result then was the massacre of 75 percent of their numbers.

To accomplish their move west, white settlers at times turned to treaties. Literally hundreds of treaties were made by various legislators with individual Indian tribes, often after the attacking white settlers forced the Indians into having to bargain from weakness. Treaty after treaty was made in good faith by a tribe, only to have the treaty brazenly violated when such violation was in the white man's best interest. Almost none of the treaties were kept.

Moreover, during the late 1800s, when the federal government realized the necessity of protecting Indians from continuing extermination efforts, they made them wards of the government and developed the reservation system. This move brought on still more atrocities. Perhaps the main one involved land. The government, in the Dawes Act, determined that property should be individually owned by American Indians, with the proviso that it could not be sold. This provision was for the Native Americans' benefit in that it prevented unscrupulous land sharks from preying on their lack of economic savvy. However, once it became apparent that this provision worked against the interests of many enterprising white land hustlers, the Act was amended three times, each time weakening the no-sale clause. The result was that land held by Indians dropped from 139 million acres in 1887 to about 47 million by 1933. And that remnant consisted of the worst, most infertile land available.

It is important that an urban pastor be aware of this tragic heritage when ministering among Native Americans who are aware of these travesties. A Caucasian pastor is a symbol of the "white man"—the Native American's historical enemy. Learning to trust Caucasians is difficult because of their history of killing Native Americans, stealing their land, and destroying their culture. The barriers are high, but many Native Americans are courteous and kind people, and many remain open to better relations.

As is the case among many minorities, contemporary American Indians are much more acculturated to the dominant culture than their forebears were. Many older American Indians tend to be more tied to the past and more docile, while their younger counterparts are hungry for pluralism and activism. Some younger American Indians, excited by the bright lights and wonders of "white" society, leave the reservations on which they were raised and head for the city. Those who survive the transition occasionally melt in with the urban society, even to the point of intermarriage. Many others, however, find themselves in the most depressed areas of the metropolis and are lost amid poverty, unemployment, illiteracy, alcoholism, and hopelessness. A growing number of these return to the reservation. In general, educationally, economically, and occupationally, American Indians have long been at the bottom of the heap among US minorities.

Over the past half century, the US government's emphasis with respect to Native Americans has been to emphasize tribal nationhood and sovereignty. Because the various tribes are legally termed "domestic dependent nations," under the US legal system many of the reservations have opened gambling casinos to generate cash. Dubious as gambling may be from a moral perspective, tribal casinos are viewed in light of the Native American movement toward greater self-determination. By the mid-1990s, this capitalistic move had already generated nearly $6 billion with 182 tribes operating nearly 300 gaming facilities. The economic value of gaming is dubious. Reservations do profit from gambling, and there are some job opportunities afforded. But there is always the risk of exploitation by non-Indian gambling enterprises that may own or manage tribal casinos, and there is an accelerated tendency toward compulsive gambling among tribe members as well as those from the outside population.

In ministering among Native Americans, then, it is important to understand the culture, history, and current needs. It is also important not to stereotype American Indian culture, for there are differences by tribe, city, circumstance, generation, and family.

Japanese Americans

The Japanese have experienced almost every form of discrimination and oppression. Yet today they are pretty much in the mainstream of American life.[11] Much of the acceptance accorded the Japanese owes to their rather stoic attitude toward hardship and injustice. This attitude stems in part from their previous experiences in Japan and the influence of Buddhism on Japanese culture. Japanese Americans come from a native tradition filled with governmental oppression, economic reverses, land droughts, and other catastrophes. Therefore, little in the United States could be much worse than conditions in the homeland. As a result, the Japanese exhibit a willingness to persevere in the face of hardship, believing that things can only get better if they are faithful and persistent. The net effect of this outlook is to make the Japanese nonconfrontive and nonmilitant in the face of discrimination. Over the decades, Caucasians began seeing Japanese as nonthreatening, decent people. That Japan now is more highly industrialized than the United States is yet another force that has prepared the Japanese to blend in with the US social system.

Acceptance by Caucasians, however, has not always been present. Most Japanese immigrants to the United States came from the agricultural class. Having suffered from agricultural disadvantage in their homeland, these farmers prospered when they settled in the San Francisco area. Around the turn of the century, the success of this group so angered and threatened Caucasian agriculturalists, however, that severe anti-Japanese rioting took place.

Jealousy over the agricultural success of the Japanese gave rise to legal attempts at disenfranchising them. In 1894, 1913, and 1920, laws were passed in California that were designed to prevent the Japanese from purchasing land. In addition, an immigration law passed by the federal government was intended in part to limit Japanese migration to the United States. These laws greatly disadvantaged Japanese Americans. The worst, however, was yet to come.

On December 7, 1941, Japan bombed Pearl Harbor, setting up US involvement in World War II. By the middle of 1942, all persons of Japanese ancestry were moved into what were euphemistically termed relocation centers, scattered about the Rocky Mountain region. This forced evacuation was done partly to protect the Japanese from white attack in response to the Pearl Harbor bombing and partly because there was some suspicion that the Japanese might sabotage the US war effort. The latter rationale is a curious example of prejudice, for even though Germany was the main adversary of the United States in both world wars, those of German ancestry were not quarantined.

In any case, the relocation experience was devastating for the Japanese. Life in the centers was more reflective of concentration camp living than political shelter. In addition, the Japanese lost all their holdings. After the war, when the Japanese were released, they had to start all over, devoid of everything from land to occupations. That Japanese now live in every state in the Union rather than exclusively on the West Coast is in a large measure a result of their World War II nightmare.

As with Native Americans, Japanese have little reason to trust Caucasians. They remain, however, very kind and genial people; by reason of the industrialization of their native country, their strong family unit, and their stoic persistence in the face of tremendous obstacles, they have overcome the disabilities placed on them twice over in the United States, surpassing Caucasians in median family income and educational attainment.

Chinese Americans

The Chinese have endured almost unparalleled amounts of discrimination in international migrations.[12] Like the Japanese, they seem to have been able to press forward nonetheless.

Chinese immigration first became significant in the middle 1800s, with the California gold rush. Men worked principally in the mines and on the railroads. The Chinese were subjected to harassment, attack, and even murder during this era, largely because of four cultural characteristics that irritated white males who worked with them. First, Chinese men wore their hair in braids down their backs—a style Anglo laborers regarded as feminine. Second, they wore skirt-like apparel, further feminizing them. Third, many were especially adept at cooking, washing, and laundering, traditionally viewed as women's work by Caucasians. Lastly, they spoke in a sing-song fashion, because in Chinese the pitch of a word contributes to its meaning. These four factors taken together caused the Chinese males to be regarded as half-men and half-feminized freaks. Hence, many received the type of treatment homosexuals have frequently endured.

Additional problems were caused for Chinese men because immigration restrictions caused the sex ratio to be overwhelmingly male. Interracial marriage was strictly forbidden, so some Chinese men were drawn into homosexuality and liaisons with white women. This led to further oppression.

Growing hatred for the Chinese brought about a series of legal attempts to disenfranchise them. In California special discriminatory statutes were enacted. One statute imposed on laundries that did not use horse-drawn vehicles a laundry license fee nearly four times higher than usual. Another law taxed those who wore their hair in a queue, the braided style. Perhaps the most outrageous of all was the cubic-air ordinance in San Francisco. Realizing that the Chinese were forced to live in the most overcrowded of quarters, the white legislators advanced several statutes that outlawed high density on the grounds that it violated cubic air space.

In addition, the Chinese were affected by discriminatory immigration laws designed to limit their growing numbers. Matters became so extreme that between 1882 and the end of World War II, more Chinese left for their native land than entered the United States.

The Chinese have little reason to be trusting of Caucasians, who have offered only grudging acceptance of them over the last century, and that not without a sizable amount of oppression. Not dissimilar to both the Japanese and American Indians, the rather genteel and low-keyed Chinese culture clashes with white America's much more confrontive and competitive way of life.

As with the Japanese and American Indians, younger-generation Chinese are more Americanized than their elders. Many are doing so well economically, occupationally, and educationally that, like the Japanese, they are ahead of their Anglo peers. Some of this success stems from the fact that most of the recent immigrants have come from the professional class.

As the Chinese continue to become urbanized, urban pastors are increasingly likely to come into contact with them. There is no way to generalize about urban Chinese, for some will live in various types of "Chinatowns," while others will, like the Japanese, be scattered throughout the metropolitan area. Regardless, the Chinese are friendly and courteous, though very private and somewhat resentful of investigations of them and their culture—this is especially so in predominantly Chinese communities.

Religiously, the Chinese have been slow to accept Christianity. The urban pastor will find that Buddhism dominates the Chinese American religious life, with religiosity being an intensely personal matter, not necessarily given to practice outside the home.

Mexican Americans

Today the various Hispanic populations (Mexican Americans, Puerto Ricans, Cubans, and others) are the fastest growing group, currently outnumbering African Americans in the United States.[13] Mexican Americans are the dominant Hispanic group, constituting slightly less than two-thirds of the total. They are a mixture of Spanish and Indian ancestry, having their origins in the Spanish overrun of the Indian cultures in what is now called Mexico. Because the Spanish were almost exclusively Roman Catholic, most of the area was quickly Catholicized, a fact that accounts for the strong Roman Catholic imprint on Mexican American culture. The strain of imagery in Catholicism appealed to the Mexicans, whose native Indian religions were also full of imagery and ritual. Hence, what resulted from the proselytizing of Mexico was, in many cases, a hybrid religion—a mixture of Catholicism and Native Indian faiths.

Mexican migration to the States became especially heavy during the Mexican Revolution in the early twentieth century.

The vast majority of Mexican Americans reside in the Southwest (Arizona, California, Colorado, New Mexico, and Texas), with much of the population in California being urbanized. Often Mexican Americans who reside in cities live in barrios, enclaves rich in Mexican American and occasionally Puerto Rican culture.

One of the historic cultural traits of the Mexican immigrants was a sense of fatalism—an acceptance of life as it is without a sense of mastery of personal destiny. This outlook was similar to the stoicism of Asians, but without the optimism and conviction that an individual can effect change. This fatalism goes back into the Mexican religious past and clashes rather dramatically with the Anglo emphasis on conquering and subordinating nature through technology. More Americanized, second- and third-generation Mexican Americans have thrown off this fatalism.

Mexican culture also favors the notion that work is to be done for its own sake rather than for economic gain. It is honorable to work, regardless of trade, and dishonorable not to. The shrewd and calculating approach to labor taken by whites is alien to this orientation. This tradition may account for the vast number of legal and illegal immigrants' willingness to work with great vigor at the most servile and menial of occupations.

There is a high value placed on courtesy and charm. Although conflict is not uncommon and may be resolved with confrontation, daily, casual interaction is nonconfrontive and marked by respect and deference.

Easily one of the most powerful Mexican American cultural traits is machismo. There has been a strong, traditional male-dominated pattern to sex-role interaction. Men have been the authority figures and obeyed. Men demonstrated machismo by pursuing women for seductive purposes, drinking heavily without losing control, and being willing to fight to defend their honor or respect. Women were expected to stand by, being both subordinate and supportive. In an era of radically changing notions pertaining to the female sex role and social identity, this male chauvinistic orientation does not facilitate communication with Anglos. Moreover, as the march toward Americanization continues, there is a growing feminist consciousness among Mexican American and other Hispanic women which militates against male dominance within their groups.

Since the 1960s there has been such an upsurge among Mexican Americans in defining themselves as a group and pointing with pride to their heritage. Cultural pluralism is usually the favored strategy in relating to the majority, with some effort at assimilation. There is a cleavage among generations here, as those younger opt for a more activistic approach to the disadvantages placed on them by Anglo prejudice, while their elders, more conditioned to the ravages of prejudice, are often more philosophical about such matters.

A major problem among Mexican Americans is the status of the illegal immigrant. A large number of Mexicans mask their identities because they are illegally in the Untied States. Illegal entrance is tempting because there is almost always a job waiting. Many US businessmen welcome illegals, offering them employment below the minimum wage and without fringe benefits. For many Mexicans, coming into a new country with work waiting is a pleasant alternative to the near-starvation conditions experienced in such places as Mexico City. Moreover, illegal entrance is very easy, as the United States and Mexico have a common border stretching 1,600 miles, devoid of natural obstacles. In addition, many have entered the United States by swimming across the Rio Grande to avoid detection by the border patrol. It is from this practice that the term "wetback" was formed.

Those in urban ministry with any Hispanic group will need to deal with the cultural traits of the population as well as with their many needs and problems. The urban worker may encounter avoidance and resistance from Mexican Americans because of their fear of having themselves, a family member, or a friend detected as an illegal immigrant. Protestants will confront the rather strong Catholic tradition operative among Hispanic groups. Although many are Roman Catholic only in the most nominal sense, the influence of Catholicism so dominates the art, architecture, and symbolism of particularly Mexican American culture that, for many, not to be Catholic is not to be truly Mexican American. Understanding and appreciating the people's culture is the most important first step toward effective ministry.

With Hispanic groups in general, there is typically minority tension under the radar. However, this tension does not receive sufficient attention because this minority is relatively "new" to the United States, few speak English fluently, and many are not citizens. As their presence grows, however, and they spread their political allegiances beyond only one political party, these groups will gain muscle and recognition in the US mainstream. Nonetheless, the temporal needs of these peoples are many. They are disproportionately represented among the ranks of the poor and the unemployed. Educationally, there is the problem of bilingualism: Spanish-speaking children enter English-speaking schools, only to fail there. Inability to speak English also accounts for much unemployment and underemployment. The possibilities for effective social ministry are myriad. Employment, education, and English language skills for all ages are crisis areas where timely aid can open lines of communication.

As is the case with any cross-cultural ministry, patience and service should characterize the effort. Establishing solid bonds of communication is not an uncomplicated process, and patience will maximize the likelihood of developing solid relationships.

African Americans

African American experience can be divided into three major epochs: slavery (1619–1865), segregation (1865–1967), and ghettoization (1967 to the present).[14] To understand African-American life necessitates a sensitivity to these eras, for the present social and economic condition of black America is largely the outgrowth of slavery and segregation.

What makes African Americans unique among US minorities is that they did not come here by choice. They were rounded up in Africa and placed on galley ships designed to bring them to the United States. The shipment of the slaves was particularly devastating. Most ships were three-decked vessels, with the slaves packed like human cargo. They were placed in a prone position with legs askew so a fellow slave could be seated in front of them. Greed hurt the shipping merchants. Overcrowding the ships made disease rampant, with frequently 30 percent or more of the slaves dying during the voyage.

Once in the United States, they were to confront one of the most savage institutions in human history. A full treatment of slavery is beyond the scope of this book; however, a review of some of its major characteristics is in order.

There was, first of all, denial of family. Slaves were not allowed to marry. Hence, every slave child born prior to 1865 was illegitimate in the official sense. Slaves were forced to cohabit and were bred, in a manner similar to the breeding of cattle, in hopes that sexual unions would spawn strong male offspring suitable for field work. In short, slave propagation was designed and controlled by Caucasians.

Along with this there was sexual violation of black women by white men. Because slaves had no legal standing, black women had no alternative but to succumb to the advances of the white slave owner. Between two-thirds and four-fifths of all African Americans have some Caucasian biological ancestry. Much of this interracial ancestry is a result of this sexual practice. Moreover, the offspring of an owner-slave union was always a slave, for any black ancestry made one black. (This incidentally is still true today. The child of a black man and a white woman is invariably classified as Negroid when, in fact, the child is most likely primarily Caucasian because of the mixed ancestry of the black parent.)

While the offspring of a black-white union was considered a slave, the lighter-skinned slaves often became house slaves rather than field slaves and had less arduous working conditions. Thus, sewn into the slave system was the principle that the lighter (or whiter) one was the better.

A second characteristic of slavery was denial of human, legal, and political rights. The slaves were totally without legal protection. They could be abused, sexually molested, attacked, beaten, or even killed at the whim of the master, who had to account to no one for the treatment of slave property.

And the slaves definitely were considered subhuman property. When the Constitution was being written, the South wanted the slaves to be counted in the population because the larger the population count, the larger would be the representation in the House of Representatives. The North objected to this, believing that if slaves were not to be considered citizens, they should not be counted in the population. After much discussion and wrangling, a compromise was reached. For every five slaves, the South would be credited with three persons in the population. In other words, a slave was three-fifths a human being. Although little noted in US history textbooks, this measure underscored the truly dehumanizing nature of the slave system.

Third, slaves were denied both education and communication. In some states it was a capital crime to teach a slave to read or write. To educate the slaves was to make them dangerous. Knowledge was power, and ignorance guaranteed an absence of communication and potential revolt. In addition, once off the galley ship, slaves were often tribally separated so that all possibilities of communication between slaves would be eliminated. Many language patterns of African Americans today derive from the clever adaptation of slaves to this vicious communication-denying practice.

Fourth, slaves had no residential mobility options. Once they were bought by a slave master, they served on that owner's plantation until they died or were sold. All power of movement was beyond their own control.

Fifth, there was massive economic exploitation. The South was built by slaves, for the Southern economy was based on what was called King Cotton. Slaves worked for nothing day-in and day-out, week after week, year after year. Yet the capitalist South today does not acknowledge its debt to African Americans, who made it what it is.

Finally, slavery was characterized by widespread violence. Because of the absence of rights and the belief by Caucasians that slaves were subhuman, slaves were regularly the objects of violence. There are numerous records of lynchings, beatings, rapes, and other atrocities that occurred during the seemingly endless 250 years of US slavery. Any paranoia blacks have developed toward whites has a solid basis in their heritage.

In 1865 slavery ended, but subjugation continued. Although African Americans were officially regarded as human beings and as citizens, it was still legal to deny political process, educational opportunities, employment, land ownership, recreational options, or public service in restaurants and hotels simply and arbitrarily on the basis of race. One example is that although major league baseball is over a hundred years old, it was not until 1947, fully eighty-two years after the legal termination of slavery, that the first black player entered the big leagues. And blacks are still underrepresented as coaches and managers.

Segregation was an era in which African Americans were legally depressed in every facet of their US existence—perhaps most importantly in the area of human dignity. To be black was to be socially inferior and to be accorded humiliating treatment. This was a century during which African American parents had to explain to their children that the reason they were unable to go to school with Caucasians and the family could not go to the museum, movie theater, recreational center, or nearby church was simply that they were black.

Often people wonder aloud why blacks have not succeeded in the same fashion as white immigrant groups.[15] Reciting the tenets of the bootstrap theory, they forget that minority groups were locked in the segregationist era while whites were moving upward. White groups came in droves during the nineteenth and early twentieth centuries when they heard of the unskilled labor opportunities in the new land. Land itself could be obtained at no cost or at a pittance. For the factory workers, unions were formed as early as 1902 to increase pay and shorten hours. Income taxes were not levied to any appreciable extent until World War II. Moreover, the standard of living was not particularly high, so the entire price structure was geared to the poor. Finally, white groups never suffered segregation and no group other than blacks spent 250 years in slavery. It is easy to talk of legal equality now, but the methods for progress available to white immigrant groups are now long gone. Unskilled labor opportunities do not exist, land is gone, income taxes are high, and the cost of living is exorbitant.

The passage of the civil rights legislation in the mid-1960s spelled the end of segregation. However, the ghettoized circumstances in which a large percentage of the 25 million African Americans live today are the result of 350 years of disadvantage. To expect any group to endure 350 years of assault and be anywhere but at the lower end of the social and economic structure is unrealistic. That African Americans have even survived is testimony to their fortitude and character strength. They have not only survived but have developed a culture in language, food, drama, sports, and music that is abundant in diversity and impact.

The African American church has a particularly rich heritage. Constituting over 40 percent of the urban congregations of some cities, the black church has myriad strengths. Worship is filled with expression, intensity, and meaning. Members are imbued with a profound sense of peoplehood and celebration of their African-American identity. Relationships within the body are celebrated and affirmed. Activities such as traveling choirs and joint worship services provide contact with sister churches in other parts of the city and across the country.

The service ministry of the black church has over the years addressed virtually every human need of black America. It was among the first institutions to do effective social work. And out of its service orientation, much evangelism has been generated.

African American urban churches have also set the pace in stewardship ministry. As the focal point of the black community, the church is the hub of social and political as well as spiritual activity. Because of its holistic approach to life and ministry, the black church has provided a host of opportunities for its members to develop leadership skills effective in large organizations. It should surprise no one that so many national African American figures, among them Dr. Martin Luther King Jr., have their roots in the church.

It is imperative that an urban minister view current black-white relations against this historical backdrop. Blacks, for the most part, are acutely aware of their US heritage; and, of course, they are reminded of them daily in their encounters with personal and institutional racism. Disadvantage and lack of respect live on for black America.

Knowledge of the history and culture of minorities is increasingly important, for, according to government data, within a hundred years whites will be in the minority in the United States. The numbers of Hispanics (Mexican American, Puerto Rican, Cuban, and South American), Asians (Japanese, Chinese, Vietnamese, Indian, Pakistani, Filipino, Korean, and Pacific Islander), and African Americans are on the rise as a result of immigration trends and birth rates. Chicago, for example, now has more Muslims (of Middle Eastern descent) than Jews. Already by 1980, the census indicated that Anglo birth rates were below replacement, while African American average 2.3 children per couple, and Hispanics 3 children per family.

Moreover, not every group is assimilating quickly. The issue for many groups is how to retain their cultural identity in the new country. They are proud of their heritages, taking particular satisfaction in their long histories and different values. As such, these groups are tied more closely to their sending than receiving culture. Contact with the culture of origin, particularly for immigrant groups, provides a greater sense of security and continuity. Ironically, however, cross-cultural studies indicate that a sense of security is necessary in order for people to assimilate. Urban ministers will need to take these changes into account.

MINISTRY AMONG MINORITIES

White evangelical Christians have not handled the issue of race well. One of the reasons is that current racism is largely covert. That is to say, that there are fewer and fewer open, blatant expressions of racial prejudice. Rather it is subtle, and—as previously discussed—embedded into the normal operation of our nation's institutions, and so largely invisible to whites.[16] Nonetheless, profound black-white racial differences continue to exist in income and net worth, health care, and life expectancy. There are race-based differences in musical expression and even television watching. Furthermore, there are substantial differences between whites and many other minority groups as well.

John Perkins has long promoted racial reconciliation. Perkins grew up in rural Mississippi in the 1930s and 40s. His mother died when he was less than a year old and his father abandoned the family. Reared by his grandmother, Perkins's brother was shot by a policeman near the black entrance of a movie theater. He learned early that whites had everything and blacks nothing. Perkins later became a believer and felt called to return to the seat of his horrors—Mississippi—and begin a ministry of racial reconciliation. Perkins, Tom Skinner (a former Harlem gang leader), and Samuel Hines (a Jamaican youth who lived in rebellion) all believed the seeds of racial reconciliation are found in the gospel of Christ, a gospel that made the eradication of racism imperative.

They believed that racial reconciliation involved four steps. First, members of different races need to have primary, face-to-face relationships. Second, there must be a recognition of and a resistance to social structures that perpetuate inequality. Third, whites must recognize their role in creating these inequities throughout history and repent. Fourth, blacks must repent of their anger and forgive.[17]

An extensive study by sociologists Emerson and Smith indicated the central problem dividing the faith and obviating true racial reconciliation is that whites simply do not see the structural aspects of racism. Most white evangelicals see no real race problem at all other than bad interpersonal relationships and individually racist behavior. In short, what racism exists is viewed as individual and not institutional. Many were hard pressed to think of examples of racism and systematic inequity. They did not see themselves as racist nor did they perceive strains of racism in US institutions. Given their individualistic view of life based on the personal, pietistic nature of their relationship with God, they saw no deeper or wider. Moreover, many believed the race problem would be better served if fewer nonwhite spokespeople and organizations agitated and created unrest over perceived inequities. These whites want color blindness to be the norm. They do not want to see society in terms of its social groups but only as a collection of individuals in need of God. They operate out of what Emerson and Smith call their "cultural tools." These include freewill individualism, relationalism, and antistructuralism. Life is about individual or personal sin and righteousness, relationships with God, family, and other believers. Consequently they do not see the influence of social structures.[18]

N. K. Clifford writes, "The evangelical Protestant mind has never relished complexity. Indeed its crusading genius . . . has always tended toward an oversimplification of issues and the substitution of inspiration and zeal for critical analysis and serious reflection."[19] Even worse, of course, is that white evangelicals are among the racial and economic beneficiaries of the current institutional system, which blinds them to the injustices. Emerson and Smith, acknowledging the healing value of personal penitence for present and past sins, state, "but before there is healing, different racial groups will also have to stop injuring each other."[20]

This creates a huge divide because it is not at all how nonwhites see and experience racial reality. Until whites grasp this larger reality, they can never be welcomed as genuine, earthly companions, laboring together toward a peaceful and just society.

To the extent that racial reconciliation ministries have not been successful, it appears their downfall relates to an inability to understand and address the reality that the issue is larger than the individual, that institutions play a major role in perpetuating a racialized society. Furthermore, white Christians must be willing to renounce some of the very practices that currently benefit them and disadvantage nonwhites if they are ever going to be perceived as serious about the matter of reconciliation.

Clifford suggests the discussion of the following questions: What are the real problems? What influences do institutions have on perpetuating racism? Why do nonwhites revere leaders that speak out and organize against the prevailing system? How do nonwhites see and experience racism? What solutions have been attempted? Why were they not successful and what issues do they raise?[21]

The problem of racism—prejudice and oppression—is indeed severe. As is evident, all too many pastors are simply unaware of its magnitude, and as a result they cannot relate effectively to its victims in the neighborhood. The first step in ministry, then, is to become aware of the devastating effects of individual and institutional racism and the problems faced by minorities. Many urbanites would be comforted if they only had a pastor who would listen to, understand, and care about their frustration.

Awareness

For any urban pastor who needs greater awareness and motivation to deal with minorities and the oppressed, there are probably two main steps to take. The first is to study the Scriptures on this issue. The Bible is filled with passages (some were pointed out in chapter 1) that indicate God's care for those waylaid by the system. In addition, Christ's life stands as a living witness to divine concern for society's rejected victims.

Christ not only took the side of the oppressed, he spent most of his time with "publicans and sinners." In fact, in the social sense, he was certainly civilly disobedient. He associated with the undesirables (the minorities) throughout his earthly ministry: his friends were the poor; he took the revolutionary step of caring about and ministering to the Samaritans (the "nonwhites" of his era, in that they were Jews of mixed ancestry); and he was perhaps the only man of his time who treated women with the respect and dignity accorded only men in that thoroughly chauvinistic society.

The second step to create greater awareness is to listen to those who claim to be oppressed. Using slavery as his example, political intellectual Alan Keyes puts it well. "It's impossible to be a Christian," he explains, "and really live out your relationship with God apart from life and action. And that action requires that you kind of be aware of and sensitive to how in fact the injustice that was involved in slavery is like one of those difficult plants where you cut off what appears on the surface but the root is still there. And it springs up again in another place, in what seems like another form, but it is the same evil. It's the same root."[22]

Once an urban pastor has logged a sizable amount of time listening, the injustices perpetrated by the daily grind of the institutional system will become readily apparent. No one can really listen to those who profess to be oppressed without returning with a new awareness of the pervasiveness of institutionalized evil.

Attitudes

Once urban pastors become aware of the problems facing the oppressed and of God's viewpoint, their next task is to examine their own attitudes and to eradicate any personal prejudice.

Minorities are peculiarly sensitive to the varied forms of paternalism, patronizing treatment, and a host of other subtly debasing forms of insincerity. Any shred of white supremacy an urban pastor carries into dealings with them is not only immoral but self-defeating. Ministry in a minority community, as anywhere else, is finally a matter of sharing, not arbitrarily distributing. Hence, the single most important principle for effective ministry with minorities is an absence of white-supremacist notions. There is no reason for any white to feel superior to nonwhites on the basis of ethnicity. Once this prejudice is controlled (and because most of it is unconscious, the control of it must be an everyday exercise), there is room to develop an identification with minorities. This eradication of personal prejudice and a growth of identification are the foundations for the development of healthy relations and effective ministry.

Identification

Identification with the oppressed, however, will have its costs. Urban workers, regardless of ethnic affiliation, must be aware that no matter how hard they push for change, there will be those who feel they are going too slow, selling out to the system, or, in the case of blacks, "uncle Tomming" (playing into the hands of white interests at the expense of black people). Charges of paternalism, patronizing treatment, and insensitivity are to be expected. They come with the task of identification. The white pastor may be the only available white symbol in the community. As such, the pastor can fully expect to be a lightning rod for much of the pain and anger of minorities. Enduring the onslaught with Christlike patience and dignity is the surest route to effective ministry.

Conversely, middle-class parishioners and certainly middle-class operators and owners of institutions will regularly accuse the pastor of pushing too hard, expecting too much too soon. Any pastor who wishes to get involved in the matter of minority issues (and it cannot be avoided if that pastor seeks to serve effectively) must take the role of peacemaker.

Communication

In addition to developing keener awareness, eradicating personal prejudice, and learning to identify with minorities, the urban pastor must develop skills in cross-cultural communication. Leonard Rascher gave sage counsel on this matter, urging first of all that the urban worker be informed.[23] It is important to be a student of the people at all times. Second, it is important to be yourself—genuine, forthright, and, above all, honest. Third, be flexible. There is too often an unwillingness to do anything in a new way, a tendency that smacks of arrogance and authoritarianism. Finally, the pastor needs to be sensitive. Learning to be alert to other groups' feelings and cultural customs is imperative.

Cross-cultural communication can be enhanced if the urban pastor learns the group's language (this can be slang as well as a recognized dialect) and its values. With this knowledge the pastor is less likely to violate a group's culture. It also enables the pastor to communicate according to the group's thought patterns and life perspective. The ability to use illustrations and anecdotes in the context of the people served is invaluable.

In communicating the gospel through cross-cultural evangelism, it is important to emphasize the universality of Christ's atonement. It must be made supracultural and stripped of its ethnocentricity. If properly done, Christianity will not be seen as just another religious option among many others.

Ministry

While it is important that the pastor develop the characteristics mentioned above, it is also important that the ministry itself be characterized by affirming the dignity and value of the person ministered to. Respecting minorities as worthy human beings who have survived the ravages of prejudice should be foremost. There needs to be openness and respect. Unless minority cultures are affirmed and respected, the church risks losing its members.

The ministry should also be characterized by placing minority persons in positions of leadership. The more committed minority persons available for ministry, the better. However, employing people, either gainfully or voluntarily, solely on the basis of ethnic background will simply aggravate the situation. It is imperative that any church worker who ministers in the name of that church be dedicated to the church's objectives and that the individual's behavior reflect that dedication. There are enough potentials for misunderstanding as it is without getting into a divided-loyalty problem.

If whites are the only ones available, then it may be better to employ a somewhat naïve but eager-to-learn person than a smooth-but-arrogant individual. When misunderstandings arise and confrontation occurs, the latter may prove stubborn in order to save face. Those with a genuine servant orientation will grow and will be respected by the community of which they are willing to become a part.

Ministry to nonwhites by white urban workers should be characterized by four additional elements. These four will serve as a summary and conclusion. First is *credibility*—trust is the watershed. No nonwhite groups really have a good reason to trust whites, given their experience with white America. It is crucial that minorities know that the pastor and church want to minister effectively, and that fact must be communicated with the utmost sincerity. Without credibility there is no ministry.

A second and related element is *servanthood.* Christ's life was characterized by a "what can I do for you?" approach. This must characterize the urban worker as well. Of course, it is vital that the worker be discerning so that the desire to serve does not carry a naïve strain, which can easily be exploited by people of any ethnic group. However, servanthood is primary. People respond to the love of God through the service of his agents. That response cannot occur if it is not preceded by the kind of service that does not demand a response of any type. No-strings-attached service, unconditional love, is God's way of dealing with humans and must characterize much of the urban ministry. This servanthood orientation is perhaps the one feature that most strikingly distinguishes urban ministry from secular programming carried on by well-paid, middle-class personnel.

A third element must be a *desire to learn.* Interacting with and being immersed in literature pertaining to the minority group are critical to effective ministry. There is no counting the number of ministries that have died simply because of ignorance on the part of those carrying them on. There must be no excuse for cultural insensitivity or ignorance. An urban worker must receive advance training in the culture and lifestyle of the minority group, along with ongoing education, identification, and involvement.

A seemingly less critical but important fourth element is *support of worthy minority causes.* Whether it means patronizing minority establishments, backing political candidates, contributing to fund-raising efforts, or visiting cultural displays, it is important that the urban minister be involved actively in advancing the best of minority life in the city. To do so is not only right and honorable, it also sharpens the minister's sensitivities and demonstrates sincerity.

Effective ministry among minorities must be characterized, then, by credibility, servanthood, desire to learn, and active support of minority causes.

SOCIALIZATION INTO VICTIM BLAMING **8**

Socialization is a process by which an individual learns and internalizes a culture. The term *culture* refers to the socially standardized ways of acting, feeling, and thinking characteristic of the community or society in which the person lives.

Culture makes an impact on each of these three dimensions. There is little difficulty in seeing how cultures differ in *acting* or behavior, for it is these variances in behavior or customs to which most people point when differentiating among cultures. However, cultures also have a powerful effect on patterns of *thinking* and *feeling*. In an industrialized country such as the United States, people are tuned to think in terms of free enterprise, money, luxuries, power, and status. They are also conditioned from childhood to have certain feelings or emotional reactions to them. Some people will scheme, steal, and kill in an effort to gain power and status. Some adults order their entire lives to attain power and dominance through leadership positions. Yet there are other societies in which individuals do not venerate leaders, but rather are suspicious of them. As a consequence, few members of such societies are inspired to be leaders of their fellows in any situations.

Culture is also analyzed in terms of norms, beliefs, symbols, and values. There is some overlap with the foregoing categories of acting, thinking, and feeling.

Norms are usually divided into folkways, mores, and laws. *Folkways* are essentially minor norms that govern day-to-day conduct. Brushing our teeth, combing our hair, bathing regularly, responding in a civil fashion to our peers, and other conventional expectations held by members of a society are examples of folkways. They are not to be underestimated in terms of the degree to which they shape behavior. In fact, the majority of the things most people consider normal behavior is not so much normal or natural as it is a matter of learning and internalizing folkways. They are internalized early in life because they are the key to social acceptance. Failure to abide by existing folkways—such as neglecting to mow the lawn regularly, missing appointments, dressing grossly out of style—is likely to bring on gossip, ridicule, and even rejection. Because folkways are not of a heavy moral nature, this gossip and rejection is often not exhibited openly by peers, but is carried on rather quietly behind the individual's back.

Mores are norms that carry considerable moral weight. These norms are devoutly held to by a society's members. They often involve the cardinal taboos pertaining to family, community, and civic matters. Violation of these almost certainly results in expulsion from the community. Mores are especially important in small towns. It would be easier for the proverbial camel to pass through the eye of a needle than to attempt to survive in a rural community after publicly violating, for example, one of its sexual mores.

Laws may be either folkways or mores. Some laws, such as those governing parking and street crossing, carry no great moral significance. Others, for example, those that outlaw murder, rape, and armed robbery, are deemed necessary for moral order. In either case, they are norms brought into existence by a recognized, organized, civil body empowered by the state.

Beliefs in a culture are very similar to thinking patterns discussed above. Each culture teaches certain doctrines formally and informally. Certainly one of the most powerful teachers of cultural beliefs is the school. Concepts of citizenship, democracy, free enterprise, cooperation, and authority are riveted in a student's mind. These beliefs underlie and justify the norms and values that people espouse and abide by.

The primary system of *symbols* of a culture is its language. Language is absolutely critical to any culture. It is the key to it. Embodied in the language of the culture are history, values, ideologies, and norms. An analysis of a culture's vocabulary reveals almost everything of the culture.

Values are a bit more difficult to define. One definition might term them a culture's cherished entities. The values taught in the culture and internalized by its members are its lifeblood. "Where your treasure is, there will your heart be also" is both a spiritual and a sociological truism.

What makes awareness of culture vital in urban ministry is that each social class constitutes a culture of its own. That is to say, each social class has its own peculiar ways of feeling, thinking, and acting—its own set of norms, beliefs, symbols, and in some cases even values. Stratum subcultures, as described previously, illustrate this fact.

Socialization of a Middle-Class Pastor

Most urban pastors have been socialized to live most comfortably in the middle class. They are largely from upper- to lower-middle income families and have lived all or most of their lives in middle-class communities.

The typical white urban pastor, most likely male, has usually been reared in an intact, God-fearing family. The family was most probably of ordinary size (certainly not containing ten or twelve children) and well controlled. It is probable that this pastor was introduced to cultural values and mores in middle-class schools. Sociological research indicates that the middle class tends to emphasize good grades in traditional academic bodies of knowledge—reading, writing, spelling, and computation—and self-controlled, self-directed conduct. The pastor's childhood leisure time was spent playing with siblings and other children in the neighborhood.

For many, their life included going to church, Sunday school, and perhaps Bible class or catechism. These programs were customarily operated by people who valued order, respect, and conscientious attention to duty. Even those wayward youngsters who misbehaved in these sessions realized they were defying the established order. If this future pastor became a full member of the church before completing high school, the decision entailed taking responsibility for personal spiritual growth.

Although all this socialization was carried on in a larger urban, suburban, or rural environment, the community that really counted, meaning those with whom the family regularly associated, was most likely quite similar to the youth's own family. That community was most probably short on violence, divorce, poverty, and rebellion, and long on order, conformity, respect, and cooperation.

After leaving the community, the future pastor headed for college. If the college was a private Christian one, then middle-class socialization was probably intensified. For there is no greater bastion of US middle-class culture than the small Christian college. The fees at such private institutions require that the student have at least a middle-income status. The seminary this future pastor then moved on to was probably quite similar. Heavy on theory, abstraction, and polite conversation, seminaries can be heart-warming oases from the real world. The high value placed on quietness, reflection, and grade-currying is extremely middle class. Colleges and seminaries are sometimes so openly middle class that they institute special programs to expose their students to non-middle-class life. These are commonly given euphemistic, academic titles, but they amount to little more than a look at how the other half lives.

Though there is nothing inherently wrong with being middle class or appreciating middle-class institutions, what is important is that the urban pastor will probably not serve a middle-class congregation or work in a middle-class neighborhood. And so, despite the growing tendency of television to homogenize the outlook of the various social classes, urban pastors are probably in for a good bit of culture shock when they encounter the urban milieu. This may be an understatement, for it is possible that almost none of their socialization prepared them for the lifestyle of the congregation they are about to serve. In fact, that socialization is probably in direct contradiction to their parishioners' culture. That is to say, it may often have used the way of life of lower-class people as an example of the kind of living that contrasts to what is viewed as virtuous Christian living.

If inexperienced pastors are to swim in the urban ocean, they will have to be resocialized. They will have to understand, appreciate, and identify with the way of life of the urban poor. It will not be easy, for almost every behavioral precept taught in their family, school, and church is rooted in the unconscious and almost certainly unarticulated assumption that the individual comes from a background with a sufficient amount of money, education, status, and, most importantly, opportunity to find this precept meaningful and constructive.

Perhaps one of the first things urban pastors will confront in dealing with lower-income people will be radically different responses to middle-class values. It bears repeating that inner-city residents do not necessarily reject, in principle, middle-class values. They simply find them irrelevant to lower-class life. What follows is a brief (in order to avoid unnecessary overlap) treatment of seven cardinal middle-class values. Although these matters have been touched on in the previous chapters, the purpose here is to demonstrate the perspectival variance of middle-class pastors from those they will serve.

MIDDLE-CLASS VALUES

Education

Few matters receive as unanimous an acclaim from middle-class people as the importance of education. They may criticize the poor quality of the schools, but they heartily agree on the value of education. In fact, many believe that education is simply good in and of itself. "The answer to the problem of _____ [fill in the blank with almost any social dilemma] is education." Such a statement regularly concludes any lengthy analysis of a social problem. Few even bother to ponder whether education cannot also be insidious—making the avaricious and power-hungry more able to manipulate their victims, the criminally inclined more able to escape justice, and the deceitful more skilled at duping their victims.

Education is so highly valued among the middle class that many young marrieds will uproot their families when the oldest child is six, saddling themselves with an enslaving mortgage and a greater commuting distance to work, in order to provide a good education for their children. In some suburbs virtually every intellectually normal child is expected to go on to college.

The lower class, contrary to the belief of many people, also places a high value on education. Lower-class adults, especially, are aware that one of the primary differences between their occupational niche and that of the middle-class professional is the amount of formal education they have had. The problem is not only that formal education of any quality is in short supply in inner cities but that other priorities may intervene.

As discussed earlier, older children may be required to tend the younger children, placing the care of these children ahead of their own education. This means that if any of the younger children is ill, an older child, usually a daughter, must stay home to babysit. In addition, the simple awareness of this responsibility often can stand in the way of children being able to devote their energy solely to educational tasks.

There is also a lack of role models. Many poor children do not see their parents rise early every morning to go to work whether or not they feel well. Therefore, there is no model to emulate in getting up faithfully and going to school under virtually every condition. Easy middle-class assumptions about the role of education in family life will prove unworkable.

Property

The love of property is a middle-class epidemic. People will purchase it, insure it, beautify it, put up signs protecting it, and become almost insane with rage when it is somehow defaced. Homes, townhouses, condominiums, and forest acreage appeal to this middle-class thirst. The condominium craze is illustrative of this property worship, for with it comes only an apartment—no land—along with continuing joint responsibility for security, maintenance, and improvement.

Property also takes the form of material luxuries. People will neglect their families, sacrifice their health, and sell their soul to obtain more things. However, equally as important is the jealousy with which the middle class will care for and protect their possessions.

Christians may call this stewardship, others simply call it common sense; but virtually everyone agrees (often at an emotional level) on the importance of taking good care of personal property. Damage to a car, building, or item of clothing could spark a colossal outburst, one much larger than the sorrow over having damaged another's feelings or emotional well-being.

To the poor, property is, of course, an abstraction. Hence, especially with housing, there is neither pride of ownership nor experience in maintaining their own dwelling. Inner-city youth, therefore, are less than meticulous in caring for their possessions. This will be particularly true of the church building. It will be used in the fullest sense of the term when city youth are in the facility.

A postscript concerning an exception may be appropriate here. Occasionally, middle-class people remark on seeing shiny cars and expensive clothes in otherwise blighted areas. One of the reasons for this is that, in an area surrounded by so much economic and material deprivation, these possessions become a symbol of affluence—something of which to be proud. In a nation where personal worth is so strongly attached to the symbols of wealth, owning a fancy suit or a new car has great meaning and does wonders for a depressed self-concept. Nevertheless, this experience is often short-lived, for economic stringency often brings default and repossession.

Work Ethic

To the middle class, work is not only a means to an end, it is an end in itself. People speak of liking their work, finding fulfillment in their work, and growing in their work. Moreover, work is not only honorable, it is necessary. Those who do not work (gainfully) have no right to eat. It is excruciatingly difficult to get middle-class workers to accept the fact that many poor cannot work. In some vague and abstract sense, they agree that some sort of welfare system is necessary. But certainly those who are healthy and able-bodied have no right to it. They should get a job.

There is a wholly different concept of work in the lower class. First of all, work is not an end in itself. The jobs the poor get are often demeaning exercises high in frustration and low in pay, jobs many of the middle class would flatly refuse to perform. Notions of personal growth, occupational goals, and life fulfillment are met with sardonic humor. In addition, last to be hired and first to be fired or laid off makes employment unstable and unemployment less stigmatizing. Attending to and understanding the radically different significance of work to the lower class is necessary in dealing with employment issues in the inner city.

Economic Savvy

In a middle-class dominated, capitalistic society, thrift and money management are central themes. Children are raised on the notion that money is nearly as critical a part of the environment as air. This fiscal socialization, then, prepares them for an adult role that is organized around financial acumen, from dealing with mortgage interest rates to paying grocery bills.

There is a wholly different fiscal consciousness in the inner city. It is utterly fruitless to expect the poor (with little money and less experience in handling it) to understand fiscal management. Protracted periods of being broke make a bit of money such a welcome sight that it is something to be celebrated rather than scrupulously saved. For while the larger society has only to wait until the next paycheck to purchase luxuries as well as necessities, the poor view a luxury like a stalk of wheat in a field of stubble.

Appearance of Respectability

There is probably no value that better highlights middle-class hypocrisy than the appearance of respectability. Middle-class people are obsessed with appearing respectable. Reputation and community acceptance are necessary for maintaining their sanity. They will go to ludicrous extremes to preserve a respectable image, even lying, covering up, falsifying records, making payoffs, and putting on façades. Soap operas watched by millions of matinee addicts are built around a series of plots that involve individual attempts to save face by duping a curious community or group of acquaintances.

This insatiable desire for respectability even extends to the law. For decades, not a word was said while thousands of poor teenagers were placed in juvenile homes for possessing and using marijuana. Then in the 1970s, when the forbidden herb began being widely used in suburbia, the cry for its legalization was heard nationwide. Why? At least partly, it was repugnant to the middle-class psyche to regard their children who used it as delinquent. If their children used marijuana, then, because they were good and decent people, marijuana use must not be wrong.

Much the same sentiment prevails with regard to abortion. With the growing concern about birth control and a rising number of middle-class women disappearing for several weeks of vacation after becoming secretly pregnant, the society began clamoring for a more liberalized set of abortion statutes. In a matter of a few short years, abortion ceased being murder and commenced being pregnancy termination. It is not my intent to take a political stance on an issue as sensitive and complex as abortion; what is central to the topic, however, is that the impetus for political and social change came when class interests were at stake.

Although almost no one is devoid of the desire for some social approval and respect, poor communities are refreshingly liberated from conventional concerns over positive social images. Therefore, although unemployment, alcoholism, and pregnancy of unwed women are unpleasant, they do not necessitate the victim's hiding from the community until the problem is taken care of. An arrest record is never welcome but not something to hide either. In short, people present themselves for who they are without undue self-consciousness about how congruent their image is with the mores of the rest of society.

It is easy for a pastor to interpret this openness as brazenness or defiance of social standards. It rarely is that. More often, it is simply life in the raw, without all the attendant pretensions and staging. What may appear to be a casual attitude toward certain sins may be the acceptance of the flawed nature of humanity and a realistic outlook on behavioral practices in this particular environment.

Future Orientation

Future orientation is so riveted into middle-class culture that not to have a five-to-ten-year outlook is adjudged irresponsible. People purchase homes, save money, buy bonds, go to college, start a business, and change residences on the basis of present sacrifice in favor of future outcomes. Eighteen-year-old youths who enter college with a commitment to become physicians know full well that this goal is at least seven years away. College, medical school, internship, and residency are all required of aspiring physicians. Yet they are undeterred, for there is no foreseeable reason, such as poor health, lack of money, or heavy family responsibilities, to slow their pace. Their goal, then, is very realistic. In fact, were the enterprising youths not zeroing in on a career objective, they might be upbraided by parents who fear they will never "make anything of themselves."

The view from the bottom is starkly different. The future looks no more bright than the present, and the past is the basis for this judgment. Federal statistics regularly reveal growing unemployment figures and increasing poverty rates rather than the amelioration of these ills. Meanwhile, inflation steadily gnaws away at the overall economic structures. As the minimum wage goes up, as automation accelerates, and as outsourcing becomes more common, the number of unemployed increases.

The result of this grim set of circumstances is that the poor protect themselves from the psychological pains of disappointment by not setting their sights too high. Not only do they not lay up treasures for the future but there is simply nothing in the way of treasures to lay up. There is no saving for a rainy day, because every day rains economic misfortune. Whereas the middle class speaks of getting ahead, the poor talk of getting by or getting over, for survival is the chief concern.

Responsibility for Personal Fate

With the topic of personal fate control, we come to perhaps the central doctrine of the civil religion of the larger US society. The ethic of individualism, and therefore responsibility for personal fate, is woven into the fabric of US society. All achievements are considered individual achievements.

If a youth who comes from a well-to-do family with well-educated parents and a firm grounding in the basic academic skills receives high grades, the youth is rewarded as if the results were based solely on personal efforts. No note is taken of the influence social class has on academic achievement. On the contrary, the youth is given honor-roll designation, faculty approval, and guarantees for a successful future.

The student who does poorly, by middle-class academic standards, is regarded as dead educational wood. This youth is eventually programmed for educational and perhaps occupational obsolescence by being routed through the lower track of the curriculum. Only the most astute school officials will note the poverty of the family, the lack of formal education of the parents, the family stresses with which the youngster copes, or the lack of academic success models available. The student will be held totally responsible.

This is tragic, for some very ordinary people are lauded for simply reaching expected heights, while some very extraordinary people are condemned because of circumstances well beyond their own control.

But this doctrine does not end there. For example, people are often led to believe that because delinquency rates are lower in the suburbs, somehow the youths who reside there are more moral. What is forgotten is that urban youth lack the space, recreational facilities, and such alternatives as travel, vacationing, golfing, and summer baseball that money brings.

This blindness to inequality of opportunity, or this adherence to total individual responsibility for personal actions, comes to final expression in the US justice system where the poor are regularly sentenced to prison terms because of higher arrest rates, poor defense, and unjust sentencing procedures.

These seven value dimensions divide the poor from the dominant society. Each class adopts a realistic view of these values with respect to social and economic position in the US stratification system. Indeed, for a middle-class person to affirm middle-class values is prudent. However, for the poor, their applicability is, to put it mildly, limited. Education may be valuable, but only in the abstract, as its quality in the inner city is thin. Property is much to be valued as a tool of affluence and power, but the poor invariably live on someone else's property, making the owner rich by their rent payments. Working hard is virtuous, and indeed, as the Protestant work ethic affirms, it is the secret to wealth; however, if there are no jobs with genuine opportunity, hard work may only guarantee early death. Thriftiness is a central skill to economic coping for many, but people must have financial resources with which to be thrifty. Appearing respectable is not only psychologically constructive, it is perhaps necessary for the maintenance of career and social position in most communities. However, such a façade may only make an inner-city resident appear uppity and insensitive. Finally, the key to much success is deferring present gratification in favor of reaping a future harvest, but this assumes there is something to sow beyond the seeds of survival.

Nonetheless, what makes these values critical here is that they are burned into the psyche of the vast majority of candidates for the pastorate. These values and their attendant attitude systems are ways of perceiving reality. And this perceptual stance leads to victim blaming.

VICTIM BLAMING

If there is one book every urban worker would be wise to read, it is William Ryan's classic *Blaming the Victim*.[1] In fact, most of the rest of this chapter is devoted to reviewing and discussing the issues raised in it. Ryan very methodically and spectacularly explodes a host of unconscious myths held by most well-meaning, well-educated, and well-intentioned members of the middle class who would seek to redress the devastating effects of what are conventionally termed social problems. Although many millions of city dwellers are victims of poverty, poor education, prejudice, unemployment, and a host of other maladies, those who seek to help these victims are victims as well. They, in Ryan's judgment, are victims of an ideology, a social perspective that renders them all but useless in their zealous attempts to heal the wounds of the obvious victims with whom they deal.

Ryan calls blaming the victim an "ideology, a mythology, a set of officially certified non-facts and respected untruths, and this ideology—which has been infused into the very cells of his [the middle-class victim's] brain—prevents him from seeing the process of victimization as a total picture."[2]

What is victim blaming? According to Ryan, it is a four-step process that begins with the identification of a social problem like poverty. Once identified, the problem is studied by focusing on its victims (the poor) in terms of how they differ from the rest of the society, that is, how they deviate from the norm. Then assuming, in the case of poverty, that the economic system is sufficiently equitable that any reasonable or average person can succeed in it, lifestyle differences are stipulated as the core of the problem. That is, the reason poor people are poor is that they do not live properly. Once this has been established, some humanitarian strategy or program is developed that is aimed at changing the victims by eliminating these differences and bringing them *up* to the level of the rest of the society.

A baseline assumption that runs through victim blaming at all levels is that it is normal to be decently educated, have a productive job, and earn a livable wage in the United States. Anything less than achieving this social status makes a person abnormal, even deviant. Failure to reach this plateau may be met with sympathy and compassion; nonetheless, it is dealt with by attempting to change the victims so that they can become productive members of society. Implicit is the belief that there is enough to go around; there need not be any losers. Institutional causes such as redlining, miseducation, economic downturns affecting employment opportunities, racism, and any other maladies that may be at the root of victimization are admitted into consciousness, but only in passing. The United States remains the land of opportunity for all, and seizing the opportunity through hard work and adjustment to the system is all that is needed. Why there are always so many millions of victims every year is rarely if ever explored, as the humanitarians zealously turn their attention to retreading the victims.

Victim blaming is as alive today as it ever has been. Shel Trapp, a community organizer in Chicago states that "whenever there is an organizing drive on any issue it turns out to be the fault of those oppressed. It never seems to be the fault of those doing the oppressing." The first words out of society's mouth when it comes to those in social duress are, "It is your fault."[3] It was much due to this attitude that states raced to the bottom of the welfare rolls once the welfare reform legislation of 1996 went into law.[4]

It is this focus on the victim that is fundamental to the failure of a host of governmental and ecclesiastical social programs. Why is it that nothing, from the Great Society to the local church program for unwed mothers, ever seems to work? Many theological conservatives chalk it all up to sin. If only everyone were evangelized, then these problems would disappear. Would they? Many evangelicals work in institutions that, albeit often unintentionally, both create and perpetuate racism, economic exploitation, and unemployment as a matter of course. Liberals take the education-brings-enlightenment view. If only the victims were better educated, they might escape their plight. What is necessary *is* an education, but it is the middle class that should be educated to circumvent it from enlisting in institutional enterprises that victimize masses of people. However, the public is often rather godless, and even the most educated are woefully ignorant of the effects of the status quo.

What this victim-blaming perspective does is cause the would-be helper to shift the focus away from the institutional injustices at the heart of the problem in question and toward the victim, who is trapped by the problem. There are two approaches taken by such helpers, both based on this victim-blaming perspective. The first approach is to volunteer to help within the very system that is itself the problem. The second approach is to find ways to change the victims themselves. Examples of both follow.

One example of the first approach is found in school volunteer helpers. People often read of the miseducation of children in a ghetto school and respond with horror at the insensitivity of the school personnel about whom they read. They quickly set their sights on helping these victimized youth escape the carelessness of the school officials who neglect them. What they pass by is the stark reality that ghetto education is an accepted, ongoing practice, carried on in virtually every major city in the United States to the detriment of literally millions of children each year. Many of the most caring will decide to take action. So, what do they do? They volunteer to help as teacher aides or in related capacities within the schools. Helpful though such service may be, the volunteers remain unaware of the school tracking system, which sorts out students on the basis of IQ and other standardized test measures, sending some into enriched classrooms, while others are doomed to sit out their educational experience until they are old enough to quit. Tragically, the well-meaning teacher aide frequently gets caught up in assisting the testing program, unaware of how the tests are used. In short, the would-be helpers become part of the problem they desire to eradicate.

Another example of the volunteer approach is seen in the various faces of urban renewal. Appalled at the quality of slum life in major cities, some would-be helpers quickly get behind the local slum-clearance effort. Again, however, the individual, while feeling good about taking action, simply exacerbates the institutional injustices at the heart of the problem: clearing space so that more affluent residents and entrepreneurs can move into a refurbished region while the poor are left to find another overly dense enclave in which to exist.

These two cases are examples of simply joining in with sweeping institutional programs that perpetuate problems by bypassing the interests of the victims and extending the power of the larger system. Often, however, the focus is directly on changing the victim. The victim, viewed with concern and sympathy if not genuine love, is seen as the cause of the problem. Poor health in slum areas is often attributed to faulty health practices. Ramshackle slum living is chalked up to a lack of adjustment to urban life. Poverty is accounted for by the inability of the poor to escape a living pattern marked by a culture of poverty. Once this focus on changing the victim has been clearly set, programs are designed to change, enrich, upgrade, or, in some other fashion, better the victim.

In education these programs are called "developmental education," "compensatory education" or "enrichment" programs. In short, these are organized attempts at elevating the low achiever to the level of the average student in the school. Absolutely nothing is done to change the structures and processes that methodically grind out millions of victims yearly. Rather than realize that much of the educational enterprise is humiliating to those who fail, that those who fail can be identified by prejudicial standardized tests in the primary grades, and that many teachers are deeply imbued with the belief that teaching the disadvantaged is really useless anyway, students are corralled, tutored, and cajoled in an effort to bring them up to standard.

In medicine, health-care information is scatter-gunned throughout low-income areas and hygienic practices are preached faithfully over radio and television. But the gross inequities involving the costs and availability of health care for the poor go unaddressed.

One of Ryan's prime examples involves lead-paint poisoning. A pharmaceutical company with social conscience and civic concern may, at its own expense, print thousands of signs warning against eating lead-paint chips and make certain that these posters are distributed throughout a major city. As humanitarian as this action may be, it diverts attention away from the real problem: that lead-paint poisoning is an outgrowth of the institution of slum landlording in the United States. The real cause is that lead-paint use (in many locales illegal for residential buildings) and mass disrepair of buildings are tolerated by city inspectors. What is really going on is that slum landlords are clearly living in violation of the legal code and contributing to the deaths of their victims. Yet the problem is addressed by informing the victims that they better beware to sidestep the effects of an illegal practice by members of the landowning class. The process begins with the use of lead paint, continues as repairs of buildings are not made, and ends with the grief-stricken urban mother looking with guilt at the body of her dead child, who she believes would be alive today if only she had protected the child from eating the paint chips.

Virtually every social problem is dealt with in some victim-blaming form. Millions of dollars have been dumped into federal programming, all designed to change the victim—for that is the

219

simplest thing to do. To change the status quo, to alter the system and make it equitable, would be to remove the advantage the dominant group has. If all the inequities were removed from the system, those in power would be in power no longer. The middle class would no longer be assured of their middle-class status, and being successful would no longer be a routine matter of effective socialization but rather a matter of greater effort.

In the church this victim blaming has a double jeopardy. On the one hand, it undercuts so many energetic service ministries; on the otherhand, the church simply becomes a supporter of the sins of institutional injustice that victimize its own parishioners. There is neither honor nor credibility in such an approach.

A key to escaping the subtle, octopus-like clutches of victim blaming is raised consciousness. There must be an ability to distinguish between victim-blaming and non-victim-blaming approaches. Figure 2 and the explanations that follow seek to provide examples of such distinctions.

Education

Looking at the institution of education, the major problem seems to be low achievement. As previously discussed, achievement has been found in repeated studies to be very closely associated with socioeconomic status. That is, the lower the student's socioeconomic status is, the poorer the academic achievement will be.

Dominant View. The conventional or dominant explanation for the association of low achievement and low socioeconomic status is fourfold. First, those who are poor economically and whose children do poorly in the nation's schools are living in a state of cultural deficiency. Though rarely stated in such politically incorrect terms, the culture out of which the children come is simply not adequate—not up to sufficient standard to assure success in the classroom.

Second, poor parents are thought to be apathetic about education. Their depressed aspirations for their children rub off on the youth, and so, over time, those in the community do not care to exert themselves enough to insure academic success.

Third, limited academic skills are also cited. The belief is that, because of a series of rather unspecified social and environmental factors, these children just don't have natural ability anyway. Trying to make scholars out of these youngsters is viewed as akin to attempting to make a bulldog run like a greyhound.

Finally, *enrichment* is usually the byword for what is needed. Head Start and other types of compensatory programs are inaugurated in the hope of surrounding the children as early as possible with the proper environmental forces conducive to doing well in school. All stops have to be pulled out to compensate for the

Figure 2. Victim-blaming versus Non-victim-blaming Approaches

INSTITUTION	PROBLEM	DOMINANT VIEW	ANALYSIS AND NEEDS
Education	Low Achievement	Cultural deprivation Apathy Limited academic skills Enrichment needed	Decentralization Money Community control Teacher-attitude change
Economics	Poverty	Poverty culture Poverty-oriented values Child-rearing differences Educational apathy Immediate gratification Hopeless situation Acculturation needed	Jobs Income maintenance Power Access to opportunities Change in the system
Justice	Crime	Crime rate highest in slums Warped personalities produced by slum living Criminals a distinct subgroup Role of police to suppress these people	Emphasis on street crime rather than on organized crime or white-collar crime Crime unrelated to socio-economic status Differential enforcement of the law Emphasis on order rather than on law Comprehensive definition of crime, adequate legal defense, fair sentencng, and rehabilitation needed

deficiencies of the students' environment and bring them into step with the middle class.

The dominant view places the blame squarely on the victim. The victim must do the changing; the school system is all right. Before turning to a non-victim-blaming perspective, it would be helpful to examine more closely the dominant viewpoints.

"Cultural deprivation" assumes a cultural superiority on the part of the larger society. It suggests not only that the poor are culturally different but also that they are culturally inferior and that the quicker that culture is undercut and replaced with a more enlightened way, the better. Such a supremacist notion is insulting and says more about the middle class than the poor who fail in the public school system.

As emphasized earlier, almost every scholarly study done on aspiration refutes the charge that lower-class people have a more apathetic view of education than the middle class. The difference is not in aspiration but in the ability to act strategically and effectively on these lofty educational goals.

Limited academic skills exist when measured by middle-class standards. Indeed, at the first-grade level, middle-class children are much more prepared for the kinds of experiences afforded in the conventional school than their less affluent counterparts. Middle-class children often know the alphabet, can do simple computation, and are able to read with considerable proficiency before entering school. That poor children do not come to school with those skills does not mean that the capacity for their development does not exist. However, when the school curricula and the expectations of the middle-class teaching personnel carry the assumption that these rather cognitive skills are already or should already be developed, then anyone who is not at that stage of academic development is already behind and will likely remain behind.

The enrichment panacea really zeroes in on the victim. Instead of taking the students where they are, determining their abilities—latent and actual—and working from there, educators deluge the unsuspecting students with "enrichment," that is, experiences assumed superior to their deficient and inferior environment. The hope is that some of this enrichment will "take" and the students will survive in the conventional academic environment. If they don't survive, then they just don't have natural ability.

Analysis and Needs. Moving from the dominant view's focus on the victim toward a non-victim-blaming analysis of the needs, the first need we might suggest is that of greater decentralization of the school system. Decentralization means more community control and, therefore, community involvement in the educational process. Too often a host of downtown bureaucrats control the purse strings and the procedures operative in the schools they rarely, if ever, visit. It is extraordinarily difficult for them to appreciate the problems and needs of the individual schools. With greater decentralization there is likely to be a greater commitment on the part of faculty and administrators, as well as parents, all making a more conscientious effort toward improving the education of the children.

The second need, money, is also important, especially in view of the fact that suburban per-pupil expenditures are greatly in excess of those in urban areas. That is, individual suburban children have much more money allocated to their education than their urban peers. In addition, the money should be spent where it is needed most: where achievement is the lowest, buildings the oldest, people the poorest, teachers and administrators most given to turnover, and so on.

The third need, community control, has already been touched on; however, it is important to add here the importance of community pride. Where there is a sense of fate control, there tends to be more energy and enthusiasm as well as a sense of responsibility.

Finally, teacher attitude is especially vital. Rosenthal and Jacobson's classic, though much-criticized, study suggests that teachers tend to get out of their students what they believe they are able to get.[5] If, in other words, the teachers expect growth, they somehow seem to get it; if the teachers believe the children are hopeless, the children vegetate academically. Other studies, as well as my own observations and experiences, lend support to this notion.

This presentation of analysis and needs is not advanced as a panacea for the eradication of the problems associated with low academic achievement. It does suggest, however, that the starting point is to abandon the notion that the system itself is just and that if children are normal, they should succeed. Instead, we need to examine the institutional process with an eye toward finding its inequities and injustices—faults that have the effect of systematically producing failure for millions of victims who, because of the system's biased assumptions and processes, are not able to compete on equal terms with their middle-class counterparts.

Economics

The major social problem in the institution of economics is, of course, poverty. Here again the public notion is that the poor develop a self-defeating culture of poverty, replete with values and behaviors that doom them to live at the bottom. This culture carries with it poor child-rearing patterns, educational apathy, and a tendency to look for immediate gratification rather than carefully storing up money and opportunity in order to succeed later.

Dominant View. The dominant view subtly suggests that the situation is really hopeless. Indeed, as Christ said, "The poor will be with you always" (Mark 7:14). If only the poor could be acculturated—socialized—into a different outlook that would enable them to lift themselves into a more productive life, the problem would be solved. As it is, however, they are going nowhere, trapped in the web of a culture of poverty. In short, America is the land of opportunity, but the poor, as a result of their own intellectual, social, and cultural deficiencies, are unable to seize the opportunity; and so they live pathetically in the economic dungeon.

Scholars cite a particular prejudice toward the poor among businesspeople. Federal efforts at eradicating poverty have met with intense opposition from the business community, which bemoans the tax burden. Most of the opposition issues from the belief that the poor must pull themselves up by their bootstraps, as did other poor before them. There is no mention as to where these bootstraps can be found in a nation that has few land opportunities, needs little unskilled labor, and suffers from continuing inflation.

Prejudice toward the poor is found also among politicians, who are probably the group most responsible for spreading antipoverty propaganda. Many do not depend on the votes of the poor—who do not vote in high numbers—to get elected. As such, they do not visit the inner cities in their states or districts. That, in addition to being socialized similarly to urban pastors (discussed previously) all but obviates any likelihood of their empathizing with the plight of the poor.

In short, the dominant view again focuses directly on the victim. The system is fine. There need be no losers in the capitalistic economy. Any person of reasonable intelligence, ability, and drive is perfectly able to garner a solid job and make a decent living. People who do not survive at a middle-class level need to change—to be rid of the faults that make them unable to compete.

Analysis and Needs. From an institutional standpoint, the problems look radically different. One area of concern is jobs. It is very difficult to succeed in a capitalistic market if a person cannot find a decent, well-paying job. With an inner-city unemployment rate frequently three to four times greater than the national rate, it is hard to imagine how people are able to survive. There may have to be some sort of much-debated family income maintenance if no plan is implemented to "put America back to work." As it is presently, unemployment compensation, aid to dependent children, disability benefits, and all other types of public aid are scarcely sufficient to keep a family alive, much less to allow them to have a decent standard of living.

A primary area of need is greater social and political power and greater access to opportunities for the poor. As discussed earlier, the poor remain politically unrepresented, and they live in areas in which educational opportunities are the poorest and where industries and other job sources do not exist. Unless there are real changes in the system, all the acculturation in the world is likely to do little good. Indeed, there may occasionally be a character out of a Horatio Alger novel that rises to the top, but such a figure is an exception and leaves millions of average people behind.

To be sure, many people chafe at welfare programs, grudgingly watching their tax dollars eaten by various forms of public-aid allotments. The only alternative to such a procedure is to change the whole institutional system by making it truly open, equal, and democratic in opportunity. In cases in which people are thrust off welfare rolls, adequate training and time is not provided. Moreover, the jobs available usually are devoid of benefits and pay so poorly that such people are unable to move beyond welfare dependency.[6]

Justice

The major problem in this area is, of course, crime. There is no shortage of concern about crime in the United States. People are particularly frightened by the extent of crime in the major cities, most notably in the slums. Why is there such a high crime rate?

Dominant View. The dominant view suggests that slum living warps the personality of slum dwellers, desensitizing them to right and wrong, law and order. Moreover, criminals are viewed as a distinct subgroup; society can be divided into criminals and straight people, the evil-doing, and the law-abiding. The role of the police in such a society is to crack down on urban crime, holding it in check with methods ranging from detection to intimidation.

Although the dominant view allows that there are some environmental factors attendant to slum living that may pressure people toward lawlessness, there is little attention focused on what these factors are. If circles were drawn on a city map around the spots in which education is the poorest, health care is the scarcest, unemployment the highest, political power the weakest, incomes the lowest, housing the most difficult to obtain, family life the most strained, recreational facilities the fewest, and street crime the highest, the same spot would be circled again and again and again. Street crime, then, is associated with a myriad of variables, quite unrelated to the skin color or personality makeup of the people who commit it.

Analysis and Needs. Most people suffer from a myopic view of crime. In reality, there are three types of crime: organized crime, white-collar crime, and street crime. Of these three, street crime is highlighted and focused on. Yet organized crime involves more money than the other two combined, and white-collar crime, especially as it is practiced in government and big business, has more far-reaching consequences for the society. Yet those involved in organized and white-collar crime are simply not regarded as criminals. The barons of organized crime are the subjects of novels, biographies, and movies, and those who commit white-collar offenses are viewed as law-abiding citizens who temporarily go astray. The prisons are built for the poor who offend on the streets.

Research attempts have indicated that crime is actually unrelated to socioeconomic status.[7] If every violation of the law (whether or not the perpetrator was apprehended) were defined as a crime, then almost everyone in the society would bear the label criminal. People who bilk the government out of vast sums of money with dishonest income-tax reporting; businesses that price fix, pollute, and defraud; consumers who shoplift for fun and profit; pleasure-seekers who illegally smoke marijuana and indulge themselves in the use of harder drugs; and that vast number of people who each week illegally bet on football games and other sporting events—all are criminals. It is not that there is a distinct group of criminals but that there is a differential enforcement of the law.

But what of street crime? It is violent and disruptive of public order. Indeed it is, and its disruptiveness is why it is focused on. The fact is that US justice is much more concerned with order than with law. White-collar crime and even much organized crime are carried on within the normal workings of major institutions. In some cases, white-collar crime not only does not disrupt order but actually cuts through bureaucratic red tape, hastening needed action. Crime of this sort is carried on by what are called productive members of society. Street crime is disorderly. It obstructs the smooth workings of the institutional system, and it is carried on by the least socially useful.

It is for this reason that an executive who is caught knowingly polluting the air and water by tolerating the use of equipment below pollution-control standards, and so jeopardizes the health and well-being of the millions of residents in a major metropolitan area, is granted 120 days to bring the plant up to standard; whereas, a city youth who is apprehended for snatching a purse containing ten dollars will go to jail that very night. The former is on balance a law-abiding citizen who necessitates prompting. The latter is a young criminal.

What is really needed is a more comprehensive definition of crime, a much more adequate defense system, and fair sentencing procedures. As it is now, the rich are defended by high-power, private attorneys who rarely lose a case even if their clients are guilty, and the poor are left with an overworked public defender who finds it most propitious to plea bargain. Overall, it is the system that needs to be rehabilitated, not just the street criminals. Without needed changes, the jails will continue to swell with the poor.

The solutions to problems in society, then, are not more programs that focus on the poor, not more victim blaming, but a reevaluation of the role of institutions in producing the problems and creating victims.

REFOCUSING URBAN MINISTRIES

Urban ministries tend to fail. Although success should not be the goal so much as faithfulness in service, it is important to examine why these failures occur. Often the ministries are based on the same victim-blaming foundations that premise so many failure-ridden, governmental programs. This is not surprising, for those who structure urban ministries have few other models than the government and the public sector to emulate. However, as long as the victim remains the focus, what occurs is the rehabilitation of a few, the loss of many, and no change in the source that is creating the problem.

With this point in mind, it is easier to understand why a church needs to refocus its ministries to include not only service ministries but also stewardship ministries. Although it is helpful to have a tutoring program, it is also important to focus on the accountability of the local school in an effort to encourage more effective teaching and learning processes. Helping residents find housing is a necessary "cup of cold water" ministry, but actively working against malicious redlining practices is perhaps even more important. Counseling and befriending neighborhood youth is necessary in building healthy relationships and modeling what adult life can be, but having a youth program that both attempts to reform and redirect the energies of the gangs and also is vigilant about ways in which the city and its officials can provide a more equitable environment for the youngsters is just as important. Directing troubled residents toward legal-aid clinics and even charitable private lawyers is a worthy enterprise, but no more so than working with community organizations and other groups toward guaranteeing more humane police treatment and fire service.

LaSalle Street Church's Young Life program developed such an effective track record that judges granted youthful offenders probation, provided they would get involved in its program. This is an example of urban workers approaching systems rather than working exclusively with individuals. Aiding an unemployed resident in an effort to find work is an honorable as well as a difficult and often frustrating venture. But encouraging local businesses and corporations within or adjacent to the community to hire the poor and indigent may provide jobs for many. It may be necessary to help some citizen who has had an unhappy experience with the city political organization, but it can be even more effective to have various political candidates and figures speak at the church in hopes of extracting pledges from them for more equitable treatment of the entire community citizenry. It may be a significant act to help one of the senior high students get accepted into the church college of choice, but if that youth is nonwhite, it might be more effective to examine why so few minorities are enrolled in these institutions. Finding companionship and entertainment for lonely youngsters is a humane thing, but so is approaching the local powers-that-be about opening more recreational space for the neighborhood youth.

It would be humanly impossible for a single pastor or even a team to address every problem at the institutional level with real effectiveness. That is not the point here. In fact, it is important that urban workers assess their resources—including time—before taking action. Then they can determine priorities and set objectives based on community and church needs.

The point here is that those who do urban ministry should refocus their efforts to include stewardship ministries and not allow themselves to be limited by a victim-blaming perspective. The victim-focusing ministries tend to help usually one person or, at most, just a few people at a time. Such relief efforts are worthy and scriptural. However, an institutional-reform approach, which can turn the tide for many, perhaps thousands of people needing relief and justice, is also scriptural in view of the many calls for justice in the Bible. Moreover, every victory carries with it an enormous sense of satisfaction because a social problem has been attacked at its root. Such a satisfying experience can pump new energy into all ministries, regardless of focus.

If urban workers keep their eyes fixed on the real causes of the ills of the poor, they are likely to be more effective in working with them. All too often the poor are encountered by well-intentioned workers who are unwitting pawns of these larger systems. Such people are of limited value to the poor and receive provisional respect. Workers who openly acknowledge the victimizing tendencies of unjust institutional systems can help those victims survive in the system by offering them personal-change options to their present way of living. Such workers are likely to develop much better rapport.

Although Ryan is singularly condemnatory toward individual-based, victim-focused programs of any sort, it is not being suggested here that all such programs be abandoned because they have a blaming-the-victim strain to them. These ministries, which work toward bringing about change in the victims such that they can adjust to and function within the system, are absolutely defensible in view of the fact that without them and without any change in larger institutional systems, these victims will remain hopeless victims. Ministries such as these at least provide opportunities to develop skills that enable those held under by the institutional system to avoid drowning.

However, knowing that such ministries are important ought not to divert urban workers' attentions away from the real causal factors at the institutional level. Any and every opportunity to address these causes should be taken advantage of. Here again, care is needed. Reckless confrontation of institutions is not only un-Christian but foolish. Moreover, it will only brand the church as the enemy of the institutional community. Diplomacy is always in order. Nonetheless, diplomacy should not be a password for cowardice or passivity in the face of a need to call institutions to a higher awareness of their social and civic responsibility.

The central issue here is awareness. The whole task of urban ministry, whether individually or institutionally focused, carries with it a plethora of problems and frustrations. However, when working in the social arena, if those in urban ministry can avoid being duped by already-duped, well-meaning officials who would shift the focus away from unjust systems and toward deficiencies in victims, they will, at the very least, have the confidence that they know what they are doing. In addition, they will be able to analyze their current set of ministries in terms of their effectiveness and inaugurate new ones with realistic expectations of what they may accomplish. Without such an awareness, urban workers are in jeopardy of blindly following the victim-blaming procedures of governmental programs, only to wonder openly and alone why nothing ever really seems to work.

THE URBAN CHURCH AND THE URBAN MINISTER 9

In this chapter we will look at the differences between inner-city churches and middle-class churches—differences in style, in expectations, in priorities, in general makeup. It is here that the sociological traits of residents of inner cities make their impact on the nature of the church. Social stratification, institutional oppression, poverty, insecurity, and victimization need to be addressed by stewardship and service ministries of the church. But the very nature of the church itself—its worship services and its programs—is affected by its urban locale. The urban pastor must know and appreciate these differences in order to minister effectively.

The chapter closes with advice to the urban minister on the psychological attributes and survival techniques needed in order to avoid burnout and instead reap the rewards of urban ministry.

THE URBAN CHURCH

Differences between Inner-City and Middle-Class Churches

There are a number of ways in which inner-city churches tend to differ from their more affluent counterparts. Some of these disparities are necessary and appropriate, given the differences between inner-city and middle-class life. Some, however, suggest deficits in one or the other's parish style. Although each of the following areas merits extensive research, here is a brief review of fourteen areas of difference.[1]

People versus Buildings. Inner-city churches tend to put their money into people-oriented ministries, while an emphasis on building size, stability, beauty, and maintenance eats up a greater share of middle-class church budgets.

Basic versus Dissertational Preaching. Inner-city pastors usually preach in a more affective domain than their middle-class peers, whose preaching often sounds more like a lecture or scholarly treatise.

Personal versus Theological. Because of the great need for basic human care, inner-city churches have a more personal style. Middle-class churches often tend toward a more theological, catechetical strain. Both elements are important in church life, but the emphasis is different. Moreover, whereas middle-class churches are often able to neatly apply their theology to most congregational issues, the complexities of inner-city life make direct theological application nearly impossible in many cases. The issue of ambiguity is discussed more fully later.

Communication and Identification versus Education and Sophistication. Inner-city pastors are judged much by their ability to communicate and identify. Academic degrees and a sophisticated style are much more highly valued in more affluent churches. This does not suggest that communication and personal warmth are not important in a middle-class congregation, but that they are all-important in the inner city.

Heterogeneous versus Homogeneous. Inner-city churches often are more diverse economically, socially, occupationally, educationally, and, in some cases, ethnically than most other churches.

Community-Centered versus Property-Centered. Inner-city parishes tend to see themselves in the context of their turf—the geographical community. Their ministries reflect this neighborhood quality. Middle-class churches tend to center their activities and ministries around the immediate building, taking a more isolationist position.

Community Service versus Congregational Nurture. Inner-city churches emphasize serving the residents of the neighborhood—socially and spiritually—whether or not they are affiliated with the parish. Middle-class churches tend to look more toward nurturing and developing their own members and fellowship.

Present versus Future. Owing to the crisis-interventionist nature of inner-city life, inner-city churches tend to respond to the immediate. Traditional, stable churches are more given to five- and ten-year plans.

Transience versus Stability. Because of poverty and community disorganization, the congregation of an inner-city church will turn over much more often than those of other churches. This transience is particularly frustrating to urban pastors, as it means not only losing the pillars of their churches but constantly having to instruct and orient new people.

Changing versus Defined. Inner-city churches are constantly experimenting and adapting. New ministries and programs are regularly being developed to keep pace with the volatile nature of the social environment. Middle-class churches usually have a more defined and routine operation.

Ambiguous versus Clear. It is difficult to describe comprehensively and accurately what an inner-city church is really like—its ethos and operation. This is partly because of the changing nature of these entities. Middle-class churches are less ambiguous institutions and, therefore, easier to get the pulse of.

Informal versus Formal Hierarchy. Inner-city churches are much more ad hoc than traditional churches. The pecking order, with more frequent changes, is both looser and more given to change than the more tightly defined hierarchy of the more stable congregations.

Anti-Status Quo versus Status Quo. This is a major area of difference. Inner-city churches view the prevailing sociocultural system as oppressive and laced with class interests. Middle-class congregations feel more comfortable with the capitalistic, economic, and social systems. While inner-city churches cry out for justice amid oppression, other churches emphasize Pauline injunctions to obey the civil authorities.

Redemption versus Avoidance of Guilt. Inner-city churches exist among so much sin and misery that there tends to be a rather positive, redemptive emphasis about them. Wrongdoing, though often acknowledged, is less emphasized than forgiveness and fresh starts. In many middle-class churches, there may be a tendency either to avoid the matter of sin—dealing with it in generalities—or to emphasize its heinousness to such an extent that burdens of guilt are carried for a long time.

Awareness of these different emphases is important for new urban ministers as well as those people from suburban or middle-class churches who are considering urban work.

KEYS TO URBAN MINISTRY

There has been much research and discussion concerning the problems facing inner-city churches, their pastors, and people.[2] The keys to urban ministry are an amalgam of ideas emerging from the literature and personal observation.

First, money, buildings, and programs are not stressed as much as people and their spiritual gifts. Heavy-handed fundraising, gaudy structures, and publicity-oriented programs are less important than the people, their needs, and having them use their gifts.

Second, in African American churches in particular the pulpit presence must be strong, with sermon messages relevant, practical, and exciting.

Third, beginning with the pastor, there must be an atmosphere of caring, one in which the parishioners are sharing their joys and sorrows, victories and defeats.

Fourth, the church needs focus and unity. It is vital that the church know what it is all about. This means defining who it is as a believing, even doctrinal community and where it is going. Is it about worship? Fellowship? Evangelizing the neighborhood? Youth? Related to its direction, of course, is that the members move beyond gossip and intramural squabbling and buy in to the identity and direction of the church.

Finally, if the church is to model Christ, it is wise to get outside itself and perform a ministry.

THE MINISTERING CHURCH

Bill Leslie died in 1993, but his ideas remain relevant today. Leslie took over a dilapidated downtown Chicago church in the turbulent 1960s. The early years were, in a word, discouraging. God, however, rewarded Leslie's faithfulness, and, by the later 1970s, his was one of the best-known urban churches in the country. Leslie himself became more and more renown, locally and nationally, for his genius in urban ministry. I had the privilege of teaching several seminary courses with him over the years and developed a deep friendship. What follows are some of his ideas for effective urban ministry.

Leslie pointed out that too much time is burned up arguing about theological issues while so much plain biblical truth has not yet been put into practice. Believers, he said, must be ready on all fronts to serve in the city. Urbanites have many more problems than just spiritual ones. They lack money, proper housing, adequate education, and legal protection. They are often plagued by relational or family problems, such as having a family member with a drug or alcohol problem.

True to other urban ministry leaders, Leslie continually stressed that programs come alive through people. A program without a real soul is dead. With people come life, commitment, and caring. Throughout his quarter century at LaSalle Street Church, Leslie repeatedly built ministries through people. Either a person would approach him with a call to minister, or Leslie would see a need and a person who could minister to it.

Leslie also emphasized the need for renewal of both the church and its leadership. A hindrance to renewal is the spectator attitude prevalent in churches. Like the sports crowd, the congregation gathers weekly at the church to watch the performance, ready to cheer or critique. The parishioners come to be entertained rather than to be equipped for carrying out the church's ministry.

He searched out some scriptural principles undergirding the ministering rather than the spectating church. First, the Bible indicates that the kingdom of God is present, even though its fulfillment lies in the future. This means that churches need to seek the *reign of Christ* presently in the lives of individuals, institutions, and whole societies. Second, throughout the Scriptures is the pervasive concept of *servanthood.* Christ's model, as expressed in Matthew 20:28, was one of ministering rather than being ministered to. People need to discover their gifts and put them to use. Third, servanthood stems from the principle that the church is the *body of Christ.* As Christ's body, it must do his ministry. When the church embodies the Spirit of Christ, results occur. Fourth, the members must be *equipped* to perform the ministry. Finally, like Christ, the church must not opt out of *difficult circumstances.* All these principles point to the pastor as a player and coach who tries to get the entire congregation on the field and into the ministry.

A renewed church will put programs into effect. But those programs need a personal touch. Bill Leslie and Keith Miller once led a meeting of about a thousand people and asked them to list the actions of a church or person that had the greatest impact on them. Not one mentioned a program. All alluded to a caring person and a caring act.

Equipping parishioners for active ministry is not an easy task. Among the impediments is that seminaries train pastors to *do* rather than to equip or to enable. This tendency, coupled with a stratification structure that places the pastor at the top of the ecclesiastical flow chart, makes it difficult for parishioners to assess their gifts and put them to use.

There is also the lethal tendency for urban workers to see the poor as those with less education, less power, and less wealth, and therefore as lesser people. However subconscious this may be, it short-circuits effective urban ministry.

Everyone has a gift with which to minister. A needy person can become healthy if the ministry is caring and relational rather than a one-way enterprise. Those who are on the receiving end should be included in a fellowship group or Bible study so they can be affirmed as persons and believers and discover the gift of ministry they have to give.

For all churches, evaluation is important. For churches involved in urban ministry, it is particularly important. From a specifically urban perspective, Lyle Schaller poses twenty self-evaluation questions for downtown, though not necessarily inner-city, churches.[3] The following questions are the ones most relevant to this discussion.

1. What is the combined contribution of the top ten and top twenty giving units? To the extent that money is an issue, it is helpful to know whether the top givers are good models or whether they are so generous that the church depends too heavily on them.

2. What types of skills are formally and informally rewarded? Growing churches emphasize creativity, dedication, and outreach as opposed to verbal and social skills.

3. What items dominate the agenda of the church's governing body? While declining churches emphasize means to ends and focus on survival questions, growing congregations look at effective ministering, caring, and nurturing as they observe community needs.

4. Is parking ample? Unless there is sufficient parking, non-Sunday-morning events will not be attended well, because of inconvenience and fear of street crime.

5. How effective is the communication network in the church? Do messages get to the members? Five of these seven communication modes should be used for important messages:

- Bulletin
- Newsletter
- Pulpit announcement
- Telephone
- Poster
- Personal visit
- Special mailing

Attention also needs to be given to the general communication level in the church and the community. Are there cliques? Is there smooth relaying of information? Good communication results from effective planning and much attention to detail.

6. What is the turnover rate? Is the church gaining or losing members? This is a good measure of how people feel about the church.

7. What is the church's image in the community? If outreach is to be at all effective, it is vital to get a good reading on this. The real image of the church may be a far cry from the intended one. It is important that the image be both positive and clear.

8. What is the attendance rate among confirmed resident members? Keeping tabs on this is valuable in evaluating the quality of corporate worship as well as the vitality of the church in general.

9. What is the age distribution of the church? Is it a young church? An old church? A changing church? Who is being ministered to and who is doing the ministering?

10. What is the attitude of members toward visitors and potential new members? Are the members service-oriented and responsive?

11. What is the nature of church leadership roles? Thriving churches place less emphasis on clergy leadership and more on lay involvement. Volunteer staff, temporary staff, and short-term specialists are common in growing churches.

12. Is the pastoral care to the members adequate? Members must be cared for in order to grow and minister themselves. Failure to perform this care gives rise to irritations, divisiveness, and stagnation.

The real goal for the urban parish is discipling whomever God sends it. This allows the pastor a tremendous sense of freedom from the usual clerical derby. Effective discipleship and personal development is the mark of the successful urban minister. In order to enjoy this success, the pastor must strike a balance between piety and action (inward, worshipful growth and outward, active thrusts) as well as between evangelism and social action.

THE URBAN MINISTER

The stresses faced by urban pastor are great. In order to live that balanced life personally, as well as model balance for their parishioners, pastors should develop particular psychological attributes that will make ministry effective. In addition, they need to pay attention to the well-being of their personal lives. The dangers of burnout are very real, but the rewards of a successful, enduring ministry in the city are very great.

Psychological Attributes

There are several psychological attributes in particular that mark an effective urban pastor or church worker. One is *respect for and appreciation of cultural diversity.* Urban communities are forever in transition and are filled with personal and cultural differences. For those who have been well socialized into the mainstream culture, this is psychologically unsettling. In fact, if they can even reach a level of toleration for this pluralism, a considerable personal victory has been won. Prospective urban pastors would do very well to immerse themselves in as many different cultural experiences as possible, so that pluralism comes to mean beauty and diversity comes to mean stimulation. It is only through this developed appreciation that the urban pastor can become truly a friend of the community. Friends appreciate, help, and serve others. To lack appreciation of the prevailing culture means to distance oneself from its practitioners and thus to be unable to serve without manipulation and conditional forms of love.

The pastor's appreciation of cultural diversity will lead to developing a pluralistic atmosphere in the church. Several brief guidelines for this are worthy of mention. One is that a rather heterogeneous principle should dominate the Sunday morning worship. Worship should be experience-centered every bit as much as content-centered. Music, meditation, and response by the congregation, in unison and individually, can facilitate the development of an experiential worship. In regard to music, people should hear their favorite kind occasionally. There should be soul music, rock, traditional hymnody, and classical sounds often enough so that the members of the congregation believe that their own preference is being presented.

Lay participation in the service is helpful. Members of the congregation can lead in prayer, Scripture reading, presentation of announcements, personal response to sermons, dramatic vignettes, testimonies, sharing of concerns, reporting on the progress of various ministries, and so on. In short, the only thing the pastor needs to do is preach the sermon. Lay involvement not only encourages the congregation to feel a part of the worship experience but also allows members of various cultures to be publicly a part of the church worship.

Preaching must necessarily be profound and presented in basic terms. Urban churches contain people who have PhDs and those who hold welfare cards, and so the preaching needs to get at profound but practical and basic issues. Illustrations should be multicultural and plentiful so that application of the message is not lost. Lengthy forays into theologically abstract matters will hold little appeal. City people want and need inputs that are usable in urban day-to-day living. Theology can be worked into other types of activities, such as evening forums or discussion groups, postworship fellowship hours, and other events.

Besides respect for and appreciation of cultural diversity, the urban pastor needs the psychological characteristic of *servanthood*. This has to be kept uppermost, for it frees a person from feeling that there must always be a return on every investment and prevents falling into the trap of cost-gain barter thinking. Knowing that the calling, like Christ's, is to serve regardless of the outcome is liberating. It removes the pressure of having to succeed and eliminates a tendency to indulge in self-pity when people do not respond.

Yet another psychological attribute involves the *tolerance of ambiguity*. A city and its people teem with diversity, complexity, and confusion. Working in the inner city, a pastor quickly realizes the depth of this ambiguity. Bureaucrats do not always return phone calls, and they often change their minds; city governments lie or stall or change policies; streets are built and destroyed; urban renewal comes and goes; and businesses come into existence and then burn down. Parishioners are unfaithful, late for appointments, dependent, and erratic. Their problems differ each day, requiring a crisis-interventionist approach. The whole environment is one of uncertainty and impermanence, and the residents incorporate a good deal of this feeling into their own lives and psyches. Being able to be calm and consistent and able to wait things out is necessary. Needing clear-cut answers from everyone, from parishioners to city officials, is not healthy.

One correlate of this tolerance for ambiguity and change is *understanding and compassion* for the temptations faced by urban dwellers. Most urban pastors will have been socialized into a middle-class ranking of sin. Although many evangelicals attest that sin is sin and that there is really no difference in the gravity of one sin or another, they tend to be particularly disturbed by illicit sex, drug abuse, alcoholism, deviance, street crime, shoplifting, and other overt behavioral misdeeds. These sins are particularly common in low-income urban environments. It would be informative to inquire from poor Christians what they consider to be the top ten sins. A pastor might find that the poor place particular emphasis on the misuse of affluence, insensitivity toward poverty and oppression, lack of concern about justice, inhospitable behavior, arrogance of power and its manipulation, and an attitude of judgmentalism and self-righteousness. These are the sins most common among the privileged.

Thus it would be helpful to adopt an attitude of understanding and compassion—grace—toward the poor and the wrongs prevalent there, just as tolerance and patience are extended for the wrongs of the middle class. Pastors need not compromise their ethics of right and wrong nor preclude calls to repentance; they need only expand his consciousness so that they deal compassionately and sensitively with inner-city parishioners, knowing the full context of their lives. For example, pastors can empathize with the rejected pregnant teenager, rather than focus on how she should have been able to avoid creating this particular dilemma. They can try to understand the reasons why some youth on drugs became involved with narcotics, rather than peel off a sermon aimed at convicting the youth of sin. Pastors can abhor the pressures and miseries of life in the crucible of poverty that drive a mother or father toward alcoholism, rather than simply condemn excessive drinking.

One particular summer urban ministries program used to begin by giving each enrollee a paltry few dollars and a ride to skid row. There they were dropped off and told to spend the weekend and to not return to the middle-class seminary until Monday. Once they had endured a weekend in the wilds of the inner city, it was amazing how empathic they became with the poor and the dubious strategies they often use to cope in the city fifty-two weeks a year.

Another correlate of this tolerance of ambiguity involves *making decisions and taking action* on issues not yet resolved by theologians. The urban pastor will deal not in a textbook but in real life with violence, homosexuality, divorce, liberation movements, radical politics, and nonmarital sexuality. Pastors will not have the convenience of confronting these matters ideologically over coffee and a textbook. Issues will stare them in the face. Pastors will need patience and the ability to suspend their desire to be doctrinaire and dogmatic so that they can come to grip with the complexity of these matters. They are even more difficult because they are encountered in the form of persons—persons who need service and ministry. Pastors will probably find themselves coming out in much different places on these matters than they did in seminary; often they will say, "I don't know," on issues to which they responded outspokenly in the past. Coping with this type of ambiguity, making decisions, and taking actions about which they will never be entirely certain necessitate a type of spiritual and psychological maturity of which they were previously unaware.

Another psychological trait is the *ability to deal with criticism and rejection.* Many urban pastors have thrown in the clerical towel because, instead of being supported by their denominations, they became objects of criticism. Urban church workers should expect to be branded a radical or an apostate by many of their denominational peers who hear of their work and style of ministry.

But this outside rejection may not be so bad, for pastors can shut much of that out. What is more painful are the breaches and cleavages likely to develop within their own congregations and the communities they serve. The pluralism of the population absolutely guarantees breakdowns of communication and the emergence of criticism and condemnation. Bill Leslie well remembered the controversy in his church over the inauguration of the tutoring program for the community children. Many devout members felt that this nonevangelistic, nonspiritual ministry of a purely social nature was a way of compromising with the soul-saving mission of the church. When the matter came to a congregational vote, it passed by one ballot. Ordinarily, Leslie would never have proceeded on such a lack of consensus. However, he was so convinced of the necessity of this type of temporal ministry that he went forward anyway.

There will be people who will be critical of the pastor for not being more socially and politically radical. Others will feel the pastor is not attending sufficiently to the spiritual needs of the church and its evangelistic thrust. Some in the community will view the church as self-righteous, while others will see it as not adequately prophetic and evangelical. With the congregation scattered ideologically, politically, socially, and even geographically, the pastor will necessarily become the lightning rod for much of this criticism. It will hurt and cause anger, but that is to be expected. In short, neither the church nor the pastor will ever be able to be all things to all people; and recognizing that is the first step to resolving much of the potential agony.

The *ability to live with compromise* is also imperative. There is a constant necessity of having to settle for second best in urban ministry. Often a pastor may wish something to go a certain way in the church, but because of the pluralism of the congregation, the lack of money for funding, the absence of sufficient workers, or any of a host of other reasons, the pastor will have to settle for an inch instead of a foot. The previously mentioned tutoring program illustrates this point. Leslie saw many other ministries he would like to have incorporated at the same time. Nevertheless, he settled on tutoring as a start, realizing the congregation was simply not ready for additional ventures. Much intrachurch compromise arises from this problem of the pastor being ahead of the congregation in awareness and vision. It is frustrating to know what needs to be done and to have to wait for the parishioners' awareness to be raised sufficiently to be supportive of it.

Compromise is everywhere in urban ministry. The needs are so pressing they cry for powerful activist ministries and solutions. However, the reason they are pressing is that economic, social, and political impediments prevent reaching a solution. Victories, then, are often limited. Tutoring programs are begun before legal-aid clinics, senior citizens' breakfasts precede counseling centers, and local youth activities come before summer camps. Vision is important to the pastor, for dreams sustain effort. But the visions need to be weighed against present realities, so that dreams for the future do not fuel frustration in the present.

One additional but often overlooked psychological trait is that of *a sense of humor*. There is an old adage that we should take our responsibilities, rather than ourselves, seriously. Humor is a guardian of sanity. If we cannot laugh, we will be left only to cry. Realizing that we are but single servants in a giant vineyard can free us to see failures and incongruities as opportunities to laugh and appreciate the delightful yet frustrating incomprehensibility of life. Laughter is a therapeutic gift, and finding as many ways as possible to exploit its use will be in the best interests of the urban pastor.

Personal Life

In addition to the foregoing psychological attributes, there are a number of behavioral guidelines that should mark the personal life of an effective urban minister. At the outset, the importance of *reading* needs to be stressed. There is a tremendous energy drain in urban ministry—reading has a refueling quality. Reading materials can be chosen to increase cultural awareness and sensitivity. Reading can fill the mental shelf with ideas and creative options for more effective ministry. In addition, reading is a very constructive way to use time alone, away from the endless demands made on a pastor's energies. A pastor who does not read goes stale.

Reading should be done in devotional, theological, and particularly social areas, for it needs to be used to develop the whole person. However, recreational reading—sports, novels, the arts, and so forth—is not only defensible but highly appropriate.

Part of the pastor's reading time should be devoted to research into local history. Studying the local community and the histories of the peoples who have settled there gives the urban minister the confidence that comes from entering a familiar rather than unfamiliar turf. Moreover, a pastor often ministers to families or clans rather than individuals. The problems plaguing the individual in Cleveland may stem from decisions made in Mississippi. It is also helpful to know the role of the pastor in the ethnic tradition of the people served. These role definitions vary greatly from one group to another. Finally, a pastor should be familiar with the local church history. Doing new things is important, but a pastor should not be too critical of the past, for it is a foundation of the present. Alluding to earlier precedents can make that foundation stronger and build a sense of affirmation and appreciation for the enduring nature of the particular church.

Another important guideline for the pastor's personal life concerns *budgeting time.* One effective way to do this is to keep a time log for a week or two, accounting for every fifteen- or thirty-minute period. From there, a pastor can assess how time can be spent more constructively and productively. Time is the urban pastor's most precious and limited resource. Ineffective use brings on guilt, depression, and despair. There is always more to do than time allows anyway. Therefore, any inappropriate use of time will have a grating effect on feelings. Time budgeting should be done realistically but with a certain amount of flexibility to account for the unforeseen.

However, the urban worker should zealously guard any free time. The tendency to feel responsible for all the ills and traumas in the community can predispose a person to skip recreational time in order to crowd in even more service-oriented activity. Other than assuaging the conscience from false guilt, such a practice is of absolutely no value. That free time is every bit as important as any other, and without it the nerves wear thin, exhaustion emerges, and soon the minister will be looking for another pastorate.

A related guideline is *establishing family priorities.* If the pastor is married, and especially if there are children, family concerns are inevitable. It is important that the entire family have a very clear understanding of the nature of the work and its demands. There may need to be a considerable amount of negotiation involved so a pastor can meet the responsibilities to the family as well as perform in the ministry. Moreover, if family matters are not of sufficient priority, the stresses that may result could ultimately undercut effective ministry anyway. So it becomes a pragmatic matter as well.

Many pastors have lost a marriage, either through divorce or because it has become vapid and lifeless, simply because the family was not a sufficient priority. It is not unreasonable to argue that if the wife does not feel resolved about moving into an urban pastorate, the husband should not feel called to such a post. It is vital to feel the support of the family in such a challenging work. If adversarial relationships develop within the home, the ministry will likely soon be over.

The most critical family problem for those in urban ministry is time. Unless pastors zealously and defensively guard family time, it will soon evaporate. Budgeting appears imperative here. Almost any type of ministry, because of its spontaneous nature, seems to work against family life. But inner-city ministry, with its additional burdens, can destroy family life unless clear priorities are set.

Finally, the urban minister needs to see the importance of *giving recognition to others.* Urban ministry is often not filled with very many strokes. If such is true for the pastor, it is even more so for other willing workers and staff members. So it becomes important that staff members regularly be reinforced, praised, and encouraged in their work. One helpful way to do this is to recognize them and their ministries periodically in the morning service. Such featuring of different ministries and their workers gives these selfless servants a bit of attention and identity. It will elicit prayers and support from a better-informed and more appreciative congregation.

Survival

Considering the magnitude of the urban-ministry challenge, it is difficult to imagine how it can be endured. Among urban workers in general, whether they are teachers, pastors, social workers, or any other professionals who work regularly with problem-plagued people, the average length of service is not much more than four years. Many experience what is called *burnout.*

Burnout is the end point of cumulative physical, emotional, psychological, and spiritual fatigue. It comes from giving when there is no more to give. The physical symptoms of burnout may include constant fatigue, backaches, and headaches. Emotionally, the person stops caring and begins to perform the functions of urban ministry as just that—functions—rather than caring service. A lack of optimism and a sense of loneliness and isolation set in. Lack of companionship contributes to a feeling like that of an Old Testament prophet, scorned by his own people. Closely related to this is the feeling of alienation growing out of the lack of denominational support and even abandonment by parishioners. While being rejected on one hand, for owning the causes of the poor, on the other hand, pastors—if they are Caucasian—may be seen as allies of the oppressors. With this dual rejection, a spiritual lifelessness develops, often accompanied by a feeling of abandonment by God.

Burnout is the result of a number of things.[4] First, there is a feeling that the ministry is cyclical rather than progressive. There is the feeling of being on a treadmill with little being accomplished. Summer becomes autumn, autumn winter, winter spring, and spring summer. The problems remain the same, and the church may not grow. In fact, it seems that for every problem addressed, there are four more to deal with. There is nowhere to hide as the mountain of need grows. There is also disappointment. Urban churches, like any organization, depend on key people. When these people are lost through death, illness, or moving away, there is a feeling of despair for many pastors, a sense of abandonment and isolation. Frustration builds and gives way to repressed anger, which in turn can lead to hostility and bitterness.

There may be a feeling of guilt over a lack of success. We need a theology of failure as much as we do success. It is difficult to draw much satisfaction from faithfulness in the absence of measurable success. Perfectionism and the inability to delegate authority and share the ministry with parishioners also lead to great fatigue. There is a need for a realistic theology of sinfulness. Such a theology would not only acknowledge the imperfection and sinfulness of pastors as well as those they serve but also equip ministers with the ability to accept themselves and their own inadequacies, rather than let those shortcomings destroy the spirit.

There is also the irregularity of the work schedule. There is no nine-to-five quality about urban ministry. Tasks are almost never as brief as they are expected to be. What looks as if it should take a half hour often stretches into a half day—especially when it includes confronting a bureaucratic system. Things to which the minister looks forward, whether it is time with family or watching a ballgame, get cancelled never to be made up. Then there is the conflict emanating out of confrontation with power structures. Finally, there is violence. The regular confrontation with and awareness of violence is also fatiguing. Violence, either potential or actual, against ourselves or a friend, breeds anger and fear. It is quietly draining.

Antidotes to Burnout. People who become involved in urban ministry need to know what they are getting into. Middle-class seminaries are not equipped to prepare a person for the crucible that is urban ministry. Internships, apprenticeships, and other forms of experiential education are critically important for readying the future urban minister.

Three major urban ministry figures—Bud Ipema, Bill Leslie, and Ray Bakke—convened to discuss ways to prevent burnout. Four main points emerged.

The first emphasizes *having a theology that keeps one in the city.* During the 1960s there was a host of churches and church-undergirded programs in poverty areas of major cities. Many were radical and spectacular in style; others were more conventional. Most of them were theologically liberal. By the mid-1970s, almost all were gone. These efforts were begun with rapid starts and high hopes. However, when those who initiated them found the going extraordinarily tough, the city political systems unbending, the problems too complex, and the publicity and glamour gone, the programs blew away. What was absent was a clear-cut theology that ordained faithfulness in serving the interests of the city regardless of success or politics.

Knowledge of the problems, compassion for the people, and a desire for challenge are not sufficient. These elements were present in the hundreds and perhaps thousands who burned out. Moreover, it is easy to rationalize leaving by pointing at different and more soluble problems, other groups in need of ministry, and alternative challenges to confront. However, those who feel called by a theological commitment to urban service become aware that they are where they should be, and therefore they are succeeding no matter what the external signs of effectiveness may be.

Urban ministry can be an extremely lonely and unrewarding task, as mentioned previously. Hence, the second point of *having a sense of community and support* is vital. Dr. Gilbert James of Asbury Theological Seminary, a sociologist who dedicated much of his adult professional life to urban ministry, was asked what bit of advice he would give to aspiring urban pastors. He responded by saying, "Find someone you can track with. You are going to need it." This is sage counsel, according to many other enduring pastors.

There is a need for support and reinforcement from others who genuinely understand the nature of the inner-city mission. In Chicago several people who do various forms of Christian urban work get together one Monday each month for a retreat held out of town. This day of fellowship, sharing, and refreshment has become a necessary monthly oasis for many of them. No longer do they feel lonely and unappreciated. There is a place to share trophies and troubles and to exchange ideas, counsel, sympathy, and support.

When the energy fire burns low, there is a special need for support. The intimacy of a support group not only provides a safe haven for blowing off steam and letting out frustration and disappointment, but it is also an excellent reality check for denial or rationalization. Ministers need ministering too, and such relationships provide it.

A third factor involves *taking time for individual development.* It is important that the pastor find other activities to provide a sense of progress, satisfaction, and accomplishment. These may be writing, teaching seminary courses, or pursuing a doctoral degree. Most people have a favorite avocation or second career they would like to pursue. Pastors are no different, and they should pursue them, for these second interests serve as necessary pit stops. One pastor spoke of his "toys," referring to his proclivity to teach courses in various seminaries, give speeches, and start new programs. Acknowledging that he is probably criticized for spreading himself a bit thin because of them, he stated that he would never have been able to make urban ministry a career without these very constructive diversions.

A pastor pointed out that just after he received his PhD in theology, he nearly burned out. He had expected to be filled with energy once the dissertation was over and he was free to pursue his parish charges unfettered, but the opposite occurred. He needed other areas of refreshment.

The reason why these diversions are so important in urban ministry is that so much of the work is cyclical. It is the same set of problems over and over. A pastor has continually to be orienting new members to the mission of the church. Such orientation can be tedious repetition. Sunday after Sunday, poverty case after poverty case, and staff change after staff change—a pastor feels much as Christ must have felt with the multitudes of needy crowding in on him. Christ needed to push out into the lake to get his bearings.

Individual development includes spiritual nourishment. Pastors are so often out doing and caring that they never have enough time to pray and meditate. They provide spiritual food and water regularly but fail to replenish their pantry or dig new wells. The result is a barrenness and an inability to minister. Setting aside a day each month or some time each week to work with a spiritual mentor can be time very well spent. One pastor has gone regularly to another pastor for "feeding" and has found that it has revitalized his power to minister.

Leslie believed a key to individual development is to keep uppermost that the primary purpose of life is to seek God's kingdom and will. It is not to horde money, get the most with the least effort, or be concerned with what others may think. Also, there needs to be personal communication with God. Leslie paraphrased a former colleague of his who said that if the devil can beat you in having a daily meditation time, he can beat you at everything else.

The fourth factor involves *getting surcease from the city*. The heat and concrete, the pains and the problems, the noises and the nuisances, and the pace and the pressure of the city have a wearing effect. Getting away from the plastic and glass to areas that are grassy and cool is a necessary change of pace. Time for reflection and rest can reenergize a person who takes a week, or a weekend, or even a day off on a regular basis.

Rewards. Despite all the problems and challenges involved in urban ministry, there are real rewards. One, of course, is that the ministry is taking place where needs are particularly acute. Simply being faithful to the call is a triumph. Any victory—through either a service or stewardship ministry—merits celebration, for it is likely that the job would not have been done without the church's involvement.

Living in the city itself is invigorating. Its diversity, stimulation, and opportunities are endless. Although the city may indeed contain the worst elements of life, it also has the best. From culture and the arts to sports and excitement, the city is the place.

For family members, the city can be liberating. The family of an urban minister is not living in a gossip-laden goldfish bowl. There are a myriad of opportunities for all family members to live their own lives and pursue personal goals and development. There are many free activities for family entertainment.

Living in the city also has economic advantages. Only one car is needed because urban mass transit is available. Keeping up appearances is less of an issue. Suburban pastors often live in tract homes and thus their children feel enormous peer pressure to dress well and have certain possessions. Individuality and diversity are much greater in the city, taking some economic and social burdens off the family. The city also abounds with rummage and garage sales, resale shops, and flea markets, further reducing economic stress.

Finally, for the urban church worker a host of professional opportunities abounds in the city—seminaries and graduate schools nearby, the finest libraries for research, and conferences pertaining to urban ministry. There are many other churches and church staffs for forming relationships and giving mutual support.

Nonetheless, it is important that those entering urban ministry zealously work to guard personal sanity. This means unflinchingly holding on to time off, hobbies, and family time, so that energy levels remain high and enthusiasm for the challenge does not abate. Urban ministry is servanthood personified. Service means giving. If workers do not minister to themselves, they may soon be so burned out that there will be nothing to give, no service to render. Soon the servant will be gone. The model of Christ is best here. His ministry was paced. It was spiced with social times, prayer alone, and person-to-person ministry. As such, it is the model of ministry and servanthood.

NEW DIRECTIONS IN URBAN MINISTRY **10**

In the original edition of this book, *Urban Ministry*, the chapters presented many practical models that attempted to address urban concerns. Many of those models were pilot efforts of various effect; some are currently obsolete. Moreover, ICUIS, the clearinghouse that enabled readers to get details on many of the models, no longer exists. In fact, there is no longer any national, central repository of urban ministry to which the reader can go for contemporary urban ministry models.

In the 1970s and '80s, most models were discrete attempts at addressing a single matter in an impoverished area. Many of them have been cited in these pages because they can still be highly effective. Others, however, including some currently in existence, are simply not replicable because they are rooted in a very specific context. Models do not abound. Most major denominations have information available on urban ministry efforts within them. Moreover, national organizations such as SCUPE in Chicago are on the cutting edge of what is taking place throughout the nation. Along with the Internet, there is much information available.

More important, however, is that models of today tend to be holistic. The 1970s used the term *whole person*. Though now a dated term, it needs to be trotted out once again with the understanding that *person* includes the individual and communal dimensions. The key to holistic or whole-person models is that they do not segment the needs of community members. The entire spectrum—economic issues, health care, employment, education, recreation, political advocacy, and, of course, spiritual concerns—is addressed.

Before reviewing some of the major contemporary models, however, we need to look at transformation.

TRANSFORMATION AS URBAN MINISTRY

Tim Larkin, an urban ministry expert who has done and observed urban ministry throughout the United States, points out that successful urban ministry is best started from the inside out. It needs to grow out of the needs of the people with whom the church deals, rather than becoming the center of the church's identity in the expectation that it will draw people to the church.

"When I was in Chicago's Uptown," he explains, "I ran into a number of people through our church who had addiction issues. I went out and got my C.A.C. (Certified Addictions Counselor) degree, rented a floor in a S.R.O (Single Room Occupant) across the street, and developed an addictions ministry."

For Larkin and many others, the driving force for successful urban ministry is personal transformation. The goal of the church is health—spiritual, mental, physical, relational, and social. The primary goal of the church is spiritual. What sets the church apart from a social service agency is not funding or staffing but that it is God's institution. It is from being ordained by God as his institution that it gains its power. Therefore its divine mission, reaching souls and speaking into the inner life of the individual, has to remain foremost. From there a direction develops that leads to effective temporal ministry.

Failure to move from the inside out is one of the biggest problems with contemporary urban ministry. "If I am involved in a church and my first step is to build a community organization or an economic development structure, it runs the risk of not having life," says Larkin. "If I work with several people who come to the church in finding them jobs, I can build off that and work toward a job-skills or employment ministry."

Larkin has put this into practice in his counseling ministry. People have come to his churches with major, untreated emotional disabilities, sexual addictions, and family breakdowns. Early on, using his health model, he plied his skills as a psychotherapist in both an urban and Christian context to help people find healthier ways to function. These same people—empowered spiritually and personally—then began to serve in the church's ministries, providing an energy and authenticity to them.

Bill Leslie constantly spoke of a whole-person theology. "The body without the soul is a corpse," he would say, "and the soul without the body is a ghost." Sound urban ministry, then, needed to be both body and soul—whole person. For Leslie, however, the key to the success of an urban church lay in its spiritual commitment. As such, he addressed the inside-out issue.

"When I came to this community (Chicago's Cabrini-Green public housing projects), there were a lot of liberals in here believing they could usher in the kingdom of God in the city."

Observing that most of them are gone, Leslie said,

"They just didn't have the toughness to stay at it—they burned out. [The spiritually centered] have resources the others don't have. One is the pietistic relationship with Christ, and another is the belief in the filling of the Holy Spirit. In short, you have a theology that can keep you there. In addition, you develop a supportive community that cares for you, loves you, and helps patch things together."

Without divine energy, a genuine call of God to reach his people in the city, the church merely apes—often unsuccessfully—the secular, social service model. Worse, when the model is an outside-in structure, it often has a professional staff quality to it, reinforcing the provider-client (or patient) status differential discussed earlier. When the model is inside-out, it becomes a natural outgrowth of the church's whole-person focus.

The inside-out issue is both spiritually sound and practically based. Its spiritual soundness resides in a theology that has an eternal dimension, one that sees humankind as spiritual beings in need of the bread and water of life. An elementary understanding of the New Testament will conclude that the central focus of the gospel is spiritual transformation of the soul—the inner life. To subordinate the church's spiritual mission to a secondary status is for the church to leave its "first love" (Rev. 2:4). We are interested in changed lives from the inside out. Moreover, from both a spiritual and practical standpoint, it gains its energy and endurance from God rather than from merely human, professional effort. From an almost sheerly practical stance, it gets much of its human capital from the people whose lives have been reconditioned spiritually.

BRIDGE CHURCH

The transformation model has its roots in the *bridge church*. A bridge church is one that accepts whoever comes through its doors wherever they are—spiritually and personally—and then offers these people a bridge from where they are to a living relationship with Christ. The fundamental difference between a bridge church and many other evangelical churches is that the bridge church puts absolutely no pressure on its people to move forward spiritually. They move at their own speed or, better, at the speed at which God takes them. This is biblically sound. Late in Christ's ministry, he asked the disciples who they thought he was. Only Peter proclaimed Jesus the Christ. After his resurrection, the disciples disbelieved reports of Jesus being alive until he appeared to them in Jerusalem. Christ allowed his followers to move toward him at their own speed, rather than manipulate them or demand that they accelerate their spiritual growth.

The reason the bridge concept is so critical to the success of the urban church is that people make spiritual and personal decisions of which they are aware and for which they take responsibility. Pressuring church attenders to receive Christ now, or to become baptized, or to join the church's official membership may, in the short term, give the church more impressive numbers in these categories, but it does so at the risk of confusion. Many of these people will not understand their decisions. This is the tragedy of so many Christian youth. Reared in Christian homes, many feel pressured into professing their faith in their teens and joining the church officially by well-meaning parents or pastors. This often produces disabled Christians—those who do not have a genuine spiritual experience undergirding their "commitment," but instead have a conflicted life in the church marked by less-than-enthusiastic involvement or by a participation driven by the hope that genuine commitment will follow.

In this context, then, the bridge church sees its congregation as consisting of three distinct groups. There are the occasional attenders, those that come to the church once or twice a month. The second group is the regular attenders. As the term implies, these people are there almost every week. The third, and smallest, group is the members. In other words, there are always more people—whether that number is 10, 30, 50, or 5,000—attending the church than there are members.

This is exactly the reverse of most mainline churches. In the bridge church, the line of accountability is drawn at membership. Membership implies not merely a vertical commitment to Christ but a horizontal commitment to the church itself, its theology, mission, and ministries. No pressure is put on any nonmember in terms of lifestyle or commitment. Each person walks across the spiritual bridge as his or her spiritual transformation takes hold. The result is a group of truly committed people. Some, of course, never move beyond occasional attendance. Others stop at regular attendance. Many, however, move all the way to full commitment.

Several points need to be added. The bridge church sees spiritual growth and commitment as being more often a process rather than an event. For every person who has a Paul-like conversion experience, there are many others who, like the disciples, come to Christ in stages. For some, serving in a church's ministry can accelerate their growth. Therefore, where appropriate, the bridge church will encourage its people to use their gifts in the church, although they may not yet be ready for membership. Also, over time people are drawn to the church through its ministries. Whether it is counseling, tutoring, legal aid, employment assistance, or housing, the urban bridge church models the unconditional love of Christ by serving whomever God brings.

The transformational model, then, is not a forced one. It is not a corporate, urban-planning entity, but rather one that allows God to direct the church toward the types of ministry he is calling it to do.

SOCIOLOGICAL GROUNDING

A problem with much contemporary urban ministry is that it lacks solid sociological grounding. It fails to use the academic tools of analysis employed in urban sociology when putting together ministry models. Too often, one new endeavor is launched here and another there without careful thought and analysis. These then pass as "models" and are even promoted as new waves in urban ministry. Many of them fail miserably, largely because they were not well thought through from the outset. "The evangelical ethos," writes Mark Noll in *The Scandal of the Evangelical Mind*, "is activistic, populist, pragmatic, and utilitarian. It allows little space for broader or deeper intellectual effort because it is dominated by the urgencies of the moment."[1]

Urban church workers need to become conversant with basic sociological realities once they begin to move in a more temporal direction. Larkin, for example, is a PhD candidate in sociology at this writing. A strong evangelical committed to the transformational model, Larkin sought his degree largely because he saw too much money and human capital wasted on ineffective efforts at whole-person ministry.

There are so many ways in which a well-meaning effort at urban ministry can pay the price of failing to do the front-end analysis. For example, a church can raise money and build staff in an effort to plant a ministry in a low-income area adjacent to the church, only to have a wave of regentrification (the movement of affluent people and businesses back into an urban area) wipe out the very existence of the poverty community the church is attempting to serve. That is now the case in Chicago's Cabrini-Green. The community, less than a mile from the super-rich along the lakefront, once had in excess of 18,000 residents. Over the years, one building after another was emptied and then razed; currently the regentrifying redevelopment in urban Chicago is threatening to render the entire community extinct. Fortunately, LaSalle Street Church saw that coming. In the 1970s the church commissioned a task force (of which I was a member) to study the future of Cabrini-Green. Though we were unable to project the long-term prospects for the community with certainty, owing to the vagaries of city politics, we were able to proceed with church planning armed with the likely options for the church's service area.

"There are three organizing principles in the sociology of contemporary society," Larkin explains, "gender, race, and class. In other words, our society is organized or structured around these principles." The problem with much urban ministry, according to Larkin, is that too many of its practitioners do not understand these principles, particularly race and class. "Some models aimed at addressing racism are really addressing class differences and don't realize it." Race and class, although overlapping, are distinct entities. Racism exists at every class level in a society with our history. Moreover, within and across racial groups, class differentials are becoming more distinct, and the evident lack of community is more due to class than racial differences.

"The goal is for the church to become the fourth organizing principle," says Larkin. He referred to a funeral held at a church in Chicago. The deceased was a feisty, yet loving, 83-year-old African-American woman named Earlene Blake. The white speaker unselfconsciously spoke of the woman's life as a black person in segregated America. "She grew up in the South," he said forcefully to a predominantly African-American assembly, "and saw firsthand water fountains, restrooms, and schools labeled White and Colored. She knew what it meant to be unwelcome in restaurants, hotels, and yes, even churches. Yet in her closing years, she hung a picture of the American flag on the door of her apartment with the words God Bless America accompanying it. The only way she could do something like that, the only way she could escape the bitterness that would be so natural was to claim the divine energy of forgiveness."

"The speaker," said Larkin, "by taking on race, was claiming the church as the fourth organizing principle. He was saying the message of the church trumps race."

In sum, the transformational model begins with the bridge church concept in which transformation is the goal. This gives rise to a larger, whole-person focus on health—mental, physical, and social. Out of this comes the call for church-specific ministries grounded in sociologically sound analysis. Again, in this model, the ministries are an outgrowth of the transformational mission of the church. They are not conceived as entities with a life of their own outside or parallel to the church. When the latter occurs, the ministries take on a secular ring, in some cases competing with the church's central purpose. They also run the risk of becoming just another professional, top-down structure. "All too often," Leslie often remarked, "the church uses the professional athletic model, in which the members pay their dues in the collection plate and then cheer or boo the pastor or pastoral team's performance. The pastor's purpose is to equip the believers to do the Lord's work" (2 Tim. 3:17).

This does not mean that community organization or economic development will not emerge. It certainly doesn't mean that the urban pastor at the small church cannot gain valuable knowledge by learning about the prevailing organizational and developmental models. It does mean that the ministries are birthed by a transformational goal emanating from the needs of the people God places before the urban church worker.

Figure 3. Transformational Model

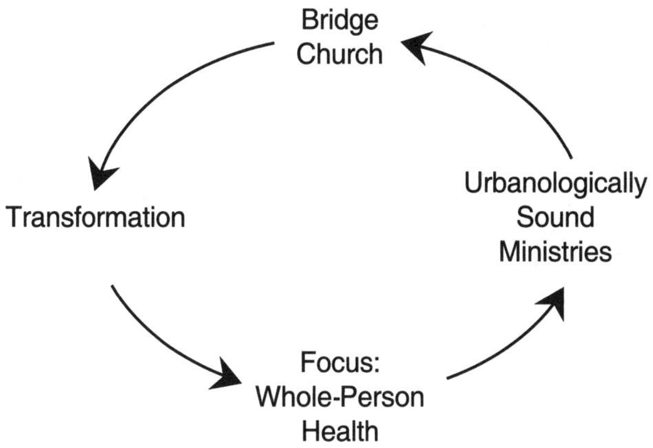

Bridge Church

Transformation

Urbanologically Sound Ministries

Focus: Whole-Person Health

COMMUNITY DEVELOPMENT MODELS

Below, three major models are reviewed briefly. Although often termed CEDs (community economic development models), they do more than develop a community's economy. In any case, any urban church worker can go to these and find hosts of ideas concerning everything from organization to implementation.

Dudley Street Neighborhood Initiative

One of the most ambitious models was developed in Boston. Called the Dudley Street Neighborhood Initiative (DSNI), this church-based community redevelopment effort transformed what was once a largely minority, heavily poor community of about 25,000 residents into a healthier model of neighborhood life.

In the 1970s nearly 60 percent of the housing stock required expensive repair that absentee landlords were unwilling to make. Rents were picked up in buildings that were under code and on which taxes had not been paid. The city had practiced a disinvestments policy by leaving large chunks of vacant land undeveloped and turning its attention away from the landlord abuse. Eventually, 177 acres of land were vacant. Soon the area became a wasteland for trash dumping, much by contractors. The quality of life of the residents declined as rats multiplied and parks and playgrounds deteriorated.[2]

Led in part by Paul Bothwell from an evangelical Baptist church, a group of residents began meeting to address immediate concerns, including a more responsive fire department and better housing. Community boundaries were determined, and the group attempted to speak with the city officials about improving life in the Dudley Street area. They were all but scoffed at and, thinking the group was focused on "gardening and stuff," were directed to the United States Department of Agriculture. Amazingly, the official from the USDA had a vision for community revitalization. He provided some funds and helped the group plan. After two years of work and community meetings, Bothwell's group of about twelve watched the city's stance move from neglect and disinvestments to resistance. The city, rejecting outright any partnership with what would be called the DSNI, all but said, "That neighborhood doesn't matter to us. What's going on there doesn't matter."[3]

Further community meetings were organized and the group expanded as representatives of disparate citizen and church groups started getting involved. From there, the organization gained funding from the Riley Foundation, and the DSNI took flight. From these humble beginnings, the DSNI developed a holistic, urban-village concept, one that encompassed all facets of community life for all resident groups, without driving out the current residents as a consequence of regentrification. The key was organization. "People say, 'I'm of the community, I'm for the community' all the time," said city official Lisa Chapnick. The DSNI people, however, were different. My experience of DSNI was that it was genuine, that this was really a community effort and that the leadership . . . were as committed to the process as they were to the product." With only about four hundred members at the time, the numbers were not the driving force. "No," said Chapnick, "it was the fact that the focus was organizing around community development, around . . . getting that circle bigger and bigger and bigger."[4]

No egos seem involved. The issue was not who was the leader but rather forging a shared vision among the community residents and its organization. A major key to the success of the DSNI was that it saw redevelopment in holistic terms. More than bricks and mortar, it included human services, economic development, and environmental dimensions ("greening" and an end to lead poisoning, for example). Moreover, DSNI did not neglect neighborhood youth. Employing focus groups of twelve- to fourteen-year-olds, among other endeavors, the organization identified problems and solutions for the community youth. In the spirit of successful community organization, the enterprise included heavy youth involvement, which helped turn the collective attitude of the community's children in a more optimistic direction and resulted in youth making an absolutely necessary and powerful contribution to the turnaround of the Dudley Street Community.

The DSNI is an example of how a well-thought-out plan became a reality. This plan, however, began with a dream on the part of church-based people. It moved from individual to community-based models; it used organization and advocacy; it took a holistic, even global perspective (given the multiethnic nature of the community, one that faced a globalistic force of regentrification through city intervention); and it employed models that emphasized small business and entrepreneurship, local human capital, and civil living for its current residents.

New Song Community Church

Mark R. Gornik was the pastor of the New Song Community Church in the Sandtown Community of Baltimore, Maryland.[5] Like many urban communities, Sandtown represents the "other Baltimore," the "second city" that has not benefited from urban redevelopment or regentrification. As with many other low-income African American urban communities, about the only aspect of the new global economy that seems to have affected Sandtown has been the growth of the penal system.

Sandtown had been systematically excluded from urban redevelopment plans and left to lie fallow and in a state of permanent disrepair with a permanent underclass. Without a vision, this would have been the fate of Sandtown.

Based on biblical and theological portrayals of the power of justice and the significance of cities in the Bible, especially those passages that speak to issues of urban space, Gornik went to work. He noted that Jeremiah envisioned a city where peace could happen even for exiles and that Nehemiah and Isaiah envisioned the rebuilding of city walls and city streets for residents upon their return.

Gornik was not interested in replicating a social-service urban-ministry model. Instead, he moved toward community revitalization due to efforts of community organizing, faith-based community economic development, and the empowerment of the people living in Sandtown. According to Gornik, community development is not "the renewal of place apart from people, but [is] the celebration of their gifts and callings in the context of the social and material world."[6] In 1992, former President Jimmy Carter helped to initiate the development of housing through the Habitat for Humanity program. The church built ten homes the first year, twenty the next, and completed the goal of developing one hundred homes for low-income people by 1997. Four years later, in 2001, a second set of one hundred homes were built. New Song was about the task of rebuilding ruins, raising up age-old foundations, repairing broken walls, and restoring streets with dwellings, as stated in the book of Isaiah (58:12).

One of the key issues in the community was job creation and job preparation. New Song Church started a program called EDEN (Economic Development Employment Network) that trained and located employment for six hundred Sandtown residents. Education was also a great need in the community. So, the New Song Community Learning Center was begun for preschoolers and the New Song Academy was initiated for middle school students. Many local residents were teachers and health care providers, so these developments also provided employment opportunities.

In short, New Song is the story of holistic community development based on the needs and assets of the residents of the community. For Gornik, a key biblical strategy found in the book of Jeremiah was the ownership and development of land (Jeremiah 32:37–41). There, as a sign of hope for the future of the city, Jeremiah purchased vacant land in the heart of an abandoned city. In this respect, peace is not an abstract biblical concept. It means to "pitch your tent" and settle down in the city. It means to relocate there with your heart and also with your talents and economic resources. The peace of the city is hard work, and it happens when a community of people work together to secure not just the security of a place but also an economically sustainable future as well.

New Song provides a practical formula for community development and empowerment based on a contemporary biblical theology of justice for the city, while also employing contemporary strategies of community organization and asset-based community economic development.

Chalmers Center

The Chalmers Center for Economic Development is a research and educational arm of Covenant College in Lookout Mountain, Georgia.[7] The center has both a practical and educational twist. It assists college students, pastors, missionaries, churches, and ministries in bringing about spiritual and economic transformation to the poor in a holistic fashion. In addition to its website, Chalmers publishes a large, extremely helpful and informative newsletter entitled *Mandate*, ably edited by Brian Fikkert.

Figure 4

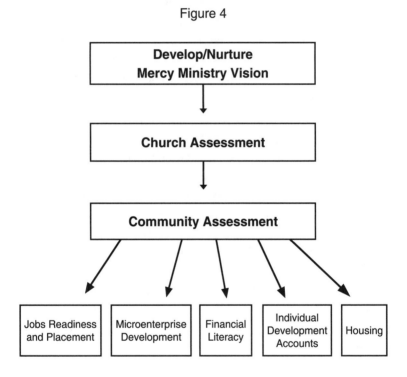

Chalmers believes that "loving the poor involves moving beyond perpetually giving handouts into ministries that restore the poor to being what God created them to be: productive human beings who are able to support themselves through their own work."[8] Figure 4 shows a flowchart to guide churches in reaching that aim.[9]

The top three boxes in the flowchart represent a vision and commitment of the church to holistic ministry.[10] According to Ron Sider, Heidi Rolland-Unruh, and Phil Olson, holistic ministry derives from balancing the nurture of the church members with outreach, developing a commitment to and love for the community, having a holistic theology and vision integrated into the church, and equipping leaders and members to action from a base of loving, healthy relationships.[11]

Olson sees the church going through three stages.[12] The first involves building a leadership team that leads the congregation through the steps of assessment of the church and the community. The second is an action stage in which plans are made, resources identified, and ministries established. The final stage involves consistent feedback and evaluation that enable ministries to be adjusted and the vision sustained. Olson warns that both a vision and a leadership team are necessary. Vision without leadership is aimless, and leadership without vision keeps the focus inward.

Once a church has worked through the top three boxes effectively, a CED becomes a possibility. The five parallel boxes at the base of the figure indicate five different ministries that can be developed.[13] The first box focuses on job training and placement, and the second teaches people how to be entrepreneurial and start their own businesses. This is a difficult but important step.[14]

Financial Literacy teaches effective money management. This is vital. An African-American educator and former colleague once told me that if the rich gave all their money to the poor, within a few years they would have it all back because of the difference between the groups in their understanding of money. Although perhaps an exaggeration, he makes an important point. Recent public policy has been aimed at increasing income, but not asset accumulation. As such, the next box moves from money management to the development of wealth.[15] The final box is concerned with the always important issue of housing development.

• • •

These are but three community developmental models. There are the previously discussed Hope for Chattanooga, Chicago's Bethel New Life, and The Resurrection Project, in addition to a growing number of ministries that have drawn from faith-based government funding.

If you have seen one church, you have seen one church. In other words, despite having certain general characteristics in common, churches and communities are unique. As creations of God they are expected to be. The challenge to the urban church is to use its unique gifts to build God's kingdom in the city.

NOTES

CHAPTER 1: URBAN MINISTRY—BIBLICAL MANDATE

1. Among the population references in this chapter are Ralph J. Alig, Jeffrey D. Kline, and Mark Lichtenstein, "Ubanization on the U.S. Landscape: Looking Ahead in the 21st Century <www.elsevier.com>; Martin P. Brockerhoff, "An Urbanizing World," introduction, *Population Bulletin* 55, no. 3 (September 2000); "United States of America 2004, Top Cities" <www.world-gazetteer.com>.

2. Lewis Mumford, *The City in History* (New York: Harcourt, Brace, and World, 1961), 573.

3. Clinton E. Stockwell, "Living in a Global City: Pedagogical Reflections from Sociological Study and Teaching" (Paper for the Association for Christians Teaching Sociology annual conference, June 12–15, 2003, Dallas, TX), 12.

4. Ibid., 2.

5. David O. Moberg, *Inasmuch* (Grand Rapids: William B. Eerdmans, 1965), 51, 75.

6. John Perkins, "Urban Church/Urban Poor," in *Metro-Ministry,* ed. David Frenchak and Sharrel Keyes (Elgin, IL: David C. Cook, 1979), 45. The *Metro-Ministry* book is an excellent compilation of timeless urban ministry insights. Out of print, it is a publication of SCUPE (Seminary Consortium for Urban Pastoral Education), 202 N. Michigan Avenue, Suite 502, Chicago, IL 60601; (312) 726-1200; <www.scupe.com>.

7. Roger S. Greenway, *Calling Our Cities to Christ* (Nutley, N.J.: Presbyterian and Reformed, 1973), 27.

8. Raymond Bakke is a major figure in urban ministry. He founded an urban ministry consulting organization, International Urban Associates, and co-founded SCUPE. His books include *The Urban Christian* and *A Theology as Big as the City.*

9. Clinton E. Stockwell, "The Church and Justice in Crisis: The Social Reality of the Church and its Role of Proclaiming Justice," in *The Urban Face of*

Mission: Ministering the Gospel in a Diverse and Changing World, eds. Harvey M. Conn, Manuel Ortiz, and Susan S. Baker (Phillipsburg, New Jersey: P & R Publishing, 2002), 163.

10. Roger S. Greenway, *Apostles to the City* (Grand Rapids: Baker, 1978), 15–96.

11. Bill Leslie, "God Loves the Inner City," *Christian Life* (July 1973), 27.

12. See Roland Allen, *Missionary Methods: St. Paul or Ours* (Chicago: Moody Press, 1959).

13. Stockwell, "The Church and Justice in Crisis," 169–170.

14. Shirley Jackson Case, *The Social Origins of Christianity* (Chicago: University of Chicago Press, 1923) and *The Social Triumph of the Ancient Church* (New York: Harper and Row, 1933).

15. Stockwell, "The Church and Justice in Crisis," 171–172.

16. Ibid. For additional insights, see Keith F. Nickle, *The Collection: A Study in Paul's Strategy. Studies in Biblical Theology*, 48 (Naperville, IL: Alec R. Allenson, Inc., 1966).

17. Stockwell, "The Church and Justice in Crisis," 163.

18. Ronald J. Sider, *Rich Christians in an Age of Hunger* (Downers Grove, IL.: InterVarsity, 1977), 85. Sider's book is a classic.

19. Paul S. Rees, "The 'Right to Food' Muddle," *WorldVision* (April 1976): 23.

20. Stockwell, "The Church and Justice in Crisis," 159.

21. Walter Brueggemann, *The Prophetic Imagination* (Philadelphia: Fortress Press, 1978), 88.

22. Stockwell, "The Church and Justice in Crisis," 161.

23. Sider, *Rich Christians*, 78–79.

24. Clark H. Pinnock, "An Evangelical Theology of Human Liberation," *Sojourners* (February 1976).

25. Harvie M. Conn, "Christ and the City: Biblical Themes for Building Urban Theology Models," in *Discipling the City*, ed. Roger S. Greenway(Grand Rapids, MI: Baker, 1979), 252.

26. Frank E. Gaebelein, "Challenging Christians to the Simple Life," *Christianity Today* 21 (September 1979): 24–25.

27. Sider, *Rich Christians*, 68.

28. "The Mission of the Church," early position paper of LaSalle Street Church, Chicago, IL.

29. Leslie, "God Loves the Inner City," 33.

30. Howard Rice, "Toward an Urban Strategy," *Cities* (Knoxville July 1981): 1–9.

31. "Mission of the Church."

32. Ibid.

33. Rene Bideaux, "Faith and Obedience for Missional Congregations," *Justice Ministries* 15–16 (Winter–Spring 1982): 11.

34. Abraham Kuyper, quoted in *The Problem of Poverty*, ed. James W. Skillen (Grand Rapids, MI: Baker Book House, 1991), 77.

35. Lowell Livezey, lecture at the Chicago Metropolitan Center, March, 2000. Excellent discussions of social capital can be found in James S. Coleman, "Social Capital in the Creation of Human Capital, *American Journal of Sociology* 94, (1988): S95-S119; Robert D. Putnam, "Bowling Alone: America's Declining Social Capital," *Journal of Democracy* 6 (January 1995): 65–76.

36. Stockwell, "The Church and Justice in Crisis," 172.

37. C. Wright Mills, *The Sociological Imagination* (New York: Grove Press, 1959), 8.

38. Stockwell, "The Church and Justice in Crisis," 176.

39. Abraham Kuyper, *The Problem of Poverty*, 51.

40. Stockwell, "The Church and Justice in Crisis," 168.

41. Mark R. Gornik, *To Live in Peace: Biblical Faith and the Changing Inner City* (Grand Rapids, MI: William B. Eerdmans, 2002), 12–13

42. Vincent P. Quayle, "The Housing Ministry in Baltimore," *New Catholic World* (May–June 1982): 102.

43. Dennis E. Shoemaker, "The Church in the City: A Strategy for Hope," *The Other Side* (October 1978): 26–37.

44. James Hefley and Marti Hefley, *The Church That Takes on Trouble* (Elgin, IL: David C. Cook, 1976), 241–42. This book chronicles the story of Bill Leslie's famous LaSalle Street Church in Chicago.

CHAPTER 2: THE GLOBAL CITY AND THE INNER CITY

1. Mary Schmich, "Pastor Keeps Big Dream Alive," *Chicago Tribune*, July 7, 2004.

2. Gornik, *To Live in Peace*, xii-xiii, xvi, 35–36.

3. Anthony Campolo, "The Sociological Nature of the Urban Church," in *Metro-Ministry,* 37.

4. Michael Harrington, *The Other America* (New York: Macmillan, 1962).

5. F. K. Pious Jr., "Three Reasons for Urban Decline," *Chicago Tribune*, September 11, 1982.

6. Ibid.

7. Schmich, "Future Closes in on Cabrini," *Chicago Tribune*, July 4, 2004.

8. Schmich, "Key Developer Also Trying to Rebuild Lives," *Chicago Tribune*, July 8, 2004.

9. Schmich, "Pastor Keeps Big Dream Alive."

10. Schmich, "Dreams Supersede Danger," *Chicago Tribune*, July 6, 2004.

11. Schmich, "Key Developer."

12. Schmich, "Buildings Stand Because a Leader Stood Her Ground," *Chicago Tribune*, July 9, 2004.

13. Ed Marciniak (orientation address, Seminary Consortium for Urban Pastoral Education orientation), Latino Seminario, Chicago, IL, September 23, 1978; Marciniak, *Reviving an Inner City Community* (Chicago: Center for Research in Urban Government, 1977).

14. John B. Calhoun, "Population Density and Social Pathology," *Scientific American* (1962), quoted in *Population, Evolution, and Birth Control*, comp. Garrett Hardin, 2nd ed. (San Francisco: Freeman, 1969), 101–105.

15. Stanley Hallett, "Strategies for Urban Reconstruction," in *Metro-Ministry*, 199.

16. <www.hope4.org/harambeehousing.htm>.

17. Hallett, "Strategies for Urban Reconstruction," 200–201.

18. Schmich, "Dreams Supersede Danger."

19. Dudley, "Churches in Changing Communities," in *Metro-Ministry*, 83–89.

20. S.A. Livingston and C.S. Stoll, "The Inner-city Housing Game," from *Simulation Games: An Introduction for the Social Studies Teacher* (New York: The Free Press, 1973), 40–43.

21. Revised and updated from seminar address by Alderman Richard Mell, North Park Theological Seminary, Latino Seminario, Chicago, IL, June 15, 1977.

22. Mark Gornik and Allan Tibbels, "Using Housing Ministry to Sing a New Song," *Mandate*, ed. Brian Fikkert (Lookout Mountain, GA: Chalmers Center for Economic Development, Covenant College, Spring, 2004).

23. <www.habitat.org>.

24. <www.iccf.org>.

25. <www.hope4.org/harambeehousing.htm>.

26. Gornik and Tibbels, "Using Housing Ministry to Sing a New Song."

27. Ibid.

28. There are a variety of websites that feature Bethel New Life; TRP can be found at <www.resurrectionproject.org>.

29. Presentation at the Chicago Metropolitan Center, March 10, 2000.

30. William Ipema, "Ministry Resources in Community Systems," in *Metro-Ministry,* 213–215.

31. "The Cleveland Covenant Concept (Papers)" (Cleveland Heights: Cleveland Covenant, 1979, 1980).

32. Gornik, *To Live in Peace,* 11.

CHAPTER 3: URBAN STRATIFICATION AND THE NEIGHBORHOOD CHURCH

1. Ernest W. Burgess, "The Growth of the City: An Introduction to a Research Project," *Publications of the American Sociological Society* 18 (1924), cited in Robert E. Park, Ernest W. Burgess, and Roderick McKenzie, eds., *The City* (Chicago: University of Chicago Press, 1967), 47–62.

2. Kingsley Davis and Wilbert E. Moore, "Some Principles of Stratification," *American Sociological Review* 10 (1945): 242–49.

3. <www.delmar.edu>.

4. Robert J. Havighurst and Bernice L. Neugarten, *Society and Education* (Boston: Allyn and Bacon, 1967), 12.

5. Two of the finest sources here are two books by Saskia Sassen. *The Global City: New York, London, Tokyo* (Princeton, NJ: Princeton University Press, 1991); *Globalization and Its Discontents: Essays on the New Mobility of People and Money* (New York: Free Press, 1998).

6. Adapted from Kurt B. Mayer and Walter Buckley, *Class and Society* (1970), 51–55, cited in David Claerbaut, *Social Problems,* pt. 1 (Scottsdale, AZ: Christian Academic Publications, 1976), 53.

7. Rachelle B. Warren and Donald I. Warren, *The Neighborhood Organizer's Handbook* (Notre Dame, IN: University of Notre Dame Press, 1977), 94–112.

8. Adapted from Ed Marciniak, *Reversing Urban Decline: The Winthrop-Kenmore Corridor in the Edgewater and Uptown Communities of Chicago* (Washington DC: National Center for Urban Affairs).

9. Saul David Alinsky, *Rules for Radicals* (New York: Random House, 1971), 52. Saul Alinsky one of the most famous and creative community organizers in the history of this country.

10. William Stringfellow, "Traits of the Principalities," in *A Keeper of the Word: Selected Writings of William Stringfellow,* ed. Bill Wylie Kellerman (Grand Rapids, MI: William B. Eerdmans, 1994), 205.

11. Michael Lerner, *The Politics of Meaning* (Menlo Park, CA: Addison-Wesley, 1996), 52ff.

12. Schmich, "Pastor Keeps Big Dream Alive," *Chicago Tribune*, July 7, 2004.

13. Schmich, "Buildings Stand Because a Leader Stood Her Ground," *Chicago Tribune*, July 9, 2004.

14. Stockwell, "The Church and Justice in Crisis," 182.

CHAPTER 4: POVERTY FROM AN INSTITUTIONAL PERSPECTVE

1. Michael Harrington, "The Invisible Land," in *The Quality of Life in America, eds.* A. David Hill et al., (New York: Holt, Rinehart, and Winston, 1973), 140–47.

2. Unpublished dissertation research by Timothy M. Larkin, University of Illinois at Chicago. Rev. Larkin is pastor of The Point Church in Chicago. I<www.thepointchurch.com>.

3. Mark W. Clark, "Job Training Program Unites Churches and the Business Community," *Mandate* (Spring 2004): 7, 10. More information on this program is available at <www.hope4.org>, <www.newcityfellowship.com>, and <www.tip.org>, as well as the Chalmers Center referenced below.

4. Barna Research, "People's Faith Flavor Influences How They See Themselves," August 26, 2002, <www.barna.org>.

5. Barna Research, "Most People Seek Control, Adventure, and Peace in Their Lives," August 1, 2002, www.barna.org/cgi-bin/PagePressRelease.asp? PressR eleaseID=68&Reference=B.

6. Jim Sutherland, "Delivering from Mammon," *Mandate* (Spring 2004): 10. The Chalmers Center is simply an excellent urban ministry resource and can be found at <www.chalmers.org> or through Covenant College, 14049 Scenic Highway, Lookout Mountain, GA 30750. Phone (706) 419-1805.

7. Sutherland points to several excellent teaching resources. One is Larry Burkett, *How to Manage Your Money Workbook* <www.Crown.org> (code HM 203); <http://216.52.177.33/LocalChurch/Counseling/training.asp>, (800) 722-1976; Reconciliation Ministries Network, Inc. <www.reconciliati onnetwork.org/financial/financialresources.htm>. <www.rmni.org/financial/church-clergy.htm>.

8. Mark W. Clark, "Matched Savings Program Makes a Difference in Memphis," in *Mandate*, 4. Advance Memphis can be reached at (901) 543-8525.

9. w<ww.hope4.org/liftinghands.htm>.

CHAPTER 5: INSECURITY AS A WAY OF LIFE

1. Marego Athans, "Psychological Poverty," *The Sun*, June 29, 1999.

2. *National Advisory Commission on Civil Disorders*, report (New York: Bantam, 1968), 35–200, 299–336, 484–93.

3. David Claerbaut, *The Reluctant Defender* (Wheaton, IL: Tyndale, 1978), 188–189.

4. Lee Rainwater, "The Lessons of Pruitt-Igoe," *The Public Interest* 8 (Summer 1967): 116–26, cited in *Spectrum on Social Problems*, ed. Jon M. Shepard (Columbus, OH: Merrill, 1973), 119–26.

5. CURE is at <www.urbancure.org>.

CHAPTER 6: YOUTH

1. John Hagedorn is among the nation's leading experts on gang behavior. His website, <www.gangresearch.net> is an excellent source for the latest information.

2. Schmich, "It's All New and It's Not Their Turf Anymore," *Chicago Tribune*, July 13, 2004.

3. Youth for Christ has a website at <www.gospelcom.net> and Young Life is at <www.younglife.org>.

4. Griffin provides an excellent discussion of effective, non-manipulative, low-key evangelism, see Em Griffin, *The Mind Changers* (Wheaton, Ill.: Tyndale, 1976).

CHAPTER 7: MINORITIES

1. Michael O. Emerson and Christian Smith, *Divided by Faith: Evangelical Religion and the Problem of Race in America* (New York: Oxford University Press, 2000), 7.

2. Eduardo Bonilla-Sliva and Amanda Lewis, 1997 "The 'New Racism': Toward an Analysis of the U.S. Racial Structure, 1960s–1990s," unpublished manuscript, p. 474 cited in *Divided by Faith*, 7.

3. Gunnar Myrdal, *An American Dilemma*, vol. 1 (New York: Harper and Brothers, 1944).

4. Based on George Eaton Simpson and J. Milton Yinger, *Racial and Cultural Minorities* (New York: Harper and Brothers, 1953).

5. The discussion on rights is taken from the film "Mythology of Racism," copyright Dr. Paul Mundy, 1968. Dr. Mundy is a sociologist at Loyola University of Chicago and an expert on majority-minority relations.

6. Egon E. Bergel, *Urban Sociology* (New York: McGraw-Hill, 1955), 9–10.

7. Adapted from a variety of materials by Dr. Paul Mundy, Loyola University of Chicago; see also Robert Ezra Park, *Race and Culture* (Glencoe, IL: Free Press, 1950).

8. George Eaton Simpson and J. Milton Yinger, *Racial and Cultural Minorities,* rev. ed. (New York: Harper and Brothers, 1958), 25–36.

9. Ibid., 23–25.

10. There are many websites that deal with the history and current status of Native Americans. Perusers will note how often they are treated in the context of specific tribal identities rather than as a collective.

11. Works treating the US histories of Japanese Americans include Harry H. L. Kitano, *Japanese Americans* (Englewood Cliffs, N.J.: Prentice-Hall, 1969); Leonard Bloom and Ruth Riemer, *Removal and Return* (Berkeley: University of California Press, 1949).

12. Books of value in tracing the Chinese American experience include: Stanford M. Lyman, *Chinese Americans* (New York: Random House, 1974); Rose Hum Lee, *The Chinese in the United States of America* (New York: Oxford University Press, 1960).

13. There are growing resources on the various Hispanic groups in the US largely because of their growing presence. It is helpful to separately research the various groups—Mexican Americans, Puerto Ricans, Cubans, along with those from Central and South America.

14. For an excellent discussion of African American experience in the US from a Christian perspective, see Ronald Behm and Columbus Salley, *Your God Is Too White* (Downers Grove, IL: InterVarsity, 1970).

15. Paul Mundy, "The Rural Past of Our Urban Present: A Sociologist Sketches the Chicago Personality," in *Leadership, Localism and Urbanism: Components in Search of a System,* monograph 10 (Chicago: Loyola University, Center for Research in Urban Government, 1968), 20–24.

16. *Divided by Faith*, 9.

17. Ibid., 54–55.

18. Ibid., 76–78.

19. N. K. Clifford, "His Dominion: A Vision in Crisis," in *Sciences Religieuses/Studies in Religion.* 1973 2:323, cited in *Divided by Faith*, 171.

20. *Divided by Faith*, 171.

21. Ibid., 171–172.

22. Alan Keyes quoted in Cathleen Falsani, "The Victory Is for God," *Chicago Sun-Times*, August 22, 2004.

23. Leonard P. Rascher, "Ministry among the Urban Indians," in *Metro-Ministry,* 185–86.

CHAPTER 8: SOCIALIZATION INTO VICTIM-BLAMING

1. William Ryan, *Blaming the Victim* (New York: Vintage, 1971).

2. Ibid., xii.

3. *Disclosure: The National Newspaper of Neighborhoods* (Chicago: National Training and Information Center, January, 2000).

4. Merrill Goozner, "Study Finds Urban Areas Lag in Trimming Welfare Cases; Illinois Among the Worst in States Faltering in Task to Cut Load," *Chicago Tribune*, February 19, 1999.

5. Robert Rosenthal and Lenore Jacobson, *Pygmalion in the Classroom* (New York: Holt, Rinehart and Winston, 1968).

6. Stockwell, "The Church and Justice in Crisis," 175.

7. Ryan, *Blaming the Victim*, 185–210.

CHAPTER 9: THE URBAN CHURCH AND THE URBAN PASTOR

1. Adapted from Anthony Campolo, "The Sociological Nature of the Urban Church," in David Frenchak and Sharrel Keyes, eds., *Metro-Ministry* (Elgin, IL: David C. Cook, 1979), 27–35.

2. An excellent source investigating poverty, race, and class in contemporary Chicago is the *Chicago Reporter*. This paper is available online at <www.chica goreporter.com>. Helpful sources for this section include George W. Baybrook, "Six Churches: Thriving on Common Ground," *Christianity Today* (June 18, 1976), 18–19; Dennis Bakke, "Churches and Energy Conservation," in *Metro-Ministry*, 104–6; William Bentley and Willie Jemison, "Church Growth in Black Congregations," in *Metro-Ministry*, 61–64; Donald L. Benedict, "Toward an Urban Church Strategy," in *Metro-Ministry*, 70–76.

3. Derived from Lyle E. Schaller, "Twenty Questions for Self-Evaluation in the Downtown Church," *Church Management* (July 1976): 17–18, 27, 29.

4. David I. Frenchak, "Urban Fatigue," in *Metro-Ministry*, 115–120.

CHAPTER 10: NEW DIRECTIONS IN URBAN MINISTRY

1. Mark A. Noll, *The Scandal of the Evangelical Mind* (Grand Rapids, MI: William B. Eerdmans, 1994), 12.

2. Peter Medoff and Holly Sklar, *Streets of Hope: The Fall and Rise of an Urban Neighborhood* (Boston: South End Press, 1994).

3. Ibid., 14.

4. Ibid., 91.

5. Mark R. Gornik, *To Sing a New Song in the City: A Book review of To Live in Peace: Biblical Faith and the Changing Inner City* (Grand Rapids, MI: William B. Eerdmans, 2002).

6. Ibid., 129.

7. You can find information on the Chalmers Center at <www.chalmers.org>.

8. Brian Fikkert, "What Can Your Church Do to Help the Poor in the U.S.," *Mandate* (Spring 2004): 2.

9. Ibid., 2.

10. Phil Olson, "So Your Church Wants to Minister Holistically?" *Mandate* (Spring 2004): 3, 6, 12.

11. From Ron Sider, Heidi Rolland-Unruh, and Phil Olson, *Churches That Make a Difference: Reaching Your Community with Good News and Good Works* (Grand Rapids, MI: Baker Books, 2002).

12. Phil Olson, "So Your Church Wants to Minister Holistically?" *Mandate* (Spring 2004): 3, 6, 12. Olson can be contacted at Network9: 35 <www.network935.org>; additional resources are available at <www.easumbandy.com>.

13. The Chalmers Center and the referenced issue of *Mandate* describe each of these ministries.

14. Fikkert cites Mark Schreiner, "Self-Employment, Microenterprise, and the Poorest," *Social Science Review* 73, no. 4 (December 1999): 496–523 as providing a helpful analysis of this challenge.

15. Fikkert points to Deborah Page-Adams and Michael Sherraden, "What We Know about the Effects of Asset Holding: Implications for Research on Asset-Based Anti-Poverty Initiatives," (St. Louis: Center for Social Development, Washington University, 1996).

ACKNOWLEDGMENTS

I want to thank Dr. Clinton E. Stockwell, Executive Director of the Chicago Semester. Clinton is a friend whose knowledge of cities and urban ministry is unsurpassed. This book could not have been done without his help

INDEX

Greenway, Roger, 4, 273, 274

Habitat for Humanity, 49, 268
Hallett, Stanley, 276
Harper, James, 21
HarperCollins Study Bible, 12
Harrington, Michael, 30, 85, 275, 278
Harris, Roy, 125
Hatfield, Mark, 9
Head Start, 116, 221
Hindu culture, 1

Infelt, Chuck, 81
Inner city simulation game, 48, 276
Institute on the Church in Urban-Industrial Society (ICUIS), 257
Ipema, William, 51–52, 277
Isaiah, 11, 15, 50, 268, 269
Islamic society, 1

Jackson, Jesse, 44, 88
Jackson, Shirley, 7, 274
James, the apostle, 13, 16, 105, 114, 136
James, Gilbert, 252
Japanese-American relocation, 174–75, 181–183, 280
Jemison, Willie, 281
Jeremiah, 5, 11, 12, 22, 268, 269
Jerusalem, 5–7, 11
John, the apostle, 16, 136
John the Baptist, 15
Johnson, Lyndon, 74
Jonah, 5
Joseph, 5
Juice loans, 95
Justice
    scriptural mandate for, xi, 5, 8–17, 20, 23, 24
    and system inequities, 23, 127–129

Kahl, Joseph, 59

Kennedy, Robert F., 59
King, Martin Luther, Jr., 23, 29, 88, 132, 193
Kuyper, Abraham, 19, 21

Larkin, Tim, 258–59, 262–64
Lazarus, 13, 18, 37, 132
Leslie, Bill, ix, 47, 126, 237–38, 245–46, 254, 259, 264
Livezey, Lowell, 19

Mack, David, 150
Malcolm X, 88
Marciniak, Ed, 276–77
Mayer, Kurt B., 70
Mell, Richard, 276
Mexico City, 187
Miami, 6, 37
Miller, Keith, 238
Mills, C. Wright, 20
Ministry (urban)
    defined and described, x
    guidelines for poverty ministry, 111–14
    and reconciliation, 15–17
    and relief, 16, 19
    refocused away from victim blaming, 229–32
    and reform, 20–21
    as service, xi, 14, 16, 17–18, 79, 102, 192, 200, 229
    stewardship in, 17, 74, 79–83, 193, 229, 230
    to insecurity of poverty, 133–39
    to institutional poverty, 86–102
    to minorities, 194–201
    to youth, 148–153
Minorities
    Asians, 186, 193
    African Americans or blacks, 3, 29, 36–7, 41, 67, 89, 91, 93, 94, 96, 97, 98, 102, 107, 149, 158, 163, 166, 168, 169, 174, 176, 185, 188–194, 198, 236, 268
    Chinese, 32, 47, 177, 183–85, 193